Yes, I'm Hot in This

The Hilarious Truth about Life in a Hijab

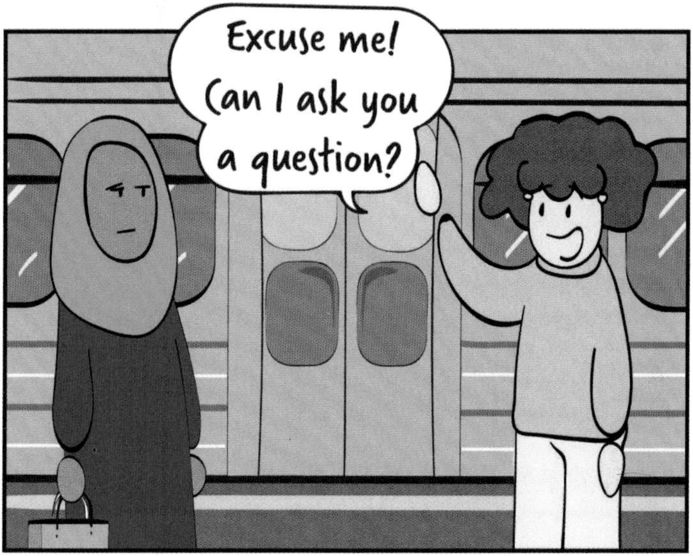
Excuse me! Can I ask you a question?

Huda Fahmy

ADAMS MEDIA

NEW YORK LONDON TORONTO SYDNEY NEW DELHI

Adams Media
An Imprint of Simon & Schuster, Inc.
57 Littlefield Street
Avon, Massachusetts 02322

First Adams Media hardcover edition December 2018

For information about special discounts for bulk purchases, please contact Simon & Schuster Special Sales at 1-866-506-1949 or business@simonandschuster.com.

The Simon & Schuster Speakers Bureau can bring authors to your live event. For more information or to book an event contact the Simon & Schuster Speakers Bureau at 1-866-248-3049 or visit our website at www.simonspeakers.com.

Interior design by Sylvia McArdle
Interior illustrations by Huda Fahmy

Manufactured in the United States of America

10   9   8   7   6   5   4   3   2   1

ISBN 978-1-5072-0934-9
ISBN 978-1-5072-0935-6 (ebook)

For my mama and baba, who built me up to be confident, independent, and strong. Thank you for all the role-playing games you made me play in the event of meeting haters in real life.

For my sisters, the strongest women I know.

For Gehad. Life is just more hilarious with you.

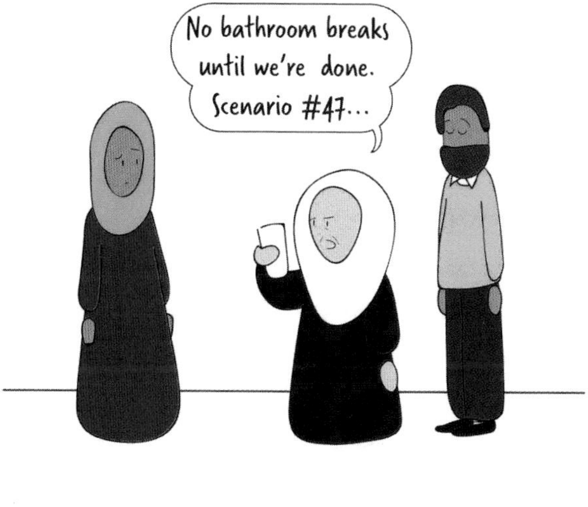
No bathroom breaks until we're done. Scenario #47...

ACKNOWLEDGMENTS

By the grace and will of God, I could not have made it this far if it wasn't for everyone who's read my comics online. To everyone who's commented on my posts, engaged with me, sent inspirational messages, given advice, pushed me to better myself, and taken the time to create beautiful fan art: THANK YOU! And to those who read my comics and wrote to tell me how much they've learned from them, you are what keeps me going.

To my big sister and role model, Duaa, this idea started out as a blog, and if it hadn't been for you, it would have stayed that way. Thank you for inspiring me to take my pent-up frustration and strange sense of humor and turn it into something I love.

Thank you, Gehad, for letting me make fun of you in my comics (because God knows you're my rock, and there's nothing to make fun of you about in real life, and I gotta get my kicks somewhere—KISSES!). For real though, thank you for supporting me in ways I didn't even realize I needed.

To my editors, Eileen and Sarah, thank you so much for taking a chance on me and for being dedicated and passionate. Thank you for giving me this stage and allowing me to speak after years of wanting desperately to be heard.

And last, but absolutely not the slightest bit least, a huge thank-you to Marzi. If you hadn't believed in me, I don't know where I'd be. I'm choking up just typing this. Thank you.

Table of Contents

Chapter 1: Yes, I'm Hot in This

Hi, I'm Huda.
Welcome to my book!

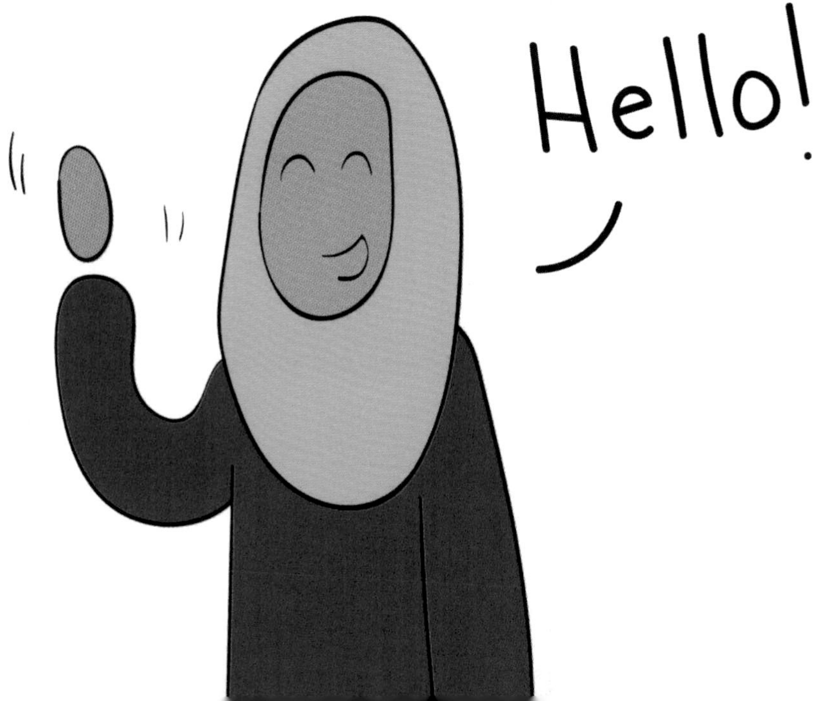
Hello!

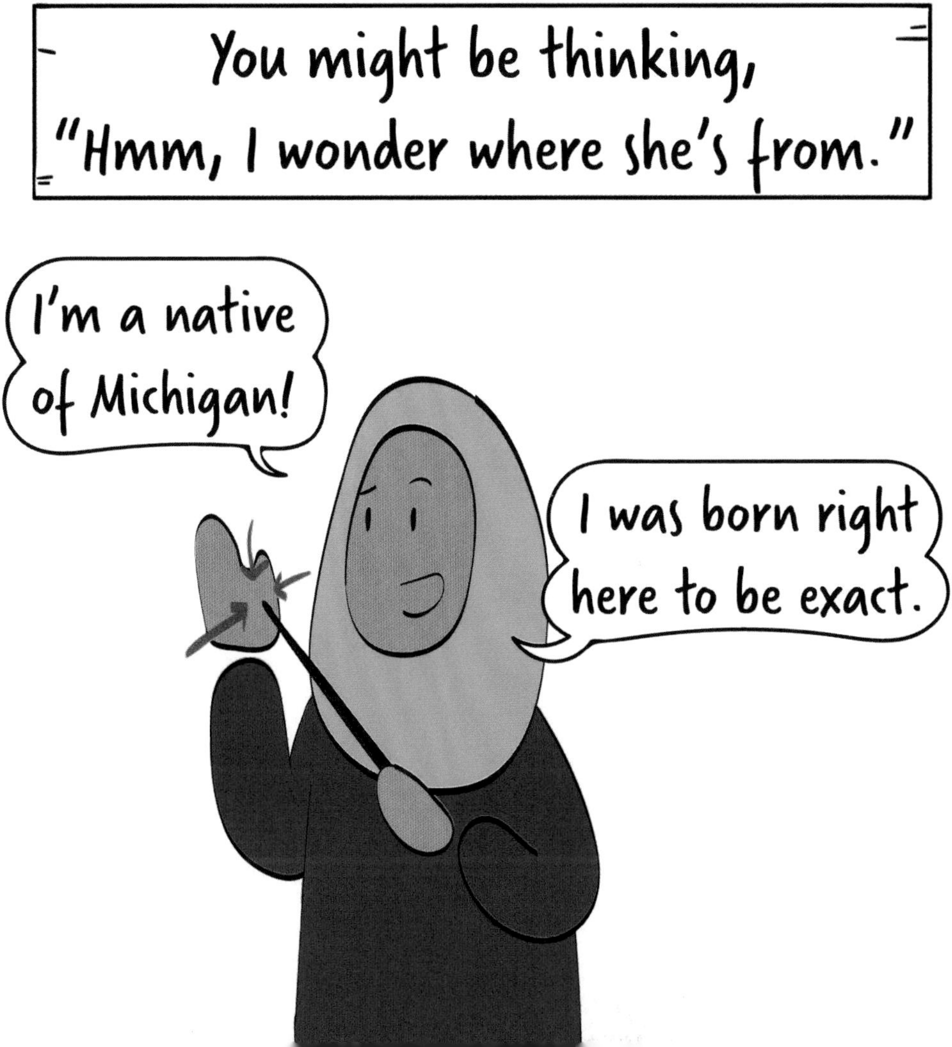
You might be thinking,
"Hmm, I wonder where she's from."
I'm a native of Michigan!
I was born right here to be exact.

Now you're saying to yourself, "Haha, no I meant *really* from."

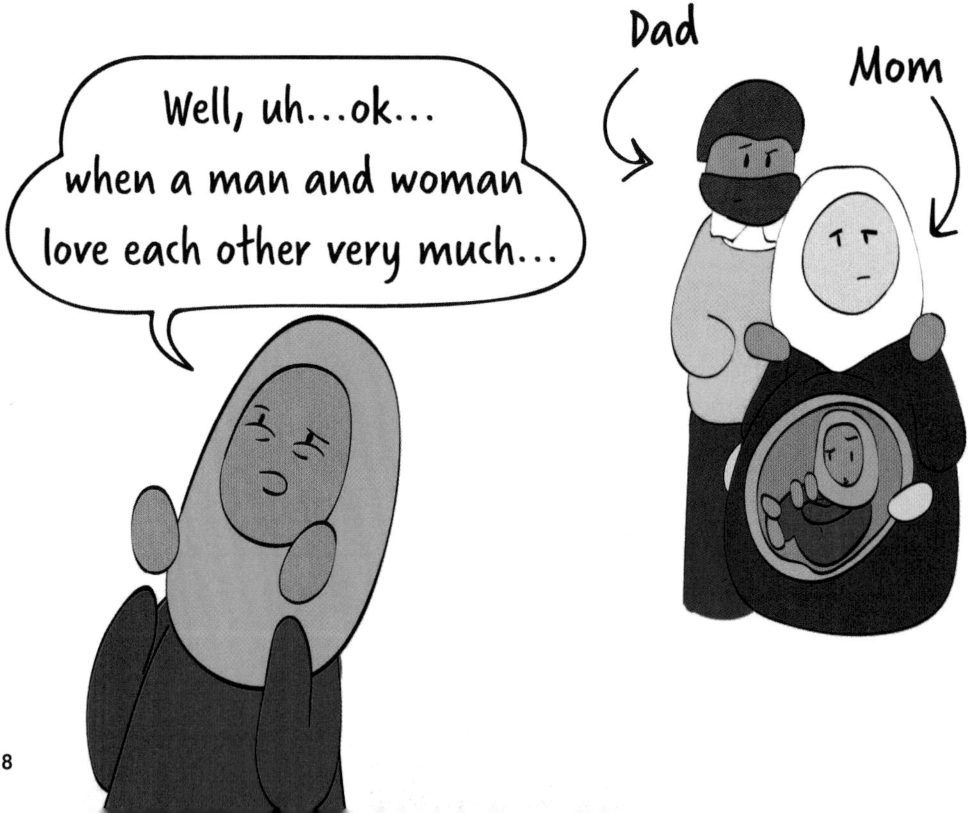

Well, uh...ok...
when a man and woman
love each other very much...
Dad
Mom

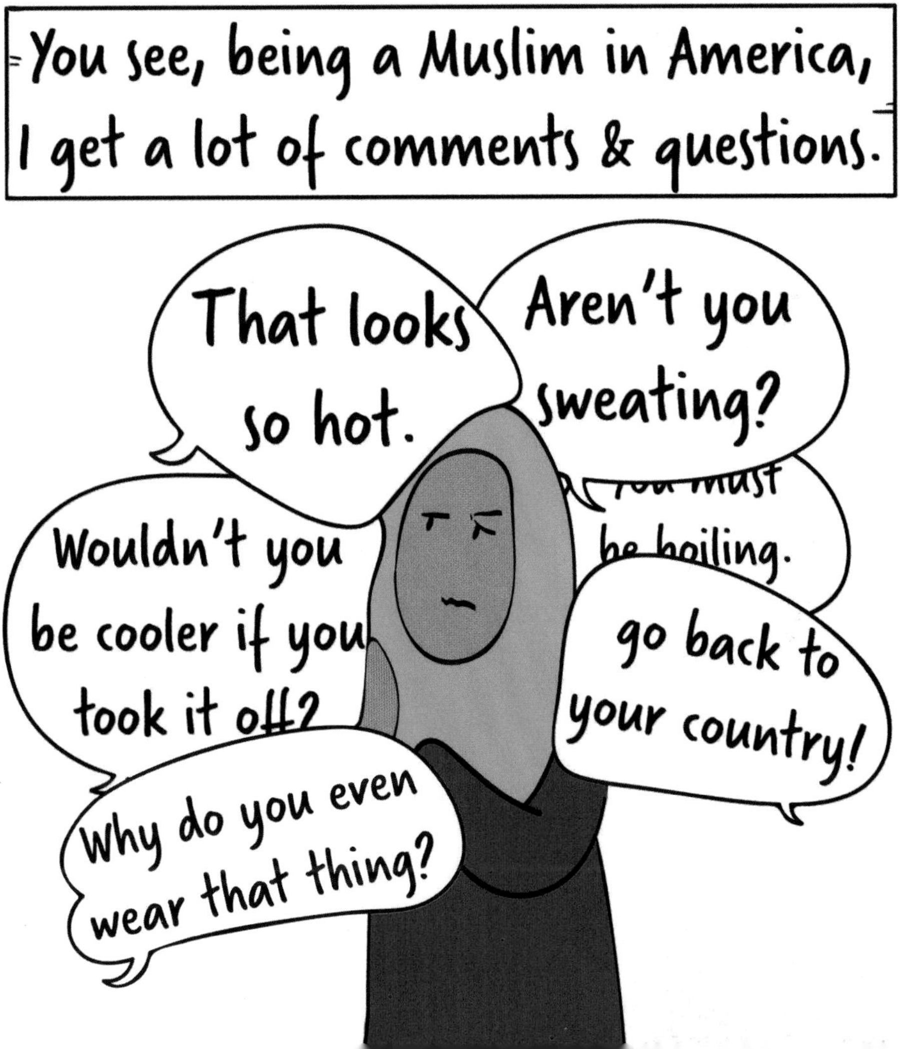
You see, being a Muslim in America, I get a lot of comments & questions.
That looks so hot.
Aren't you sweating?
Wouldn't you be cooler if you took it off?
be boiling.
go back to your country!
Why do you even wear that thing?

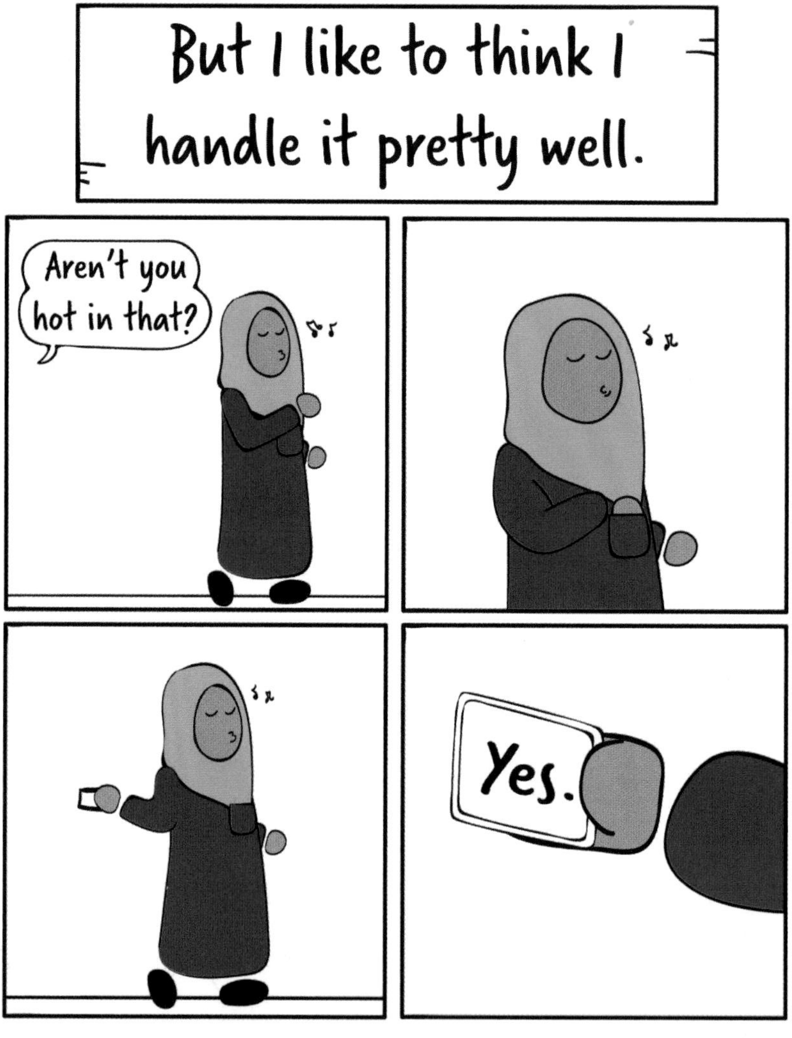
But I like to think I handle it pretty well.
Aren't you hot in that?
Yes.

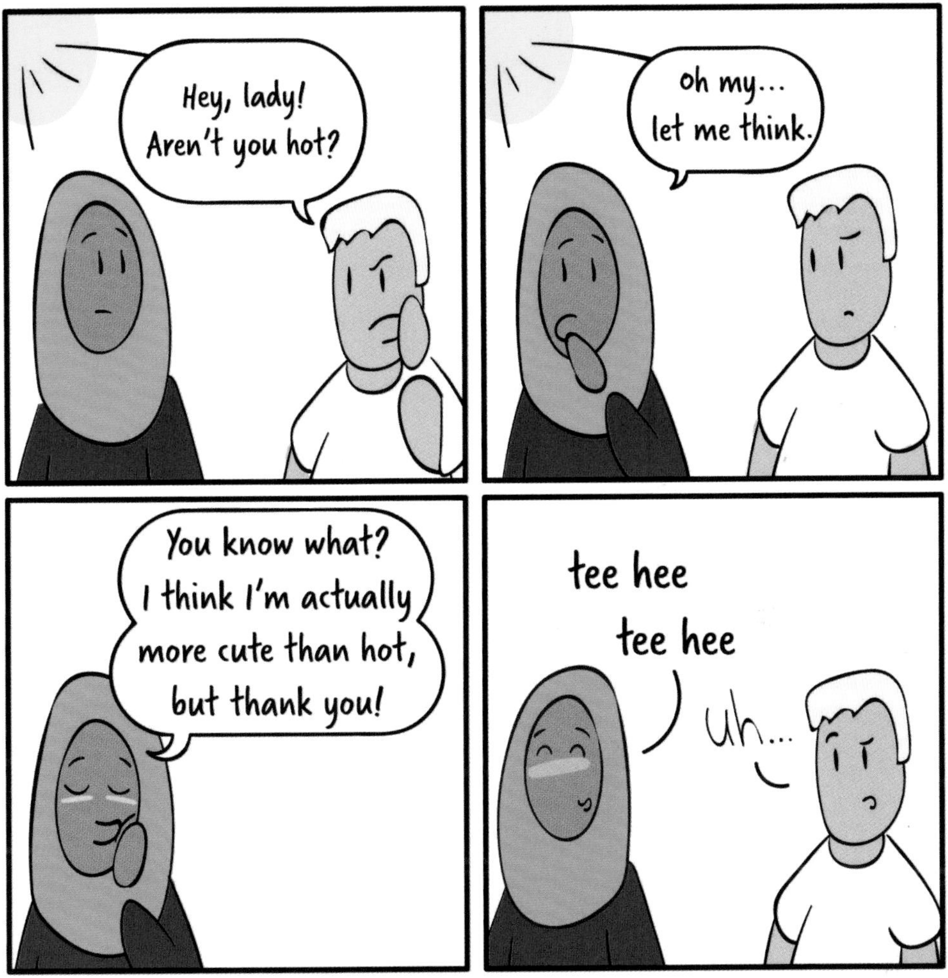
Hey, lady!
Aren't you hot?
oh my...
let me think.
You know what?
I think I'm actually
more cute than hot,
but thank you!
tee hee
tee hee
uh...

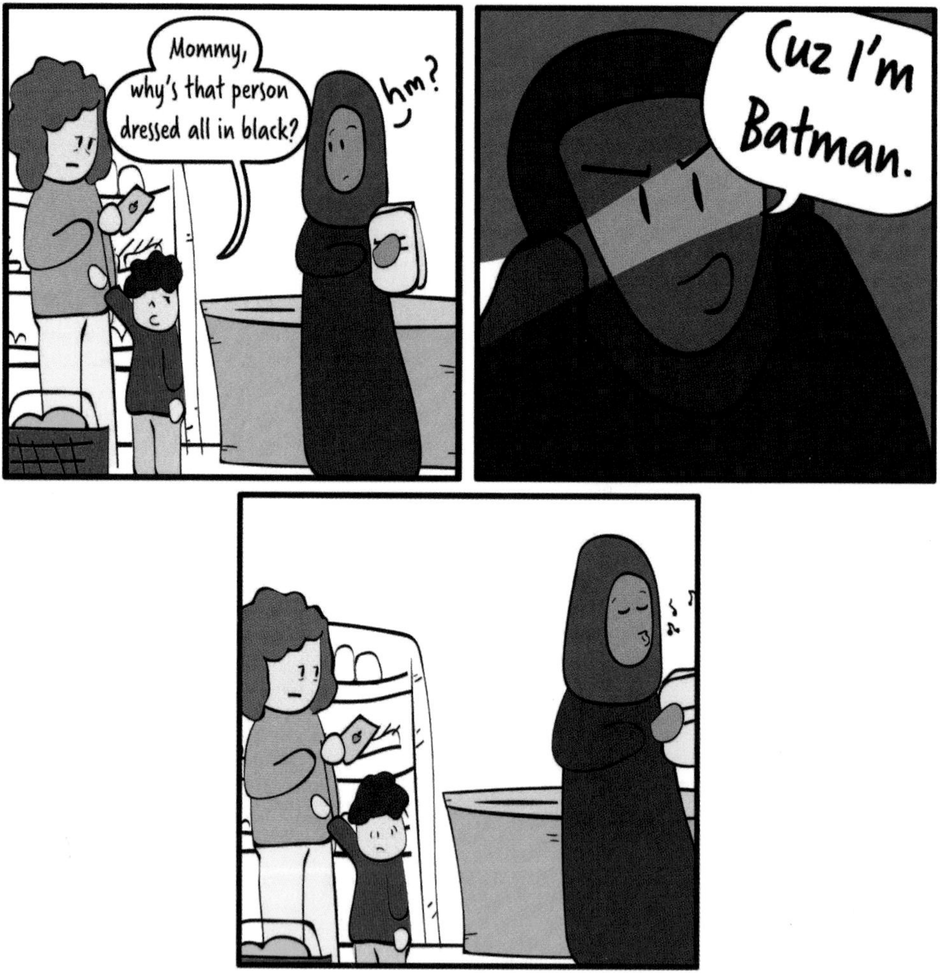
Mommy, why's that person dressed all in black?
hm?
Cuz I'm Batman.

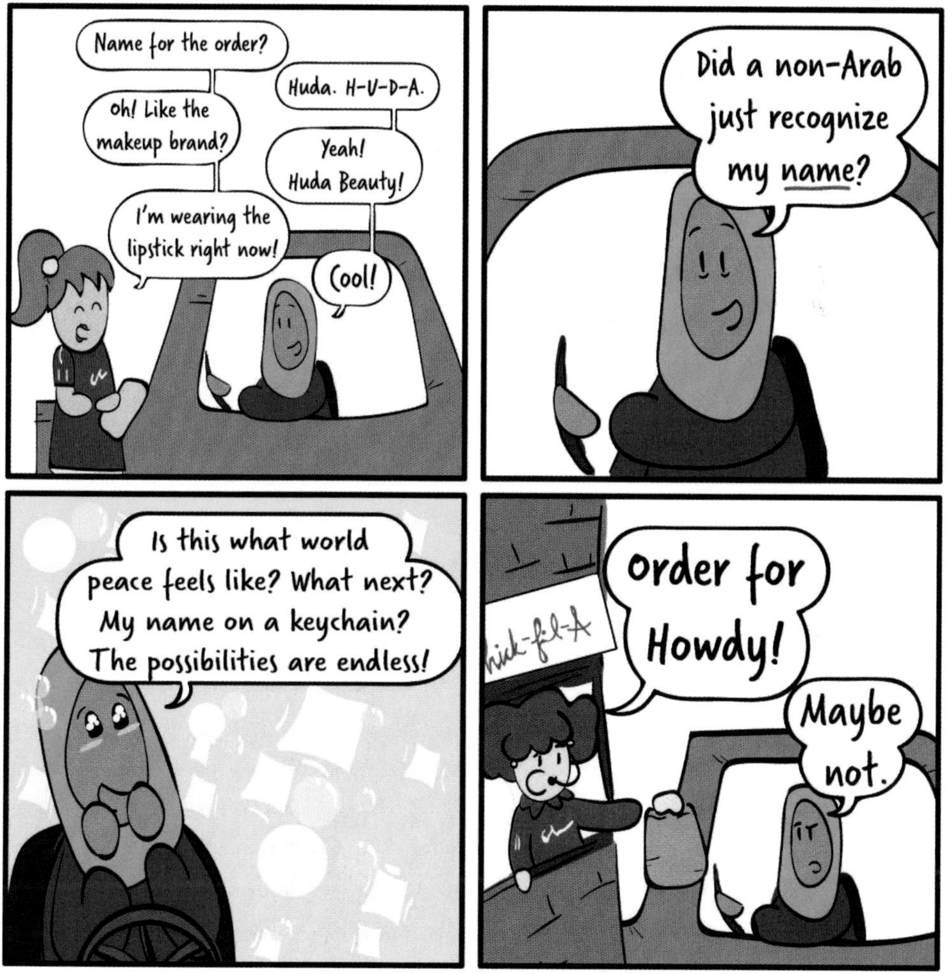
Name for the order?
Huda. H-U-D-A.
Oh! Like the makeup brand?
Yeah! Huda Beauty!
I'm wearing the lipstick right now!
Cool!
Did a non-Arab just recognize my name?
Is this what world peace feels like? What next? My name on a keychain? The possibilities are endless!
Order for Howdy!
Maybe not.

Society made me feel like the odd one out...
What is she wearing?
She must be so hot!
And then came the male romper.

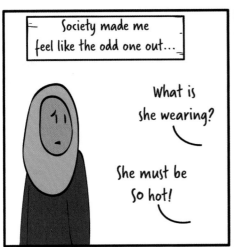

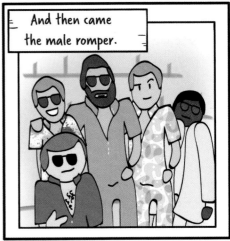

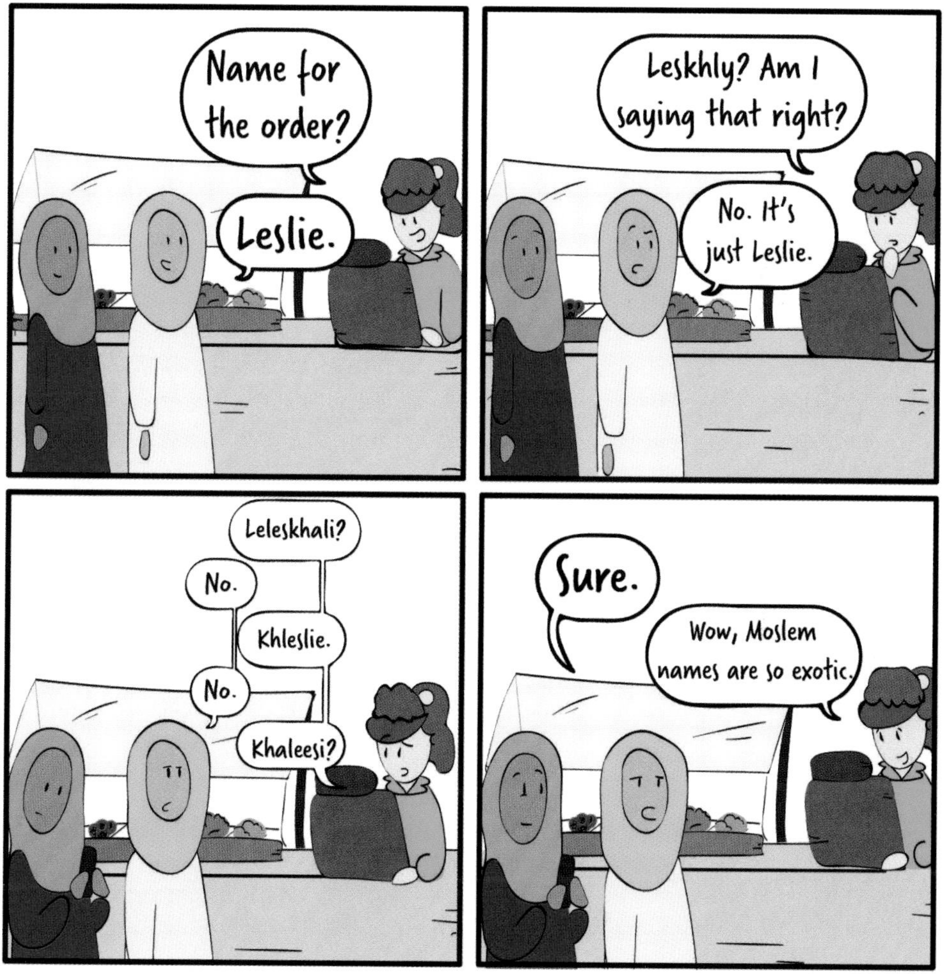
Name for the order?
Leslie.
Leskhly? Am I saying that right?
No. It's just Leslie.
Leleskhali?
No.
Khleslie.
No.
Khaleesi?
Sure.
Wow, Moslem names are so exotic.

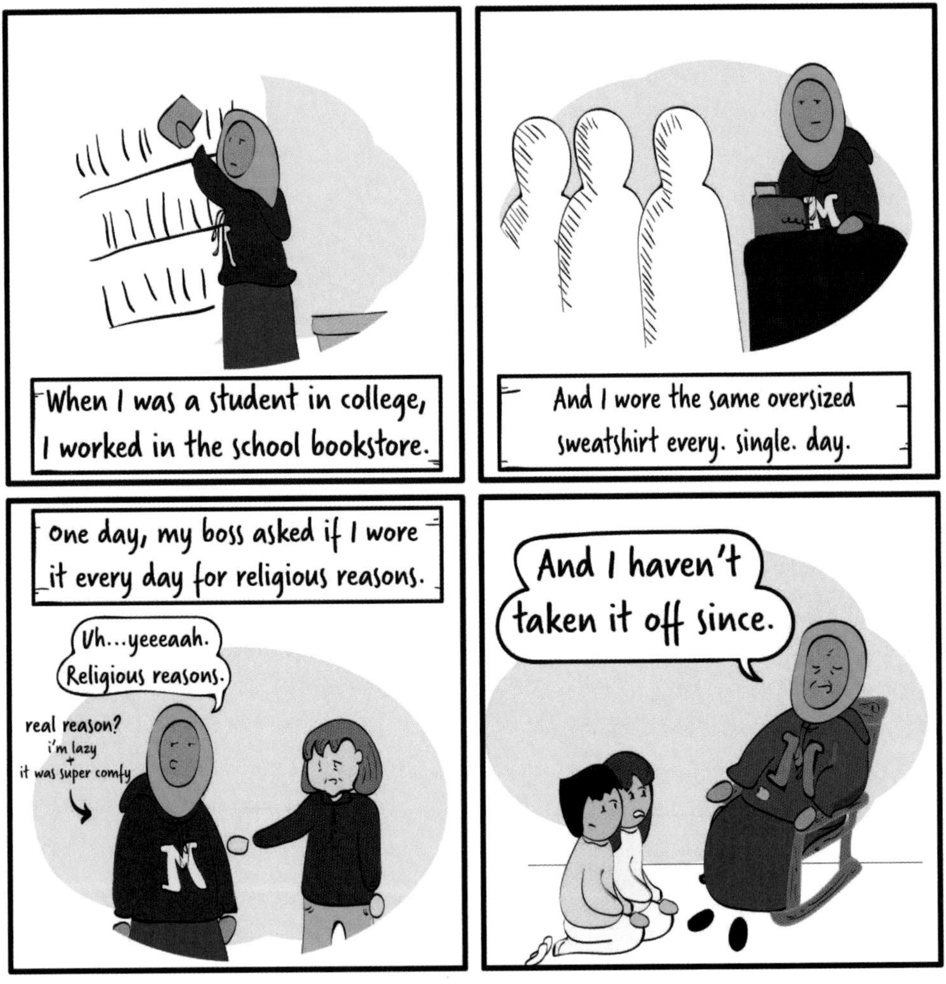
When I was a student in college, I worked in the school bookstore.
And I wore the same oversized sweatshirt every. single. day.
One day, my boss asked if I wore it every day for religious reasons.
Uh...yeeeaah. Religious reasons.
real reason? i'm lazy + it was super comfy
M
And I haven't taken it off since.

Makeup Tutorials

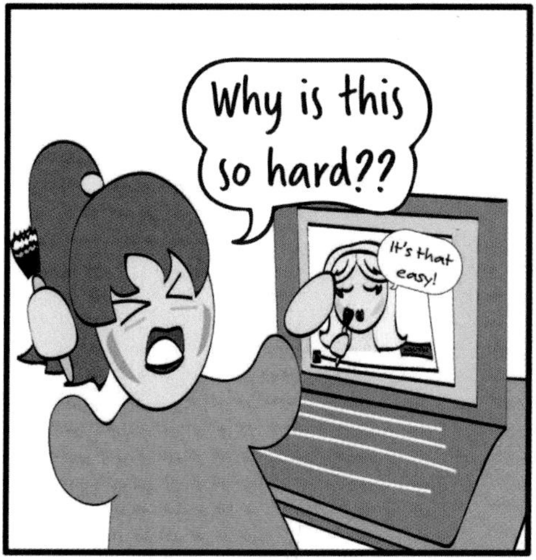
Why is this so hard??
It's that easy!

Hijab Tutorials

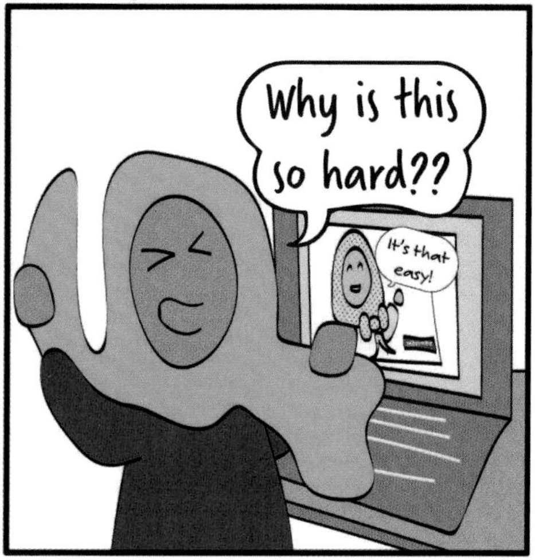
Why is this so hard??
It's that easy!

ME

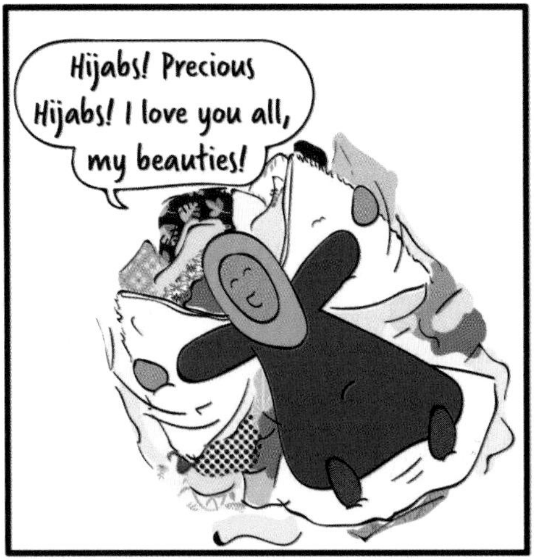
Hijabs! Precious Hijabs! I love you all, my beauties!

ALSO ME

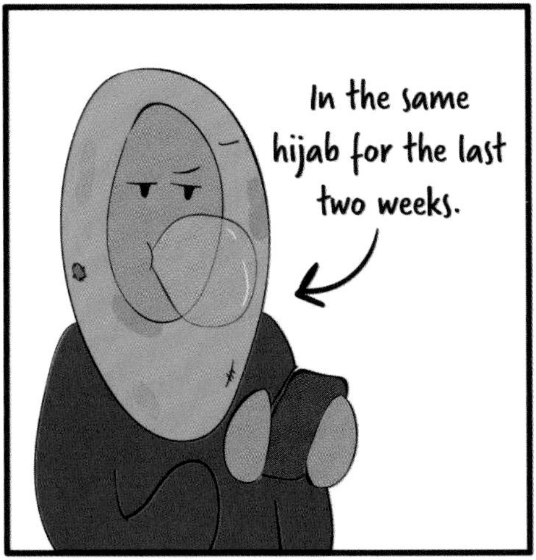
In the same hijab for the last two weeks.

Your scarf is so exotic. Where'd you get it?
Uhhh...
Earlier...
SALE
$5
SCARV
oooh don't mind if I do!

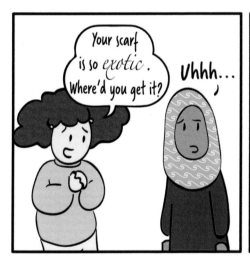

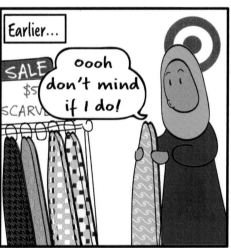

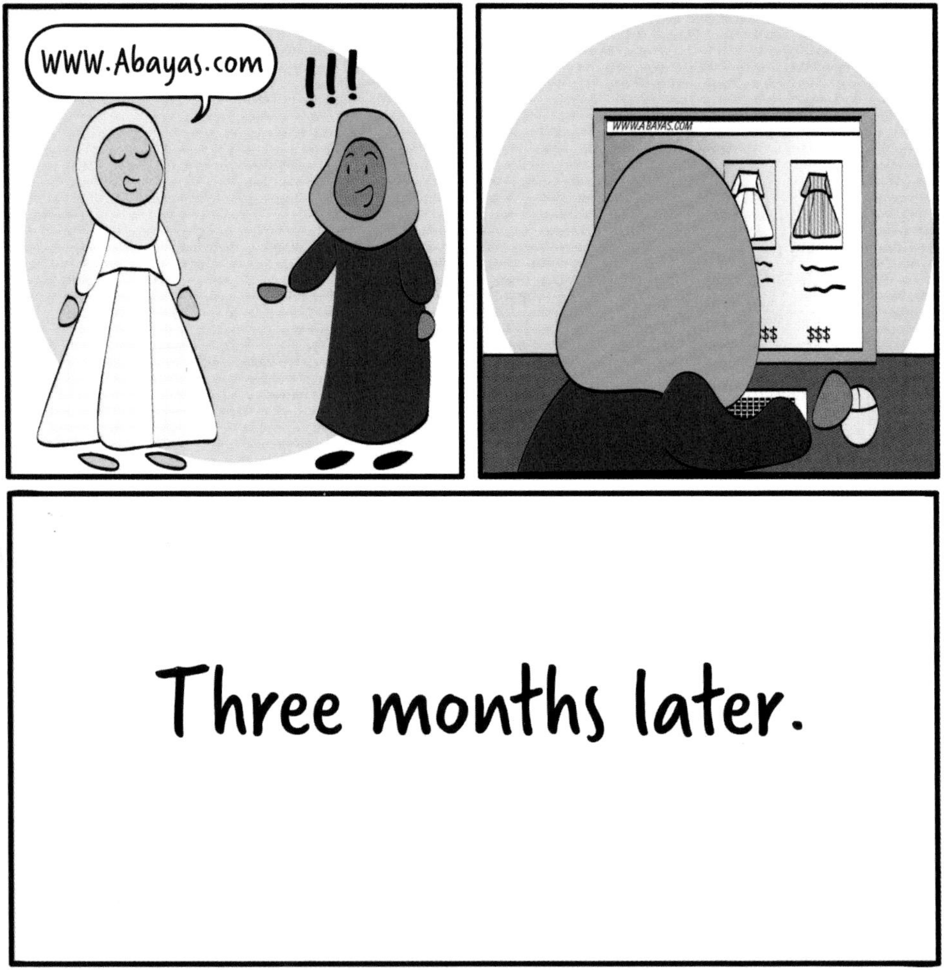
WWW.Abayas.com
!!!
WWW.ABAYAS.COM
$$$
Three months later.

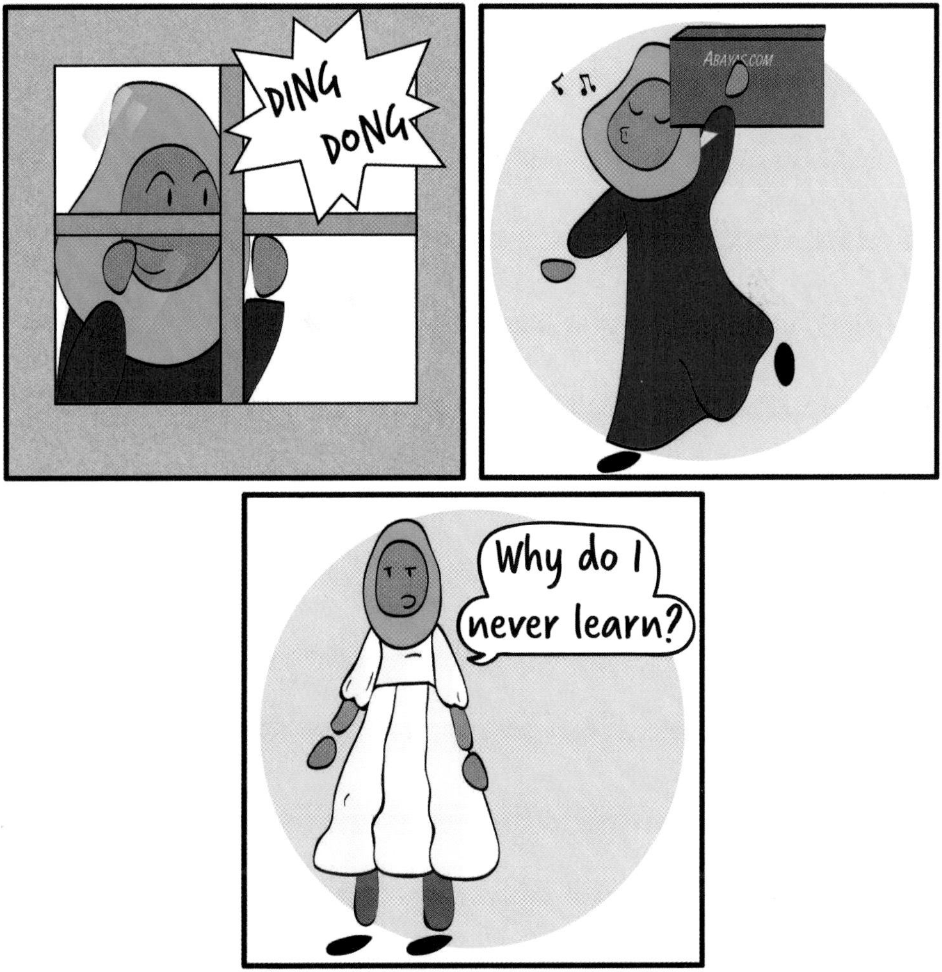
DING DONG
Why do I never learn?

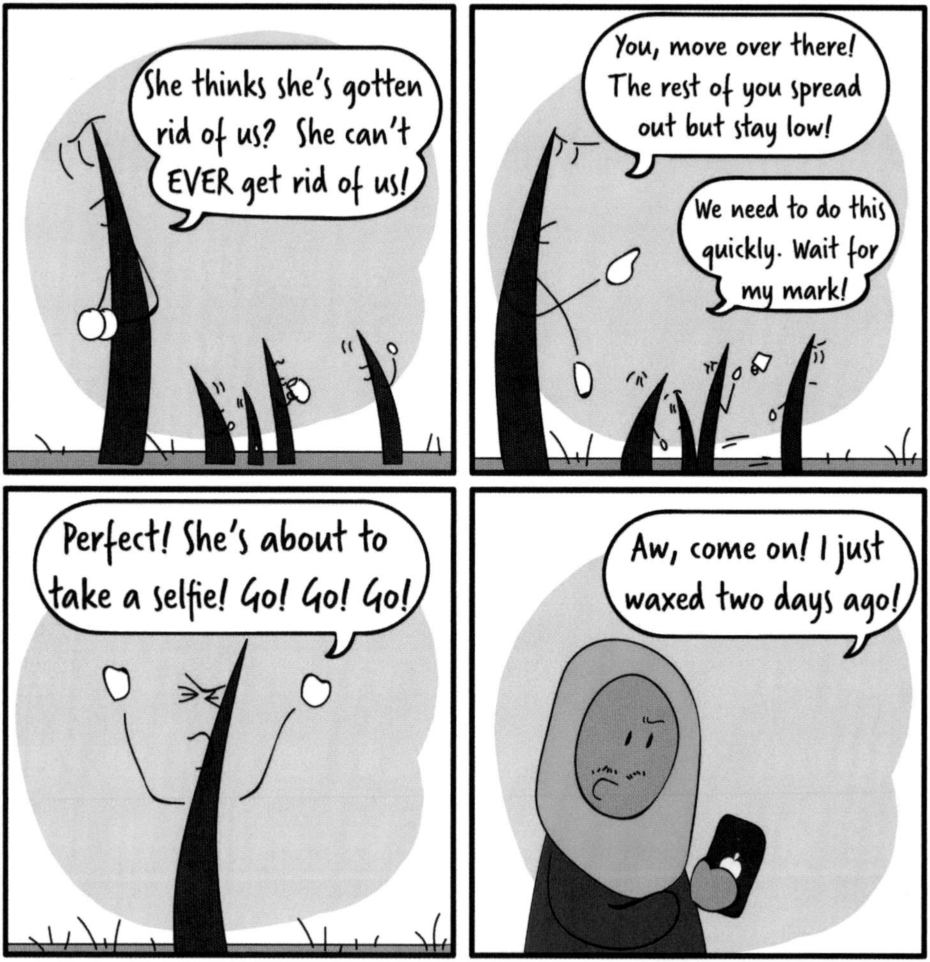

She thinks she's gotten rid of us? She can't EVER get rid of us!
You, move over there! The rest of you spread out but stay low!
We need to do this quickly. Wait for my mark!
Perfect! She's about to take a selfie! Go! Go! Go!
Aw, come on! I just waxed two days ago!

Mirrors at the store

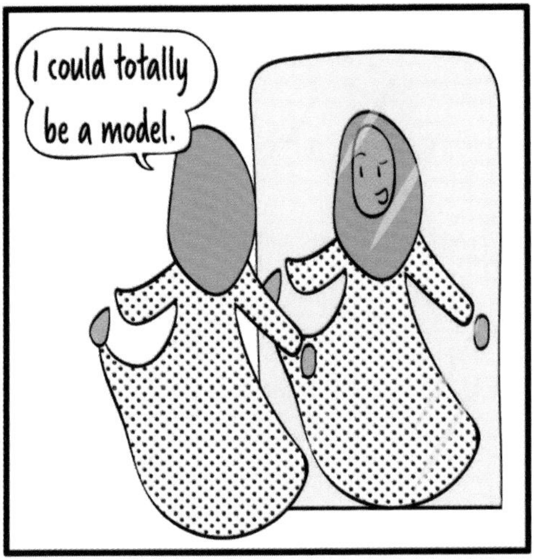
I could totally be a model.

Mirror at home

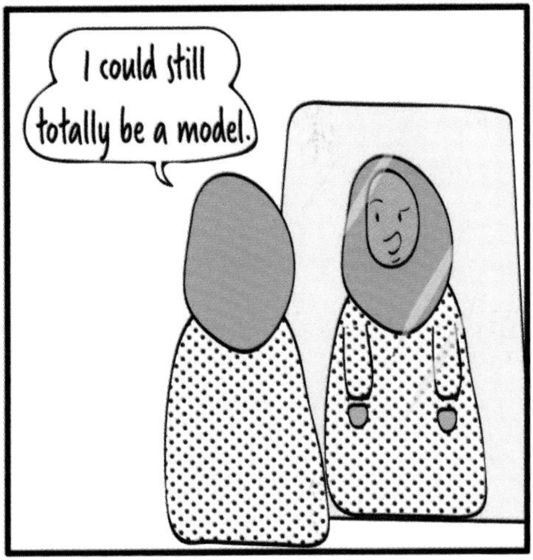
I could still totally be a model.

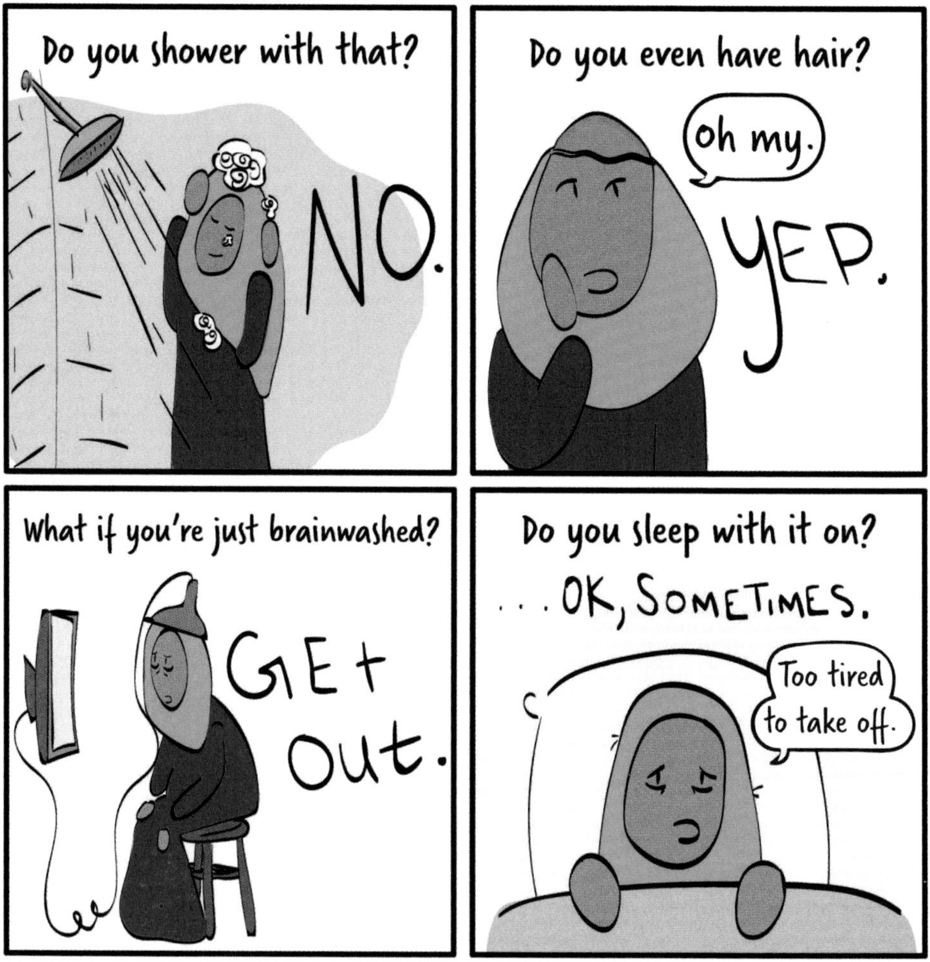
Do you shower with that?
NO.
Do you even have hair?
Oh my.
YEP.
What if you're just brainwashed?
GEt out.
Do you sleep with it on?
. . . . OK, SOMETIMES.
Too tired to take off.

Good for him covering up and protecting his skin from the sun's harmful rays!
She must be so hot in that! How oppressive!

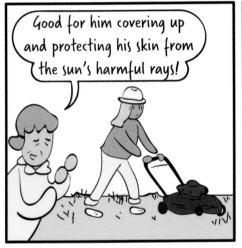

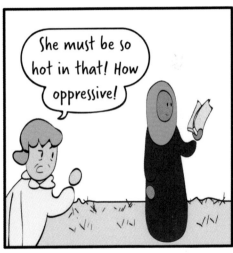

Scenario: You're introduced to a dude, and he goes to shake your hand.

He does not know that you do not shake hands with just any rando guy. Time slows down. Do you:

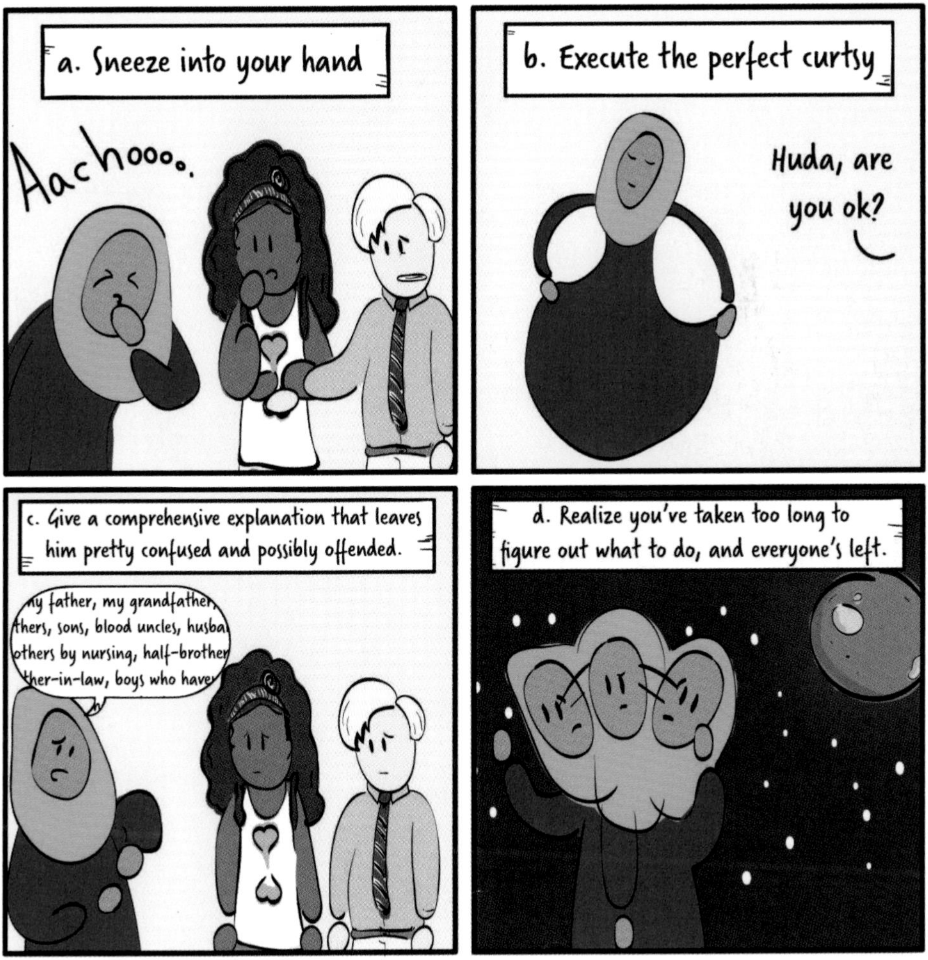
a. Sneeze into your hand
Aachoooo.
b. Execute the perfect curtsy
Huda, are you ok?
c. Give a comprehensive explanation that leaves him pretty confused and possibly offended.
father, my grandfather,
hers, sons, blood uncles, husba
others by nursing, half-brother
her-in-law, boys who have
d. Realize you've taken too long to figure out what to do, and everyone's left.

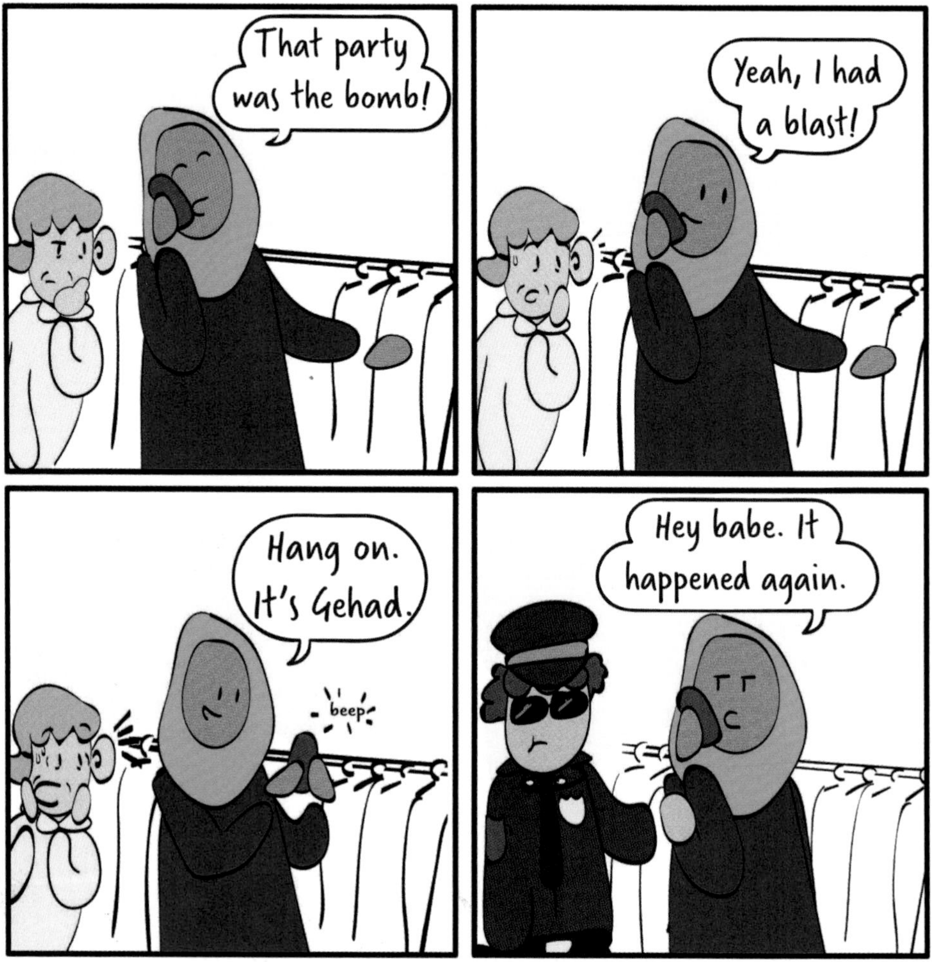
That party was the bomb!
Yeah, I had a blast!
beep
Hang on. It's Gehad.
Hey babe. It happened again.

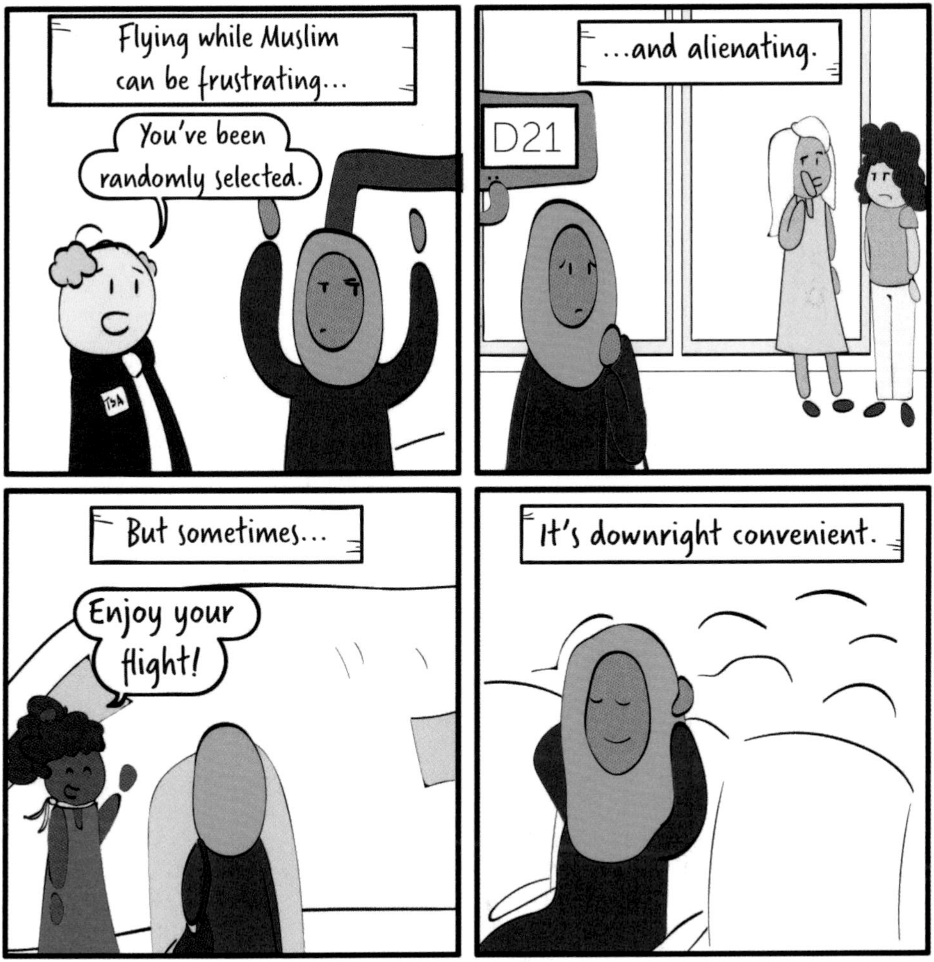
Flying while Muslim can be frustrating...
You've been randomly selected.
TSA
...and alienating.
D21
But sometimes...
Enjoy your flight!
It's downright convenient.

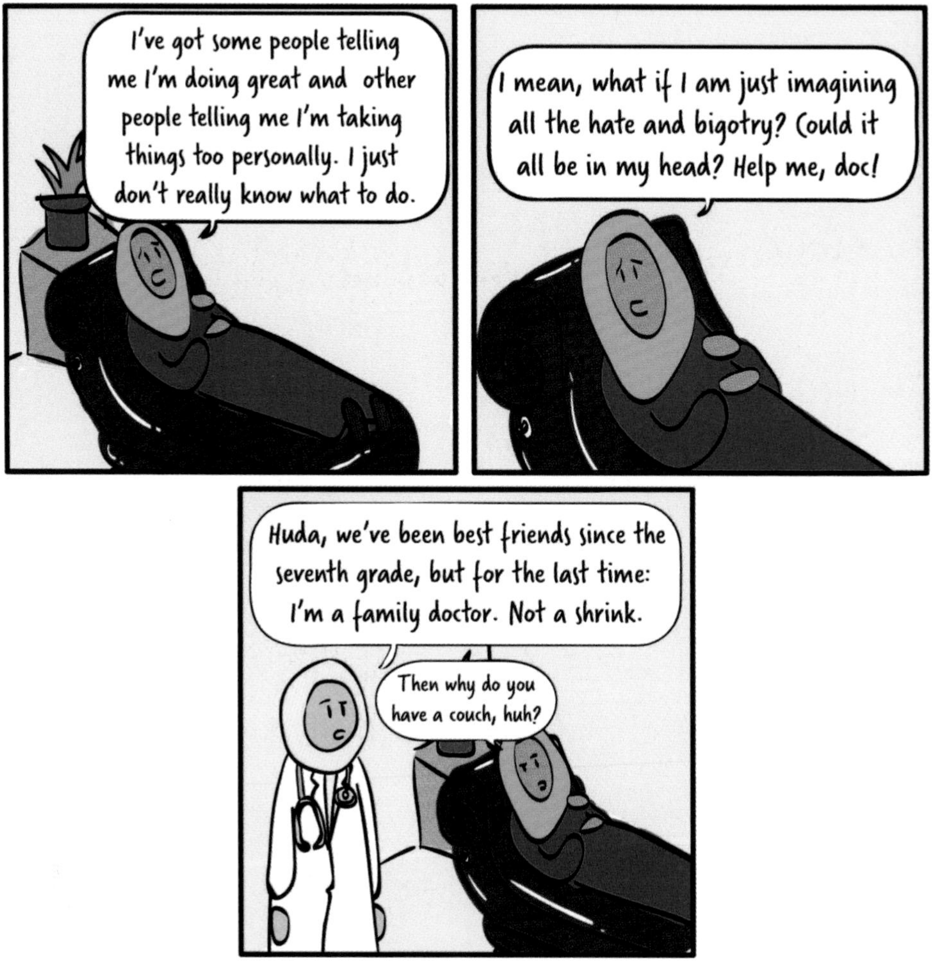
I've got some people telling me I'm doing great and other people telling me I'm taking things too personally. I just don't really know what to do.
I mean, what if I am just imagining all the hate and bigotry? Could it all be in my head? Help me, doc!
Huda, we've been best friends since the seventh grade, but for the last time: I'm a family doctor. Not a shrink.
Then why do you have a couch, huh?

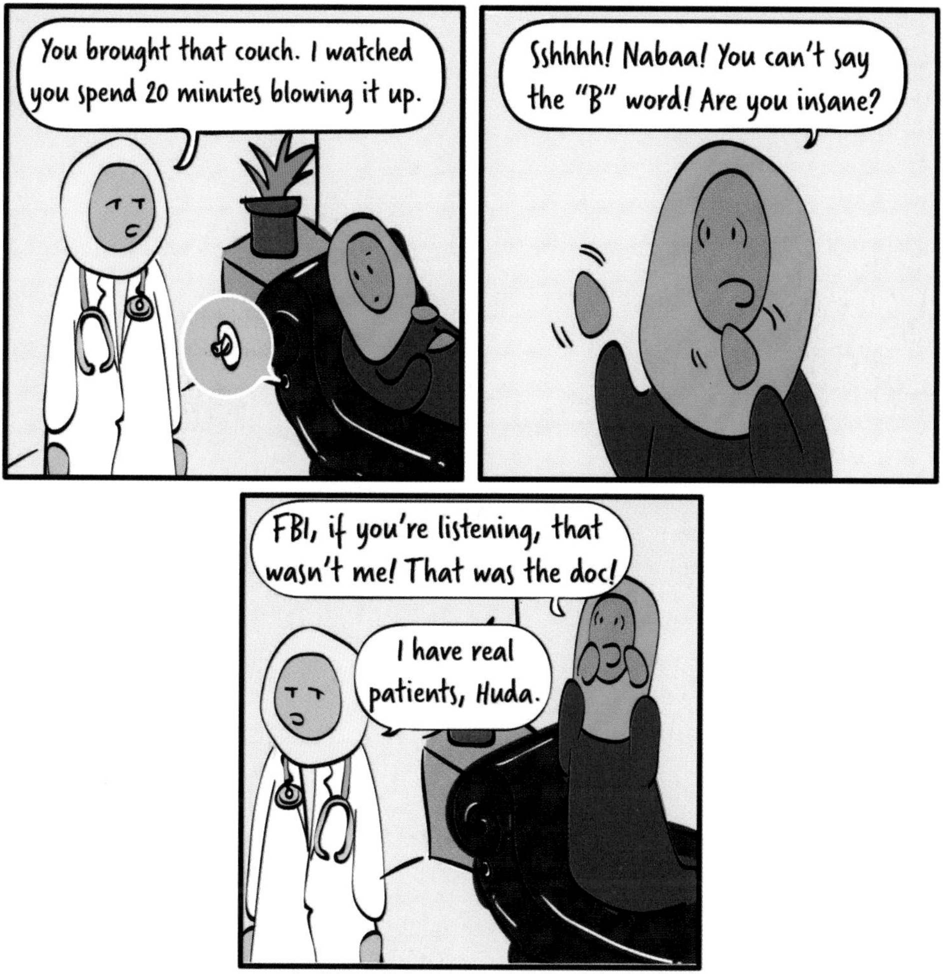
You brought that couch. I watched you spend 20 minutes blowing it up.
Sshhhh! Nabaa! You can't say the "B" word! Are you insane?
FBI, if you're listening, that wasn't me! That was the doc!
I have real patients, Huda.

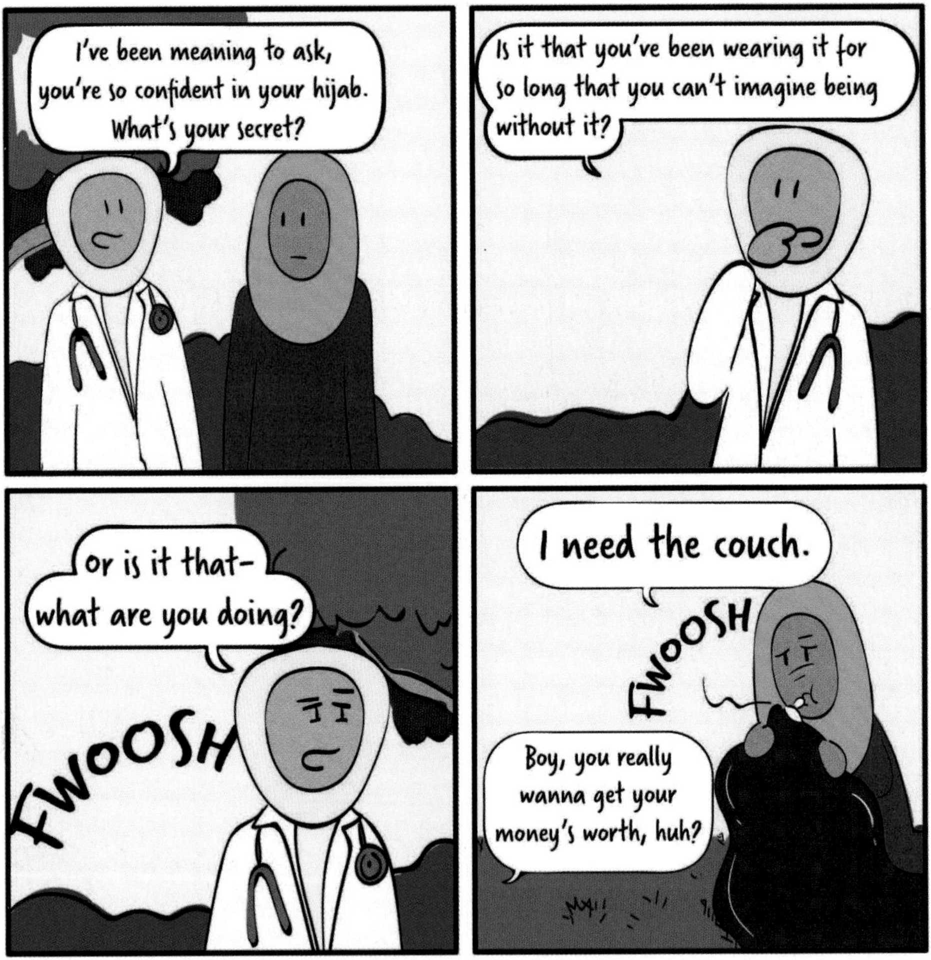
I've been meaning to ask, you're so confident in your hijab. What's your secret?
Is it that you've been wearing it for so long that you can't imagine being without it?
or is it that-
what are you doing?
FWOOSH
I need the couch.
FWOOSH
Boy, you really wanna get your money's worth, huh?

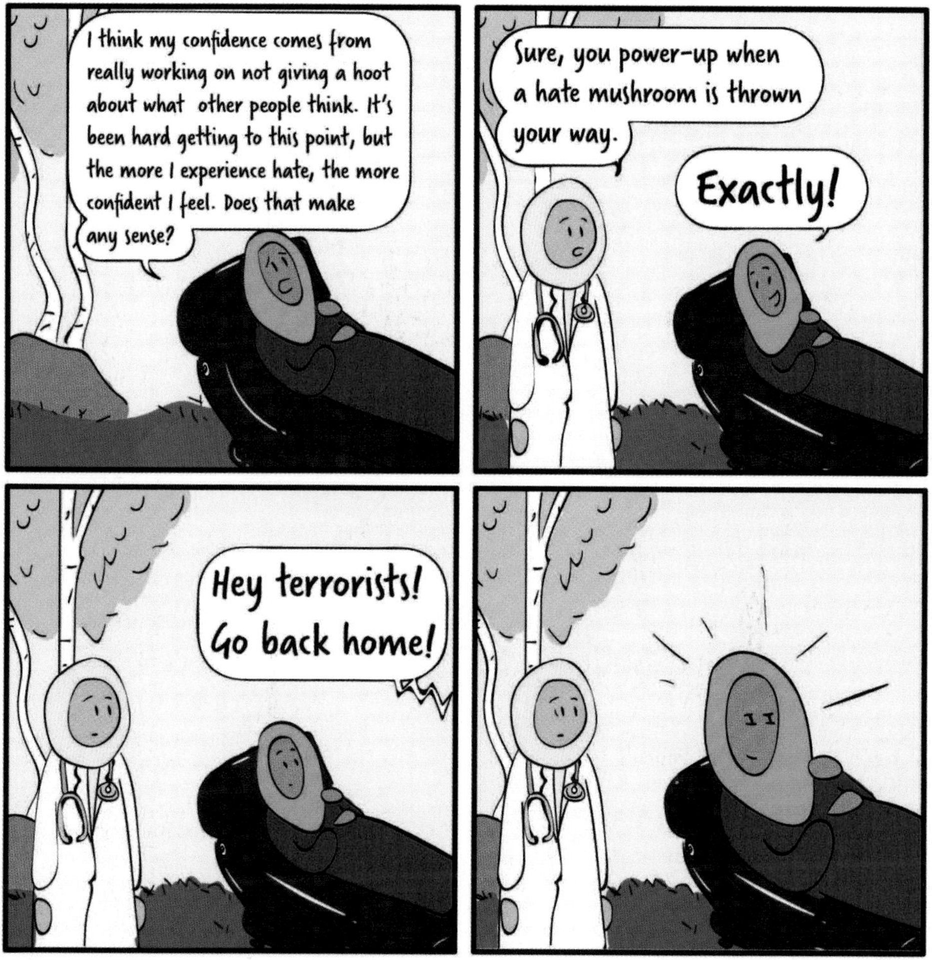
I think my confidence comes from really working on not giving a hoot about what other people think. It's been hard getting to this point, but the more I experience hate, the more confident I feel. Does that make any sense?
Sure, you power-up when a hate mushroom is thrown your way.
Exactly!
Hey terrorists! Go back home!

Let's play the "Guess Your Weight" game!
Let's go on the water ride first!
Why?

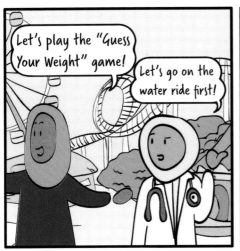

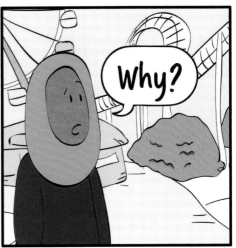

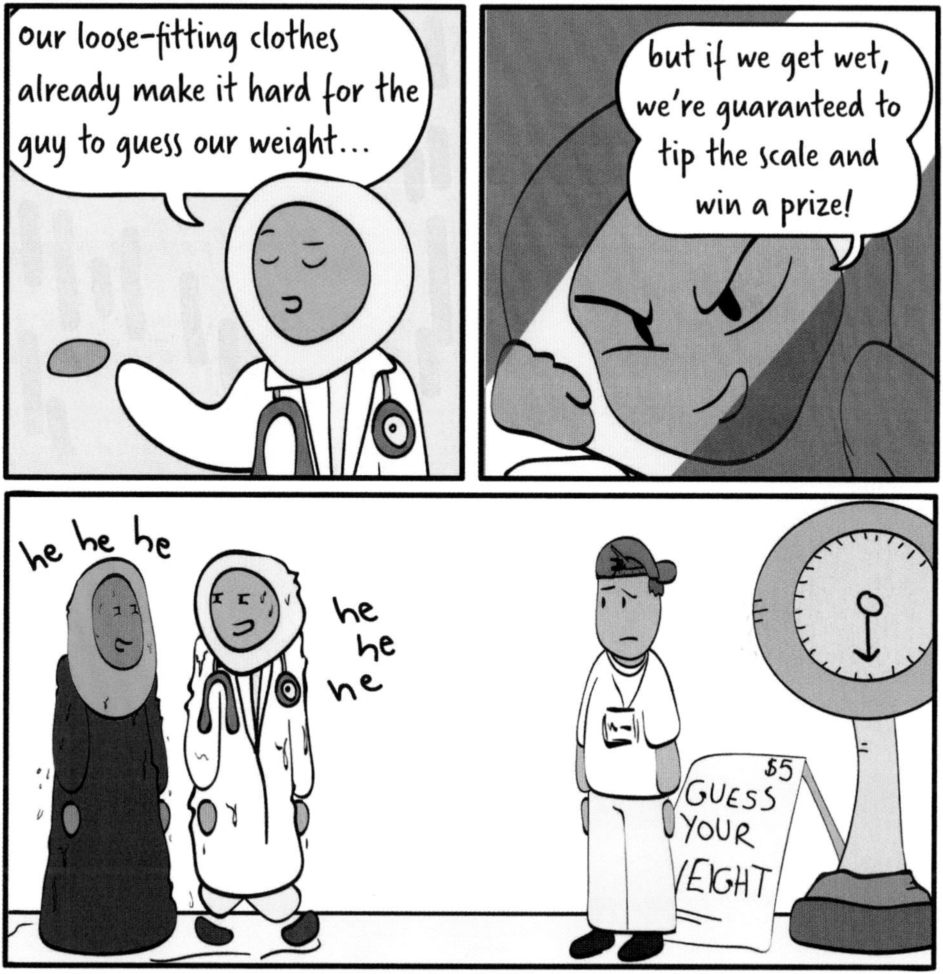
our loose-fitting clothes already make it hard for the guy to guess our weight...
but if we get wet, we're guaranteed to tip the scale and win a prize!
he he he
he he he
$5
GUESS YOUR WEIGHT

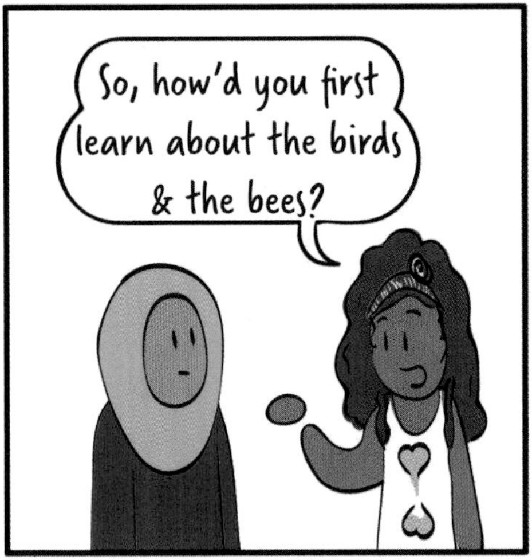
So, how'd you first learn about the birds & the bees?

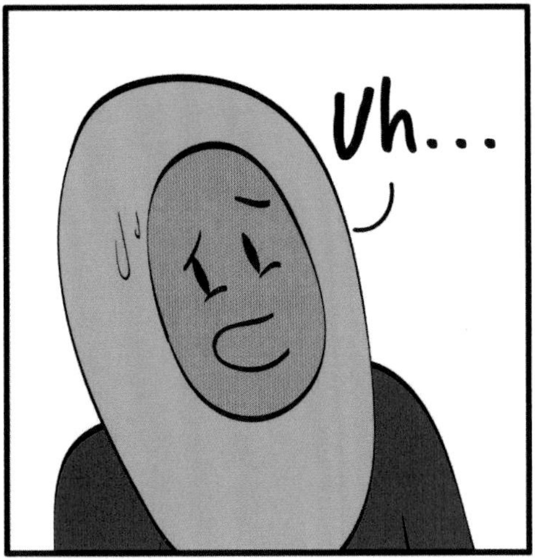
Uh...

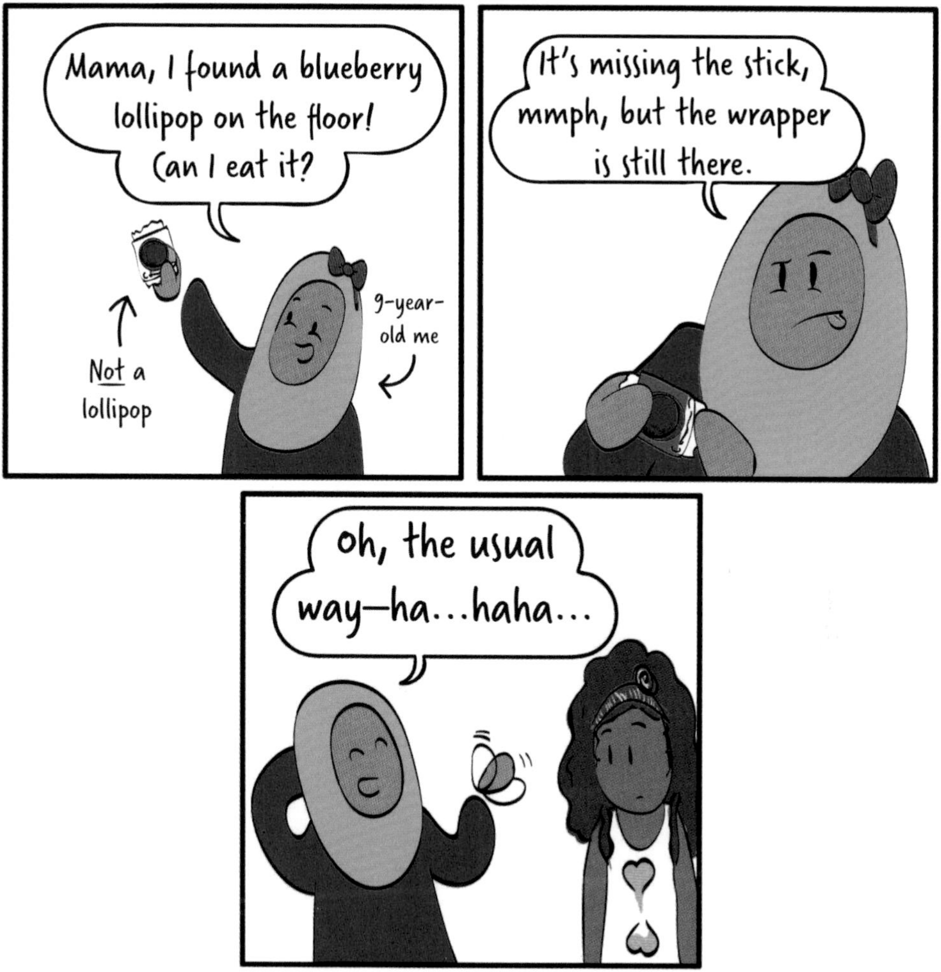
Mama, I found a blueberry lollipop on the floor! Can I eat it?
Not a lollipop
9-year-old me
It's missing the stick, mmph, but the wrapper is still there.
Oh, the usual way—ha...haha...

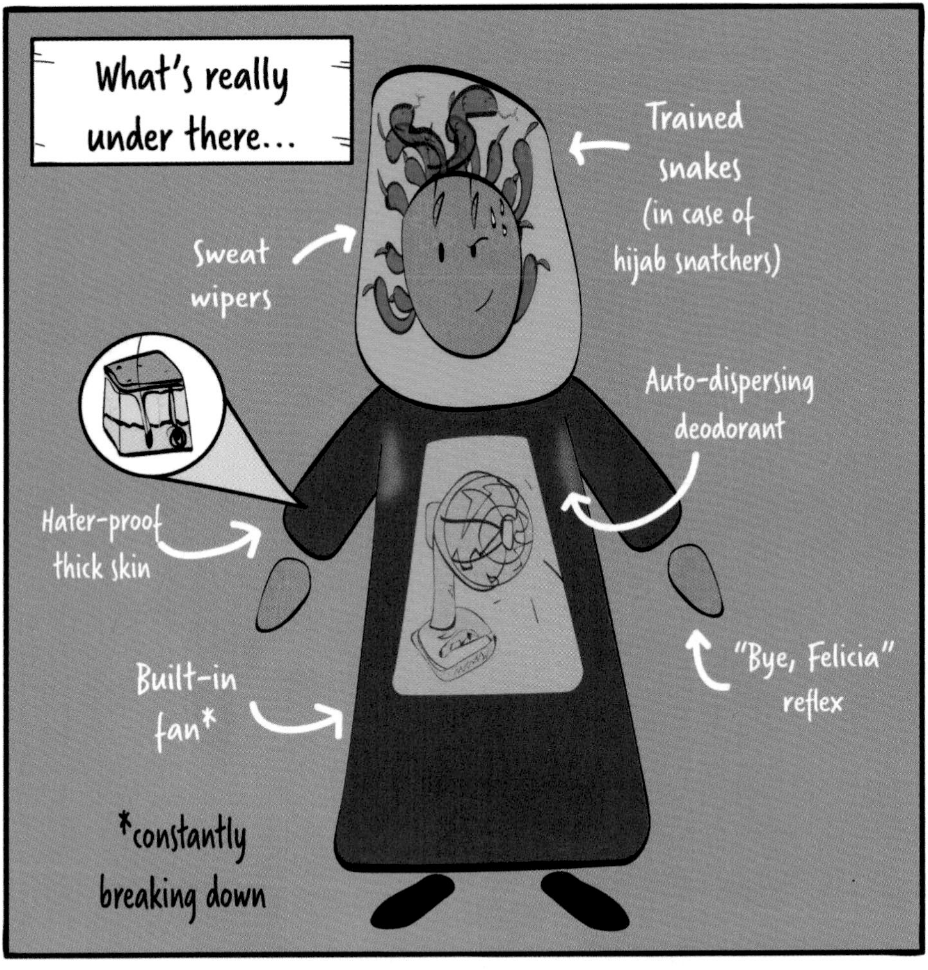
What's really under there...
Trained snakes (in case of hijab snatchers)
Sweat wipers
Auto-dispersing deodorant
Hater-proof thick skin
"Bye, Felicia" reflex
Built-in fan*
*constantly breaking down

Chapter 2: My Born Identity

I'm a first-generation American.

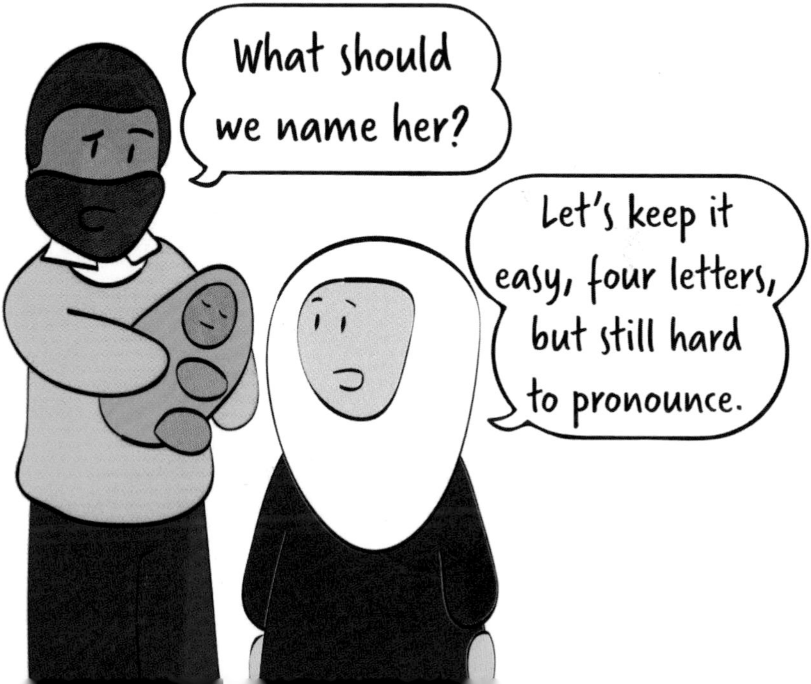
What should we name her?
Let's keep it easy, four letters, but still hard to pronounce.

And my family will not let me forget my heritage.

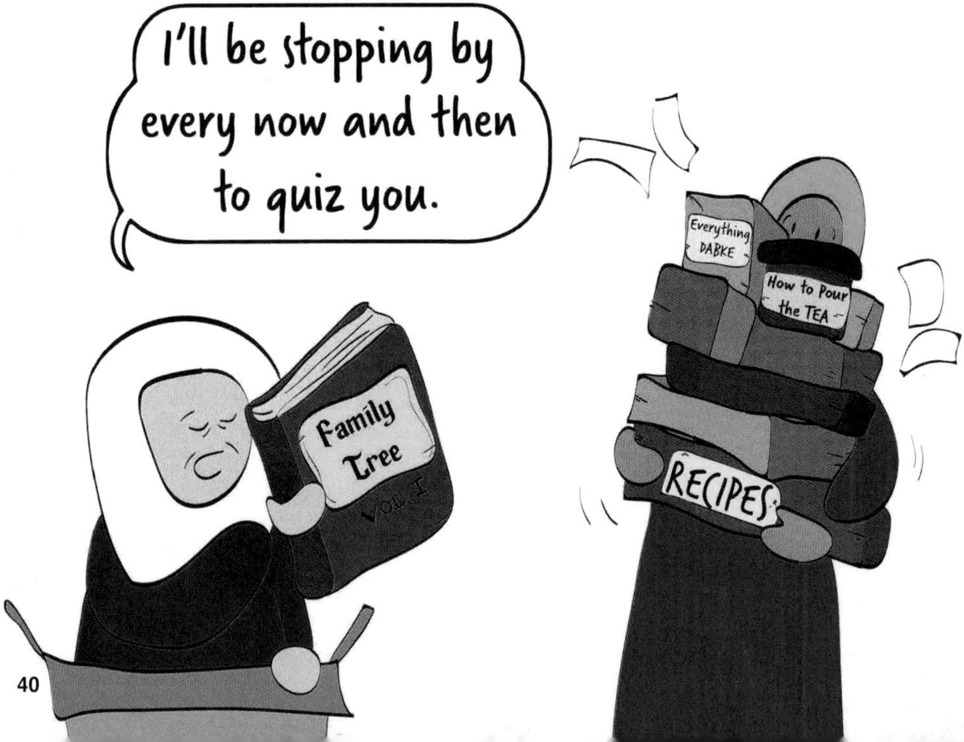
I'll be stopping by every now and then to quiz you.
Family Tree
VOL I
Everything DABKE
How to Pour the TEA
RECIPES

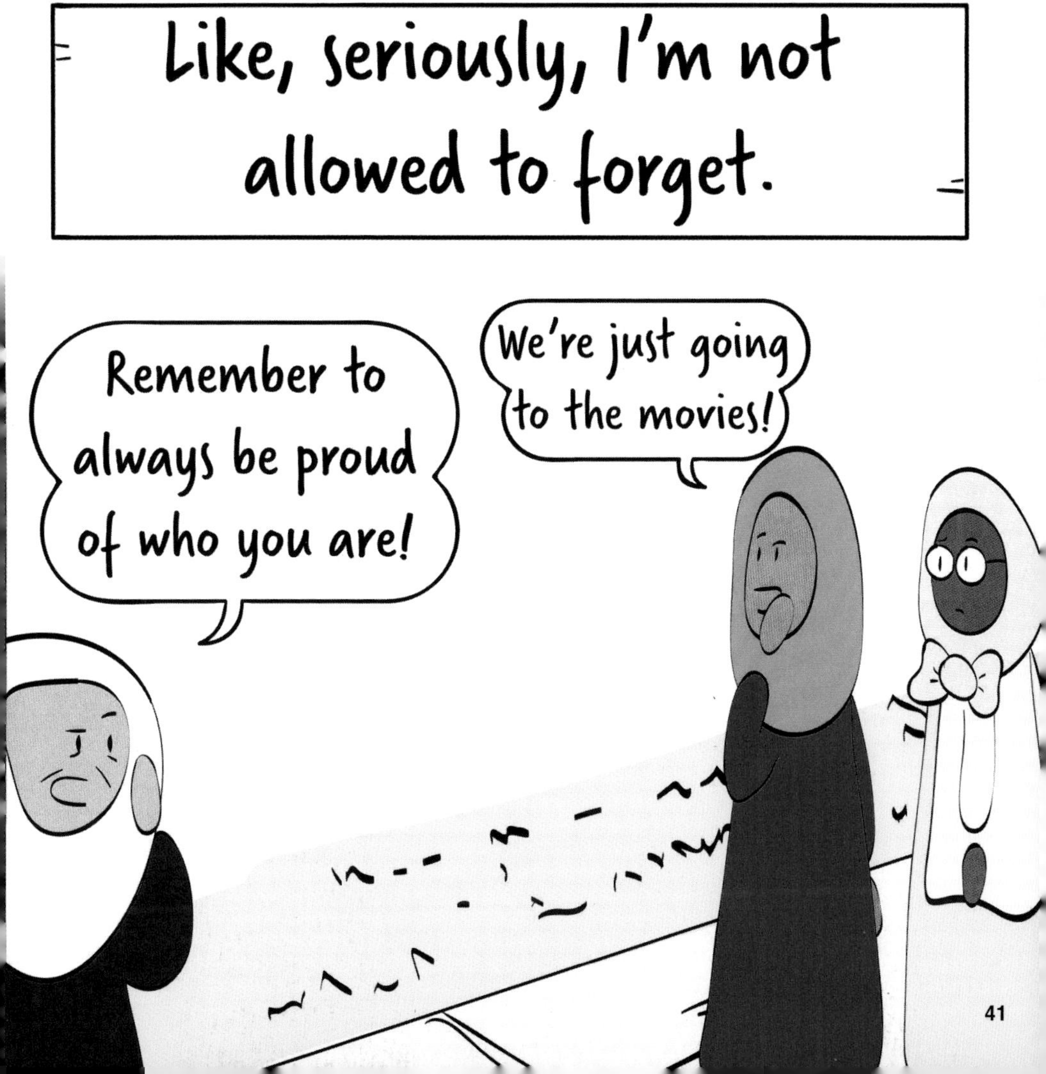
Like, seriously, I'm not allowed to forget.
Remember to always be proud of who you are!
We're just going to the movies!

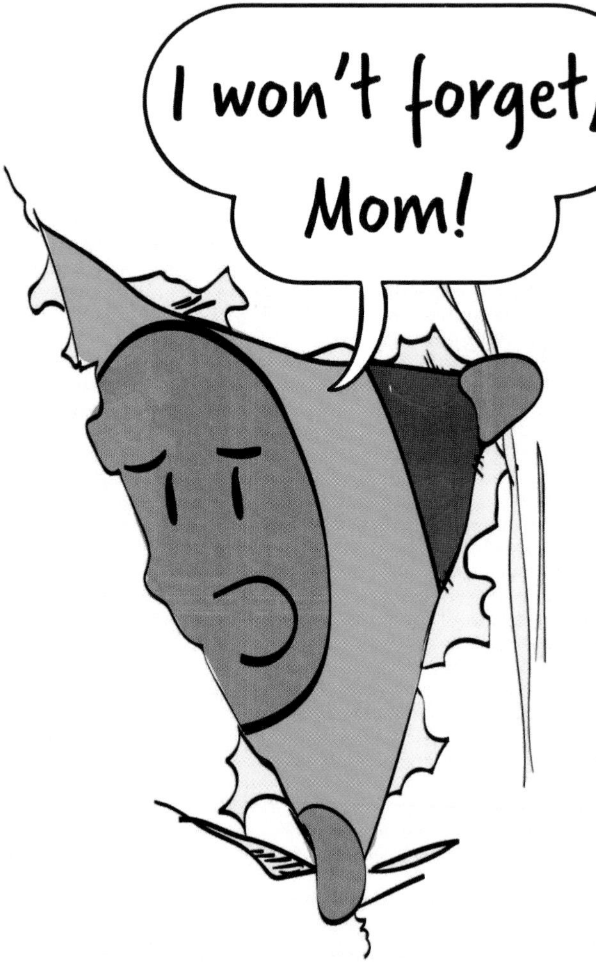
I won't forget, Mom!

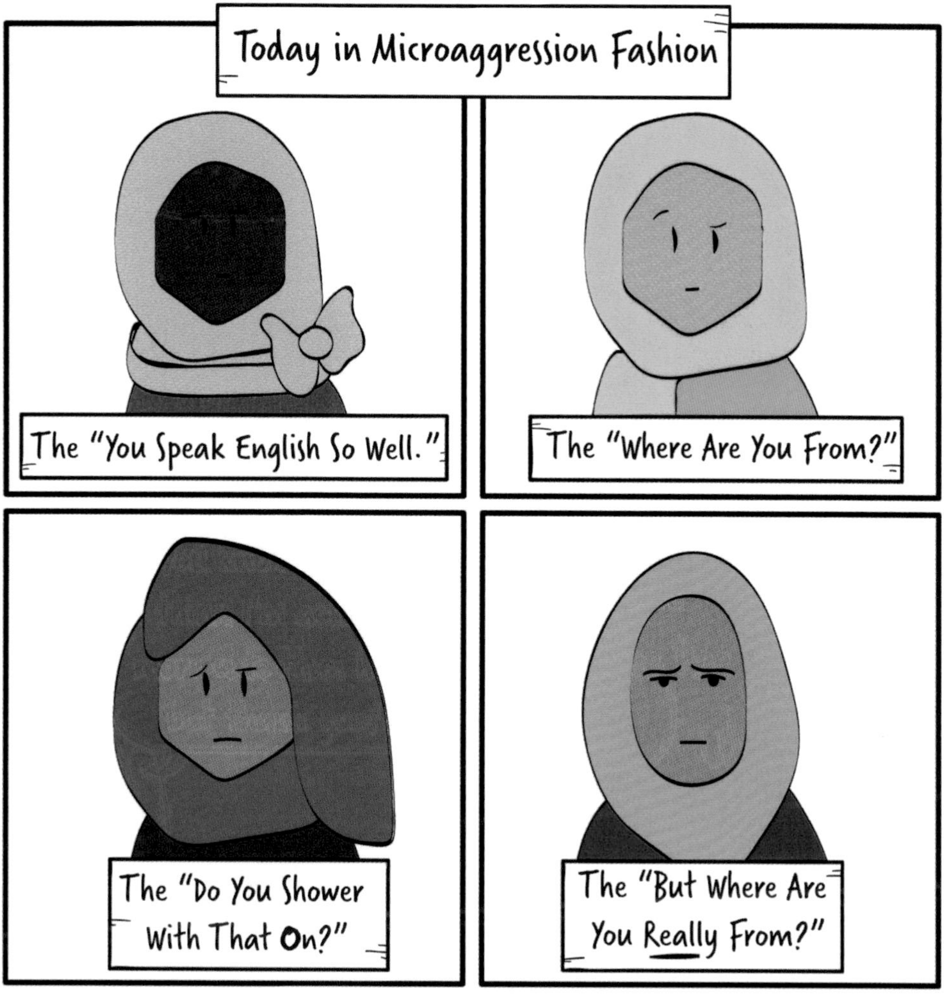
Today in Microaggression Fashion
The "You Speak English So Well."
The "Where Are You From?"
The "Do You Shower With That On?"
The "But Where Are You Really From?"

What do you want to be when you grow up, Huda?
5-year-old me
I wanna be a writer!

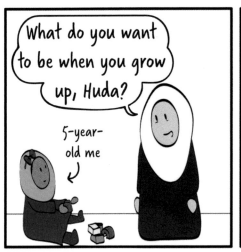

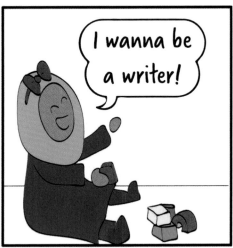

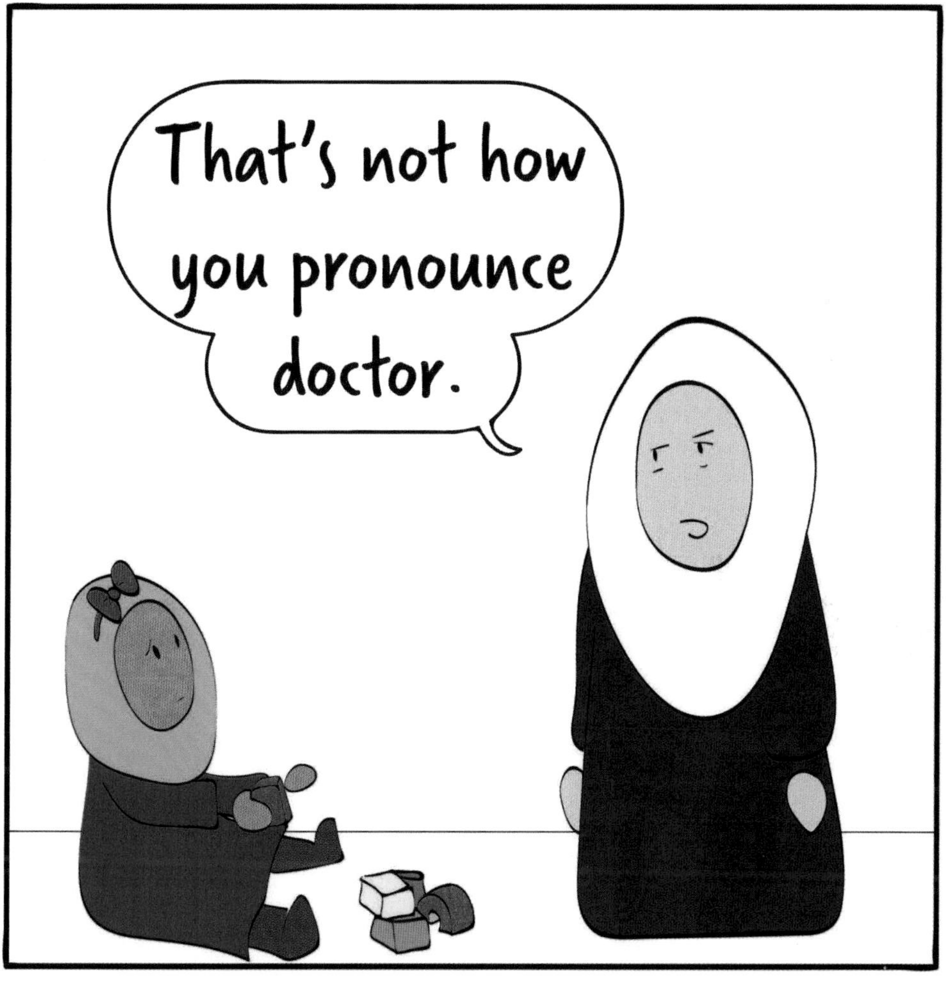
That's not how you pronounce doctor.

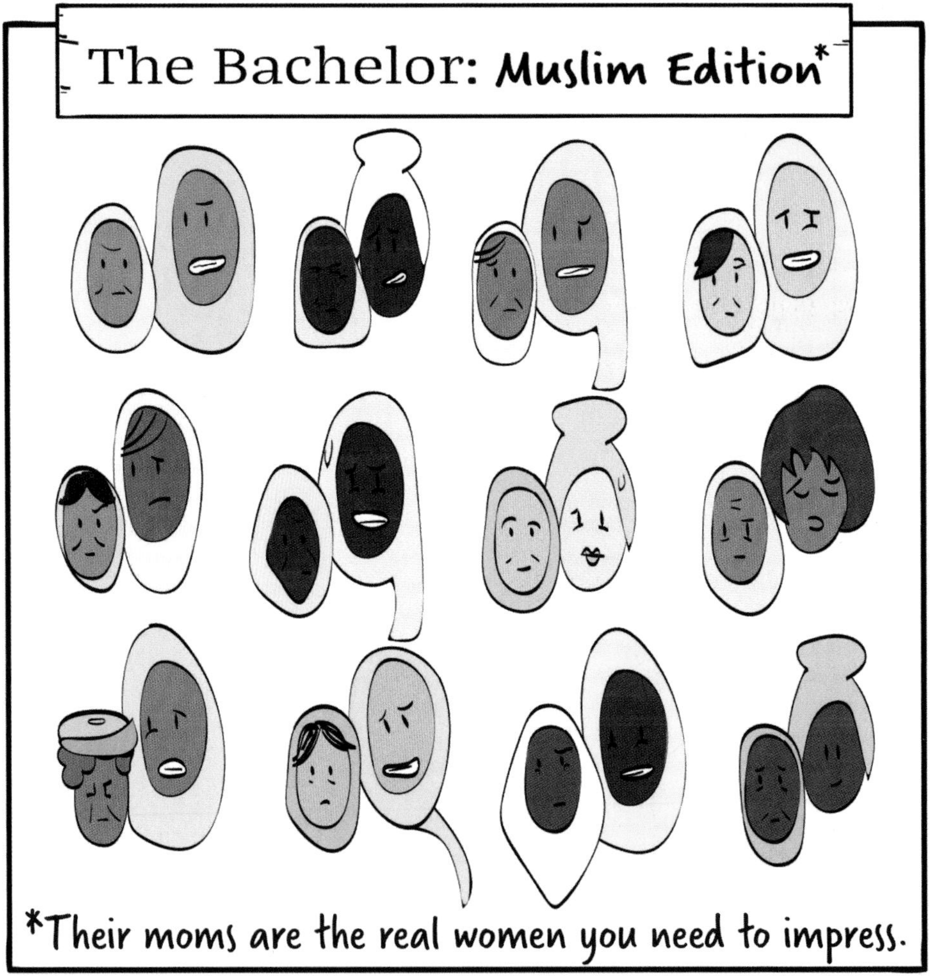
The Bachelor: Muslim Edition*
*Their moms are the real women you need to impress.

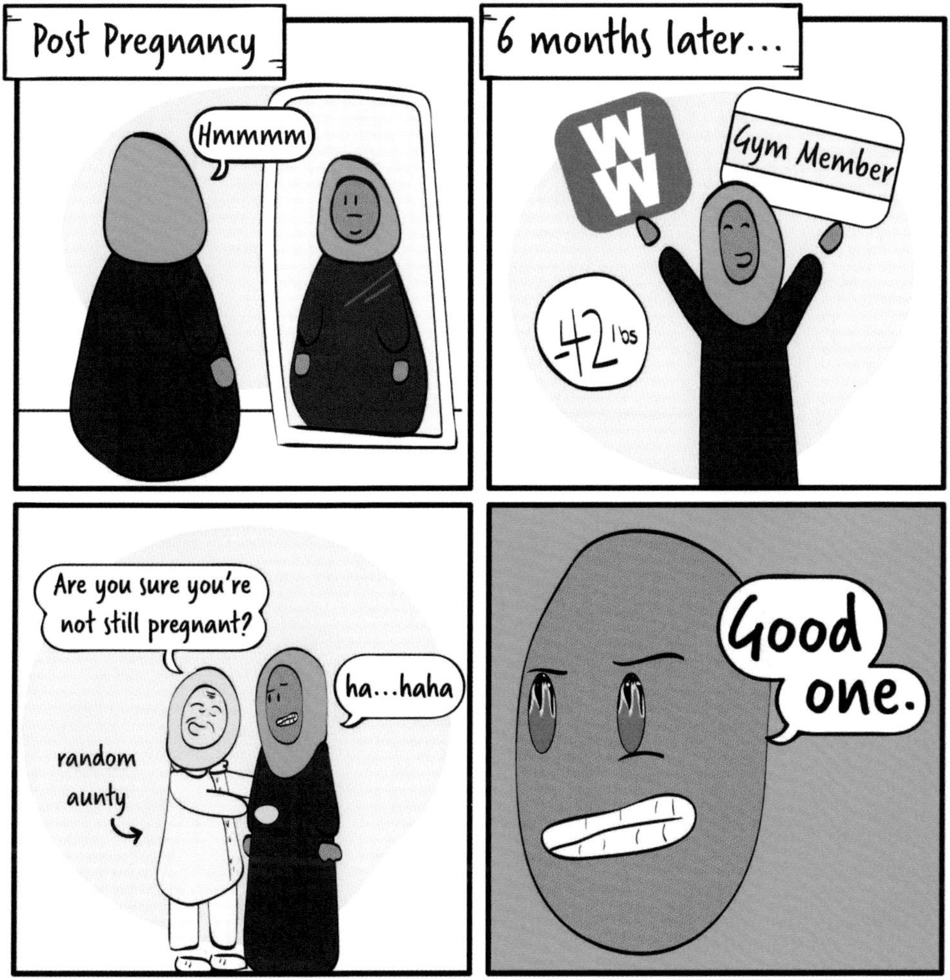
Post Pregnancy
Hmmmm
6 months later...
WW
Gym Member
-42 lbs
Are you sure you're not still pregnant?
ha...haha
random aunty
Good one.

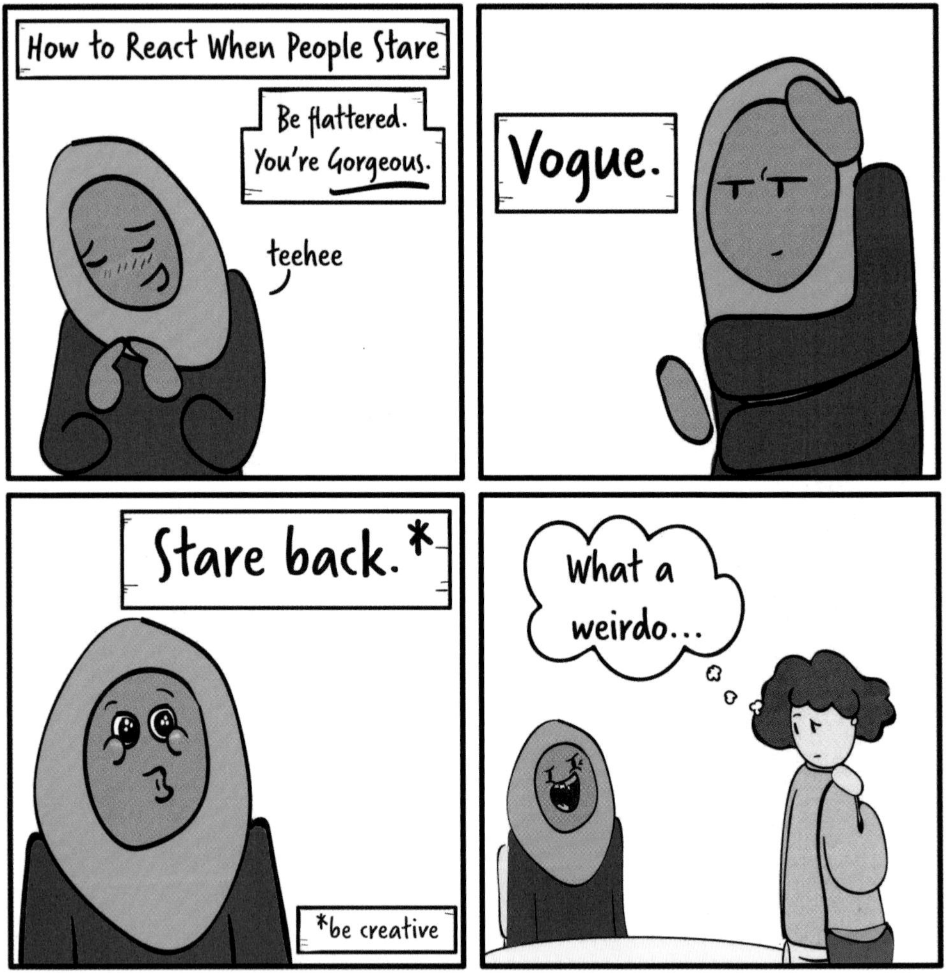
How to React When People Stare
Be flattered. You're Gorgeous.
teehee
Vogue.
Stare back.*
*be creative
What a weirdo...

Turnabout

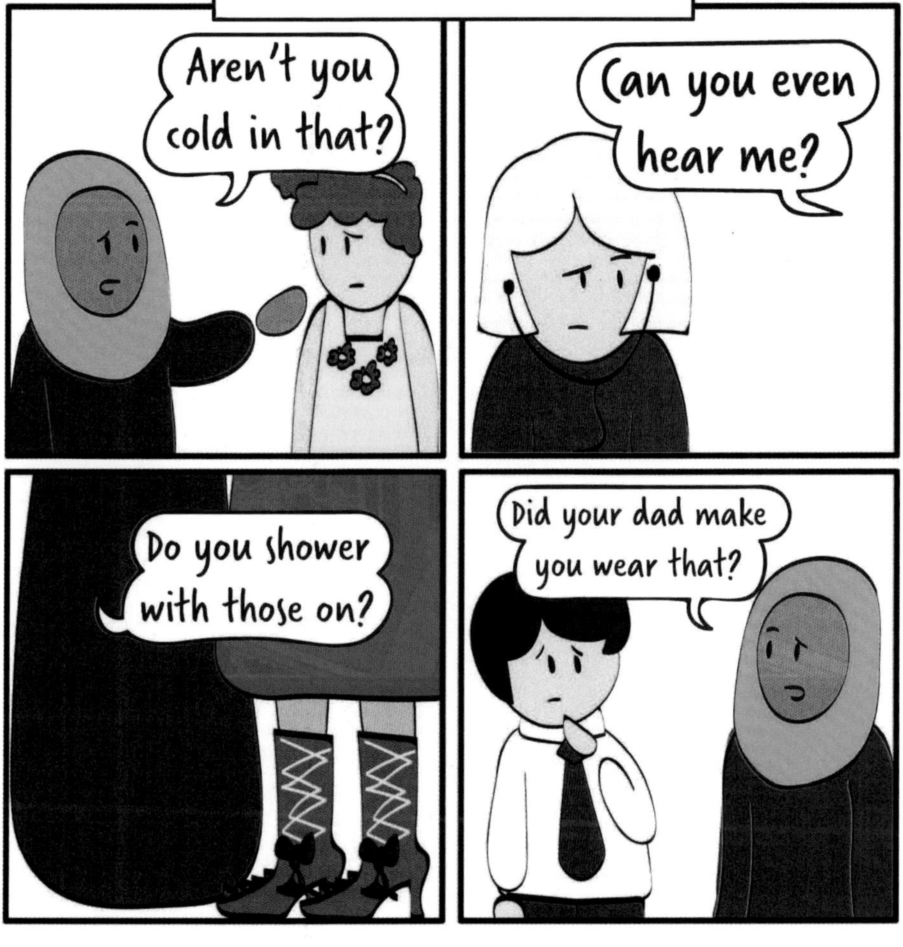

Aren't you cold in that?
Can you even hear me?
Do you shower with those on?
Did your dad make you wear that?

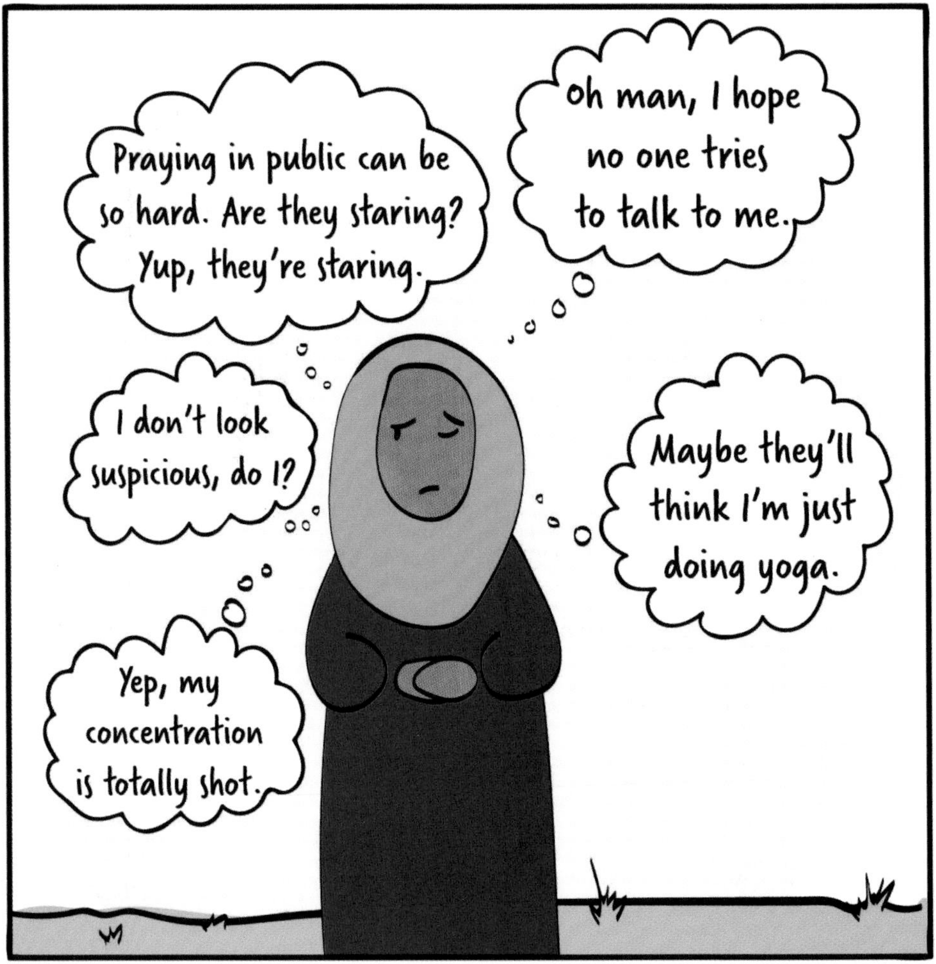
Praying in public can be so hard. Are they staring? Yup, they're staring.
Oh man, I hope no one tries to talk to me.
I don't look suspicious, do I?
Maybe they'll think I'm just doing yoga.
Yep, my concentration is totally shot.

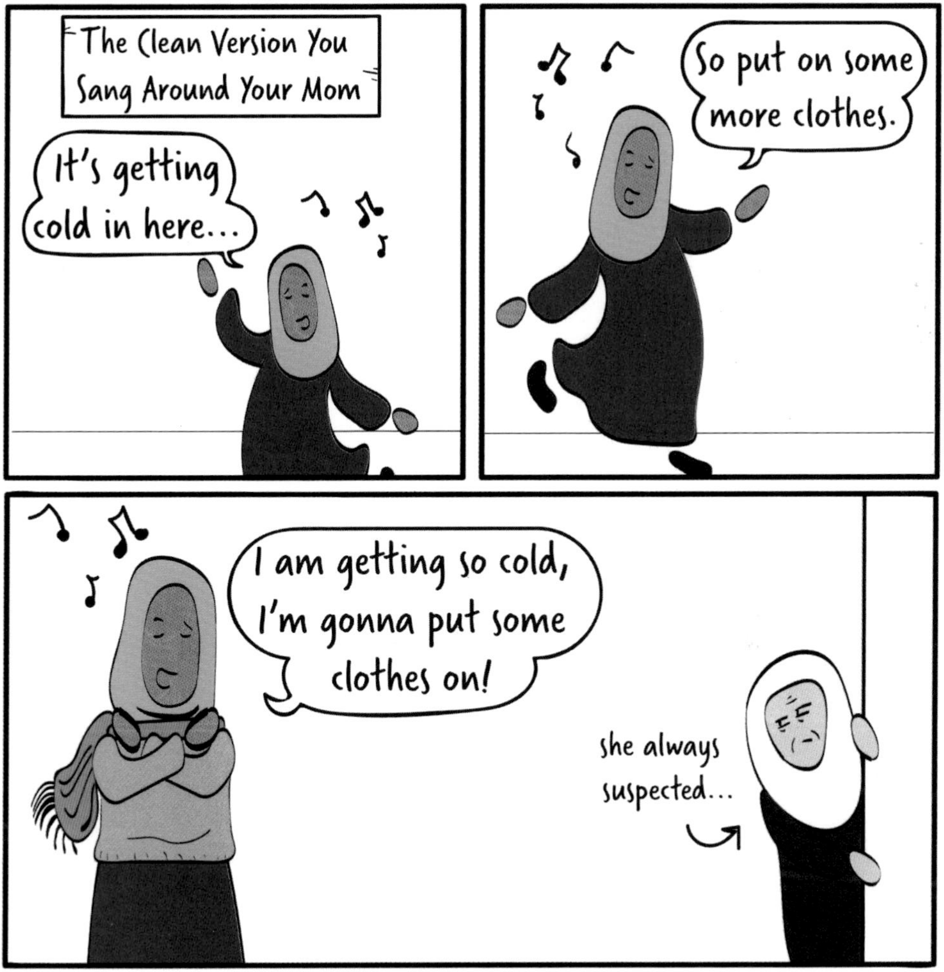
The Clean Version You Sang Around Your Mom
It's getting cold in here...
So put on some more clothes.
I am getting so cold, I'm gonna put some clothes on!
she always suspected...

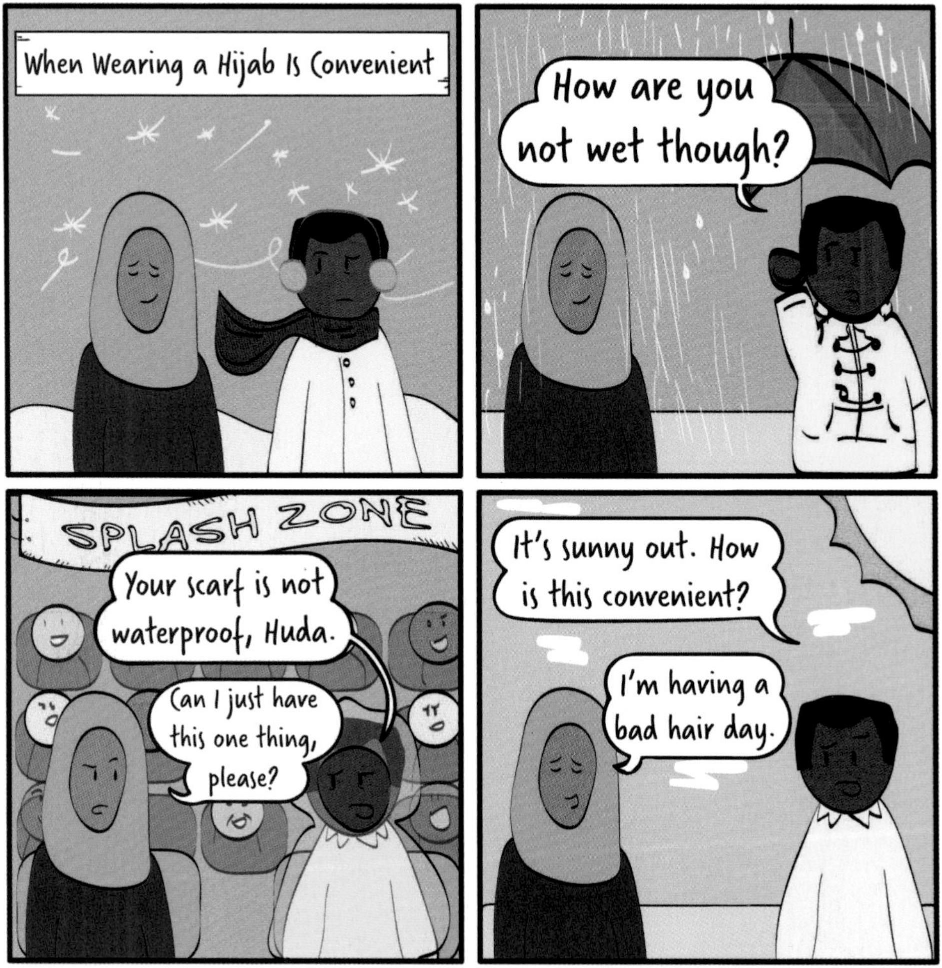
When Wearing a Hijab Is Convenient
How are you not wet though?
SPLASH ZONE
Your scarf is not waterproof, Huda.
Can I just have this one thing, please?
It's sunny out. How is this convenient?
I'm having a bad hair day.

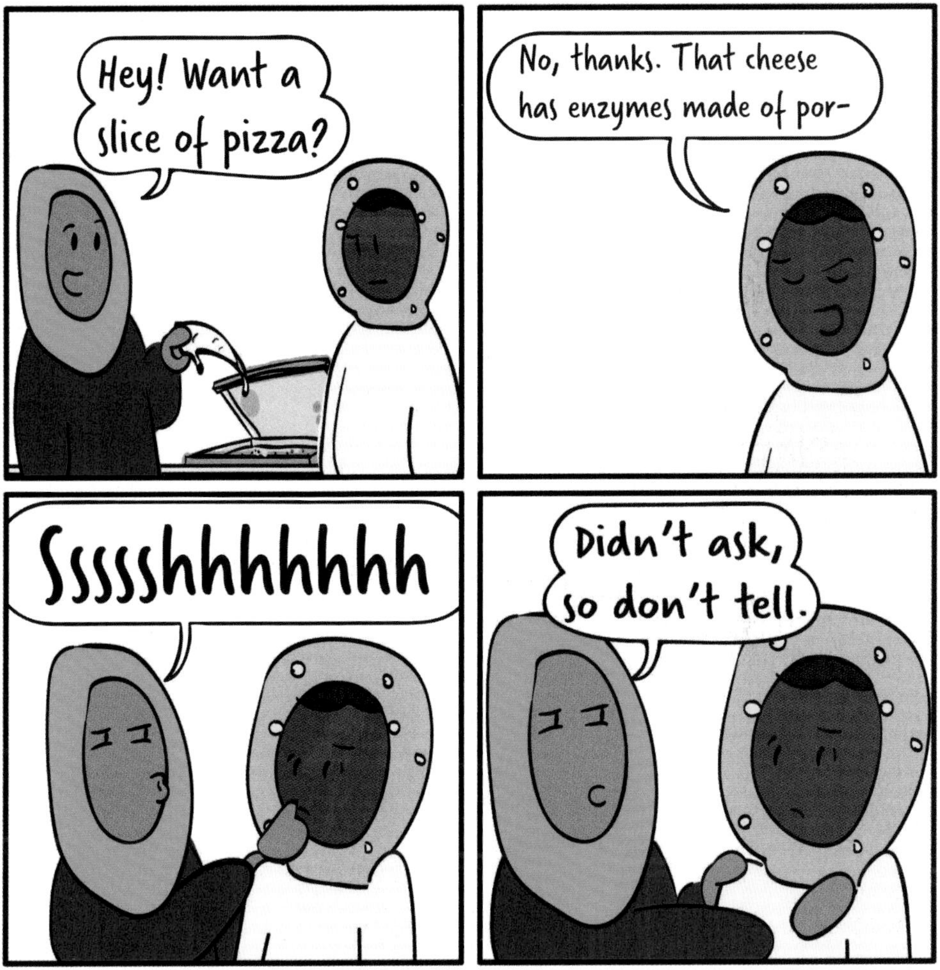
Hey! Want a slice of pizza?
No, thanks. That cheese has enzymes made of por-
Sssssshhhhhhh
Didn't ask, so don't tell.

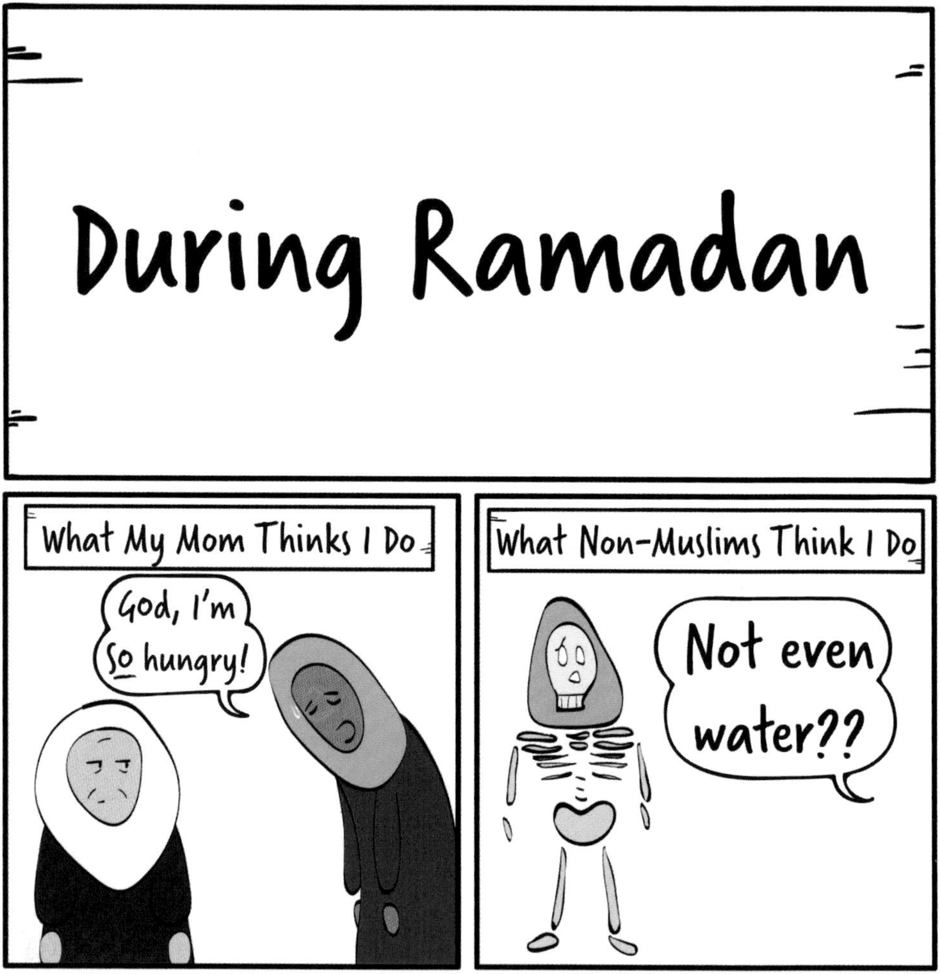
During Ramadan
What My Mom Thinks I Do
God, I'm So hungry!
What Non-Muslims Think I Do
Not even water??

What I Think I Do
What I Actually Do
still not Maghrib

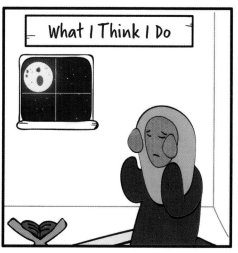

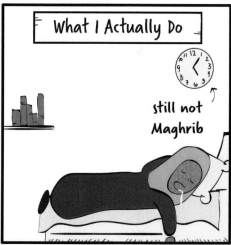

Halaloween

(ha-la-low-een) n. [arabeesi]:

the day after Halloween
when all the candy goes on sale.

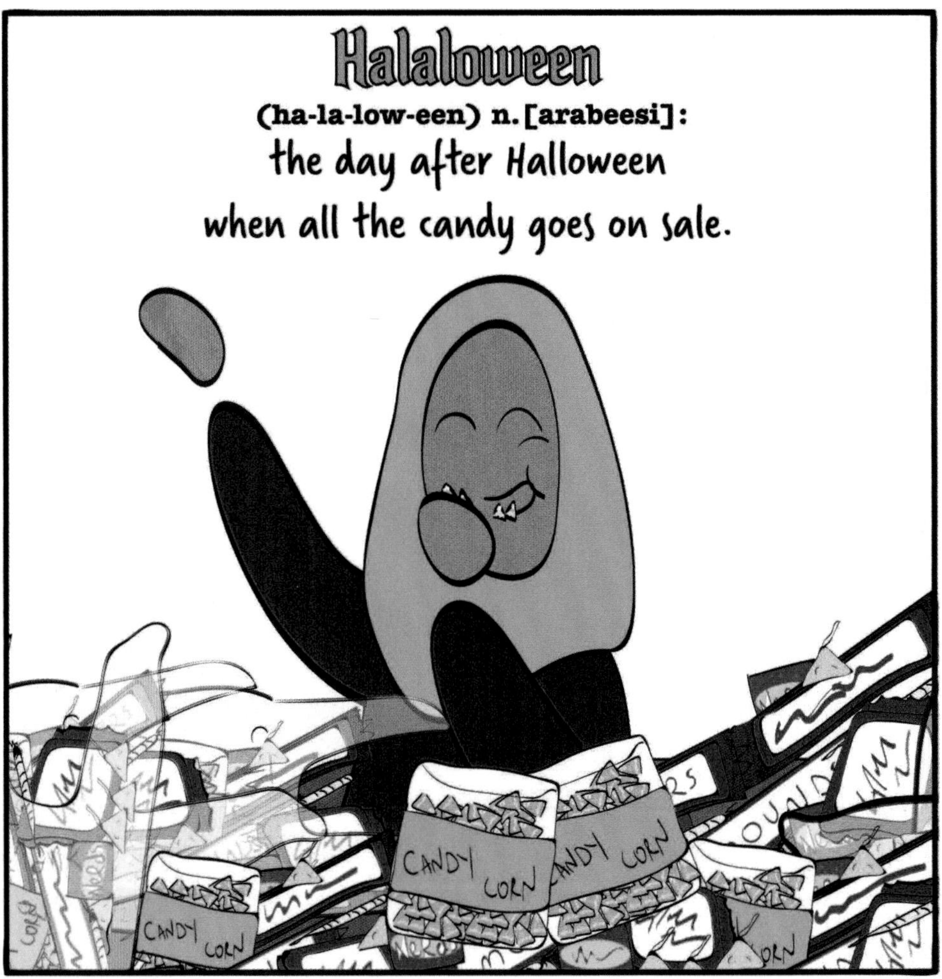
CANDY CORN
CANDY CORN
CANDY CORN

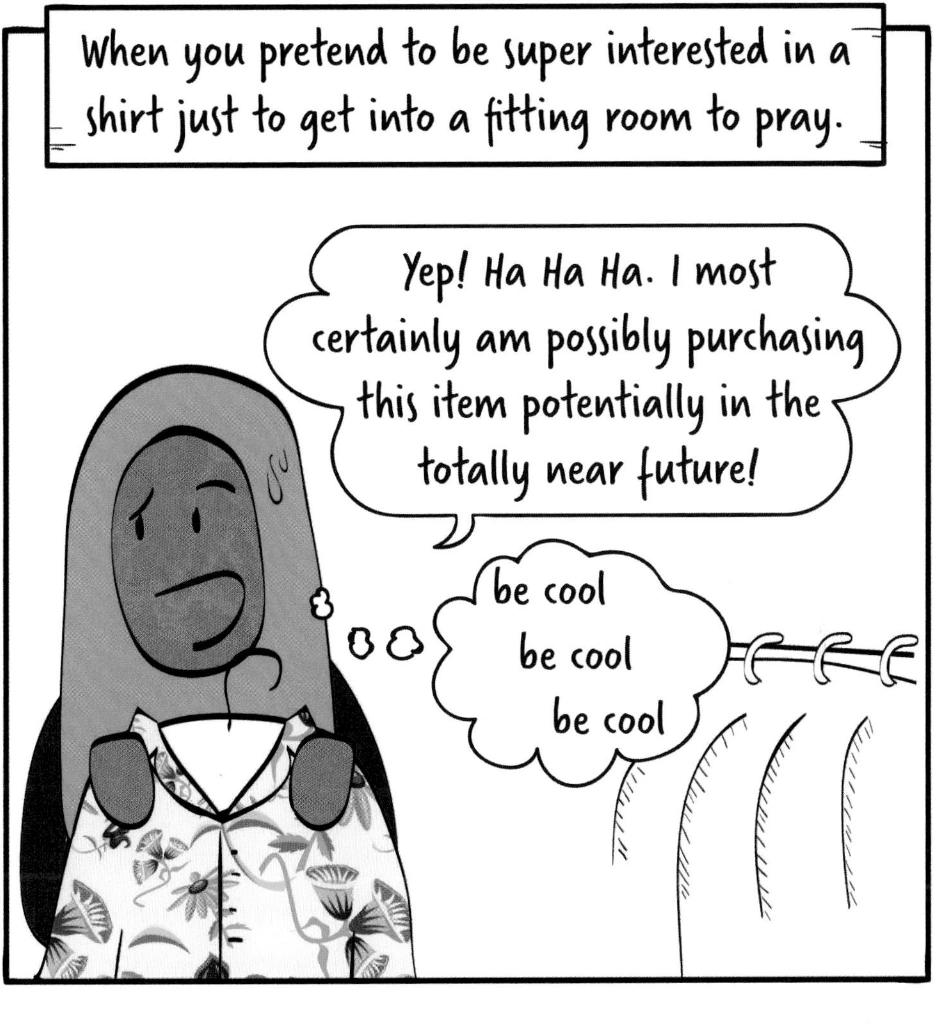
When you pretend to be super interested in a shirt just to get into a fitting room to pray.
Yep! Ha Ha Ha. I most certainly am possibly purchasing this item potentially in the totally near future!
be cool
be cool
be cool

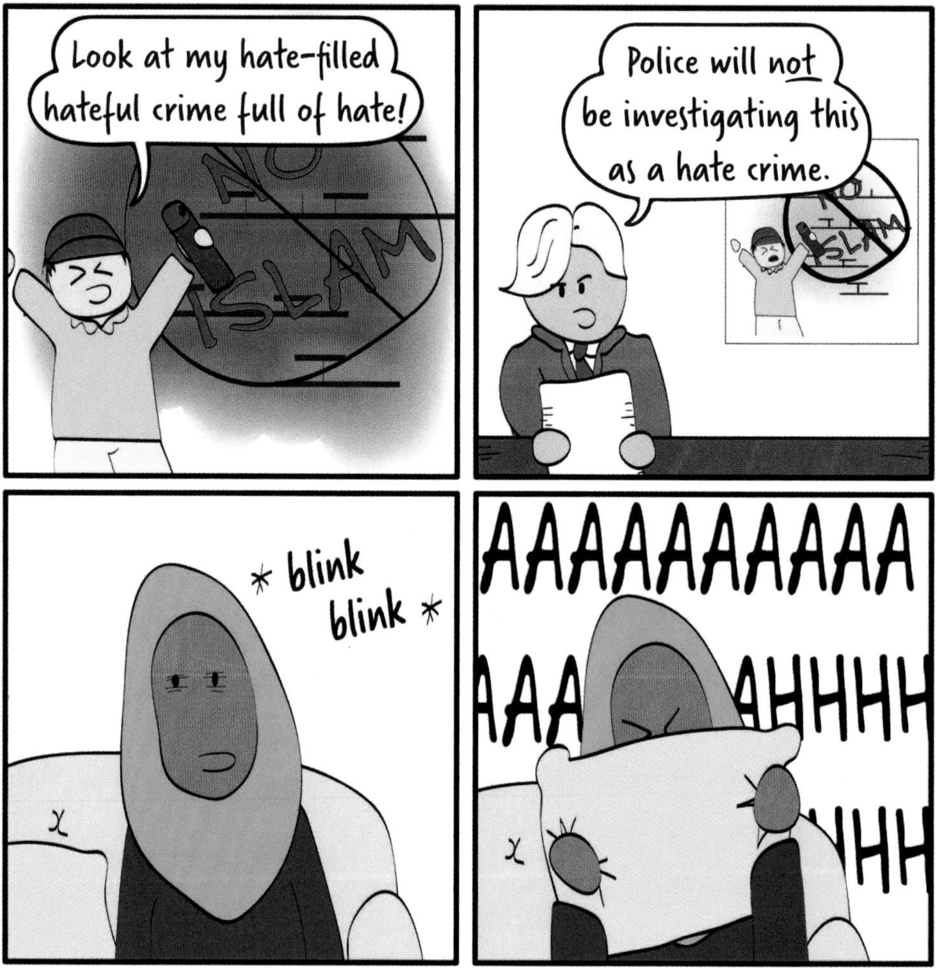
Look at my hate-filled hateful crime full of hate!
NO ISLAM
Police will not be investigating this as a hate crime.
NO ISLAM
* blink blink *
AAAAAAAAAAA
AAA AHHHH
HHH

In other news, there has been an increase of Muslim-on-pillow crime.
Could this be a new terror on sleep? Up next.

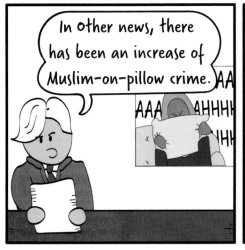

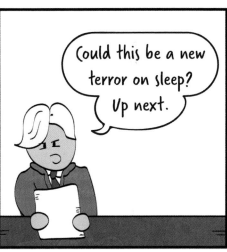

When You Try to Teach Your Friends New Words

So, have you filed your taxes yet?
InshaAllah.
That's not what that—
InshaaaAllah.

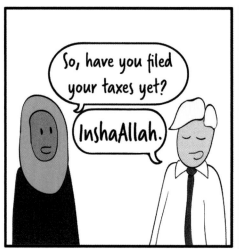

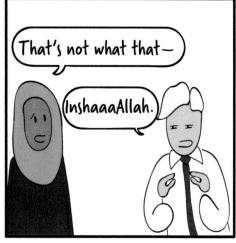

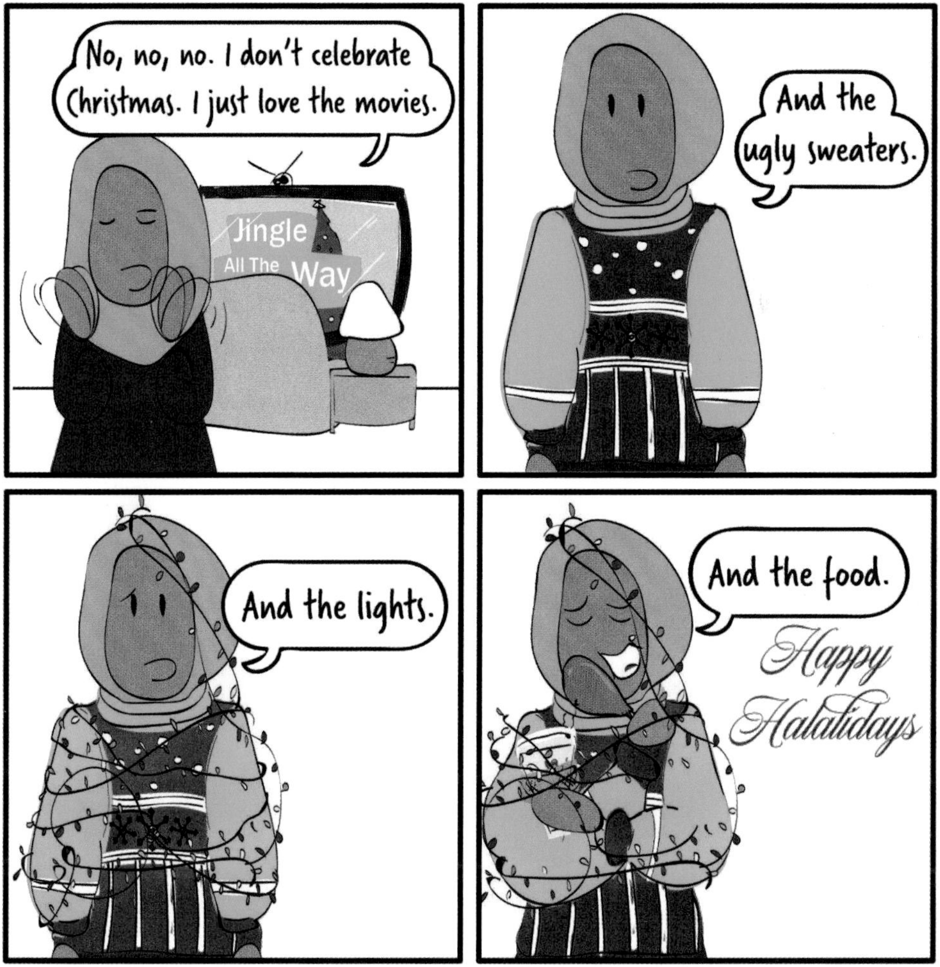
No, no, no. I don't celebrate Christmas. I just love the movies.
Jingle All The Way
And the ugly sweaters.
And the lights.
And the food.
Happy Halalidays

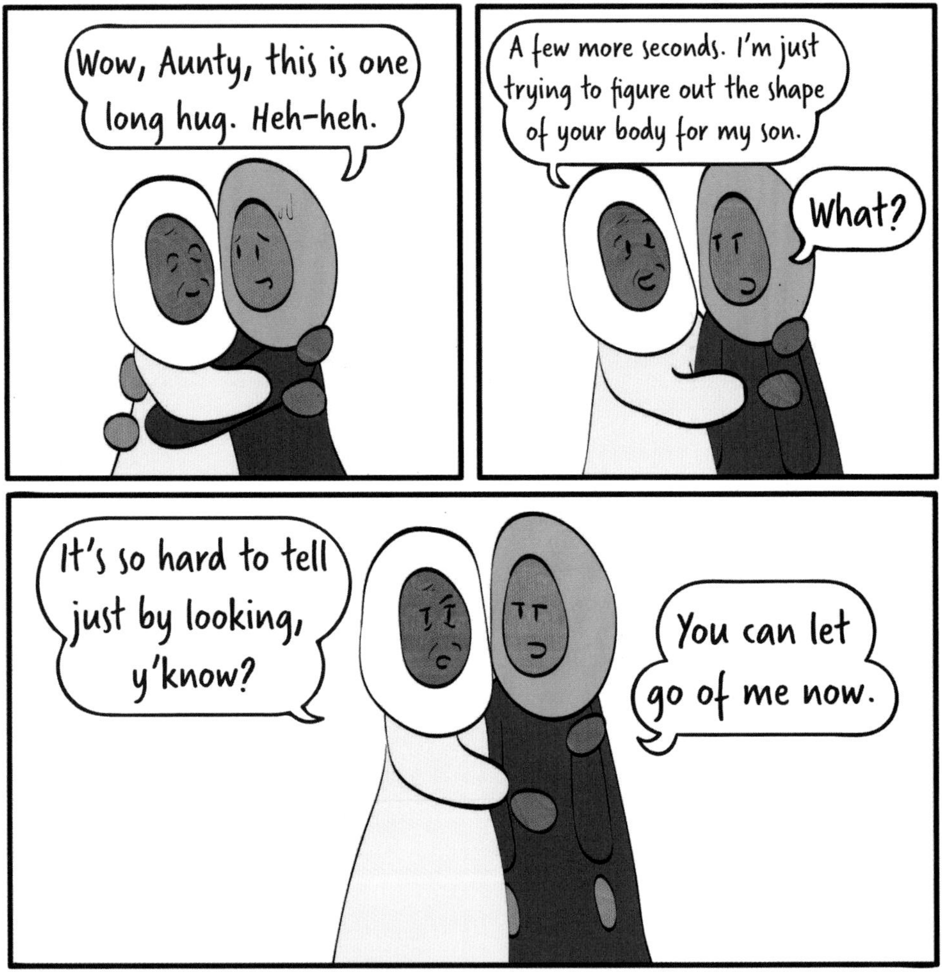
Wow, Aunty, this is one long hug. Heh-heh.
A few more seconds. I'm just trying to figure out the shape of your body for my son.
What?
It's so hard to tell just by looking, y'know?
You can let go of me now.

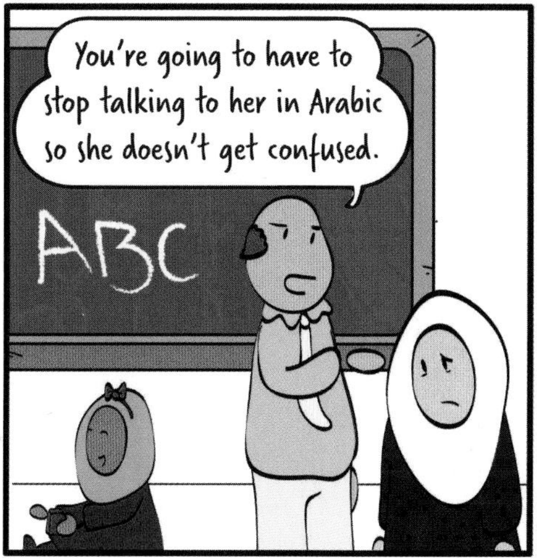

You're going to have to stop talking to her in Arabic so she doesn't get confused.
ABC

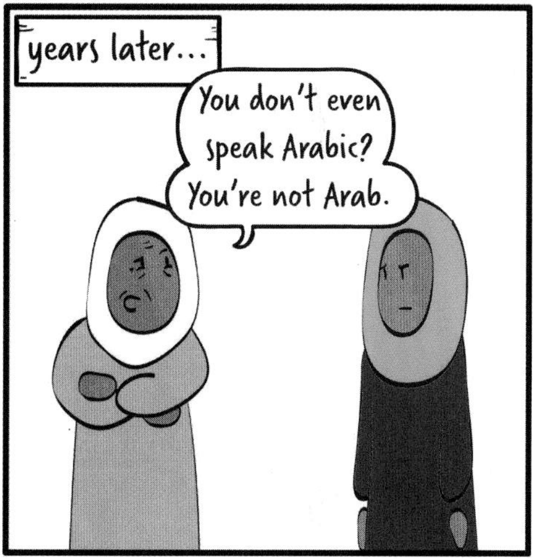

years later...
You don't even speak Arabic? You're not Arab.

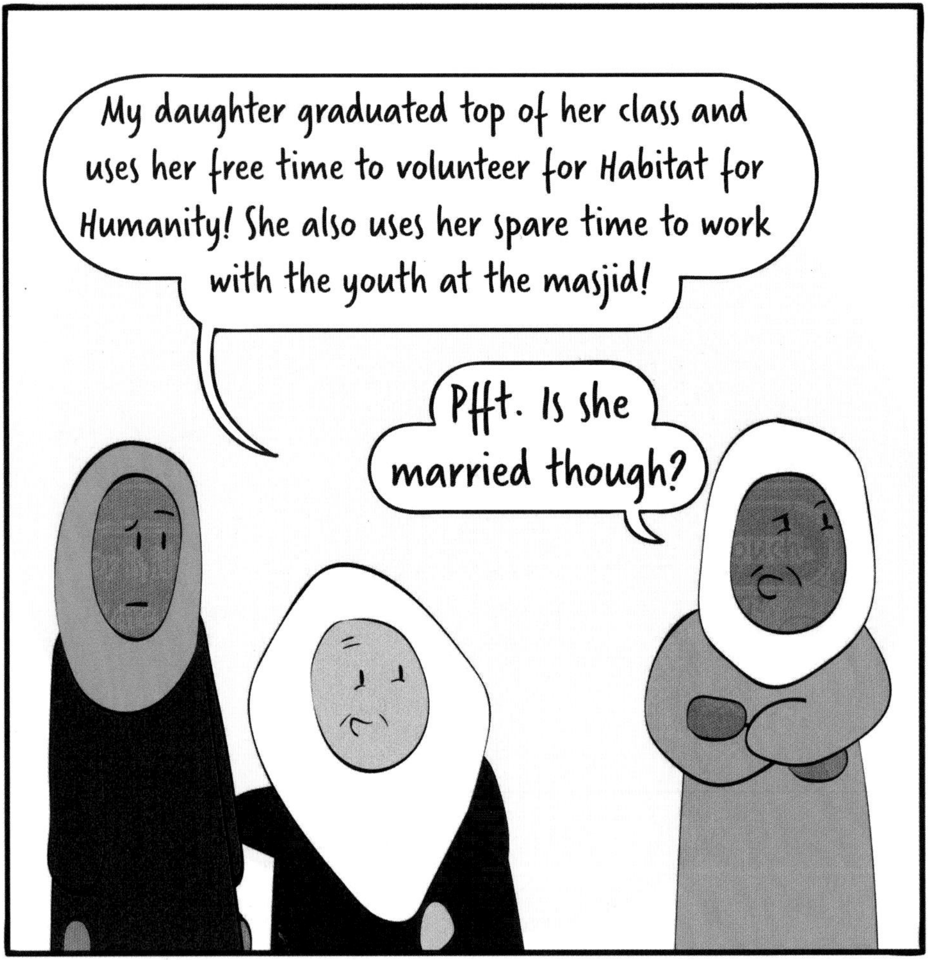
My daughter graduated top of her class and uses her free time to volunteer for Habitat for Humanity! She also uses her spare time to work with the youth at the masjid!
Pfft. Is she married though?

Chapter 3: Married to the Struggle

This is my husband, Gehad.

It's like Jihad, but with a G!

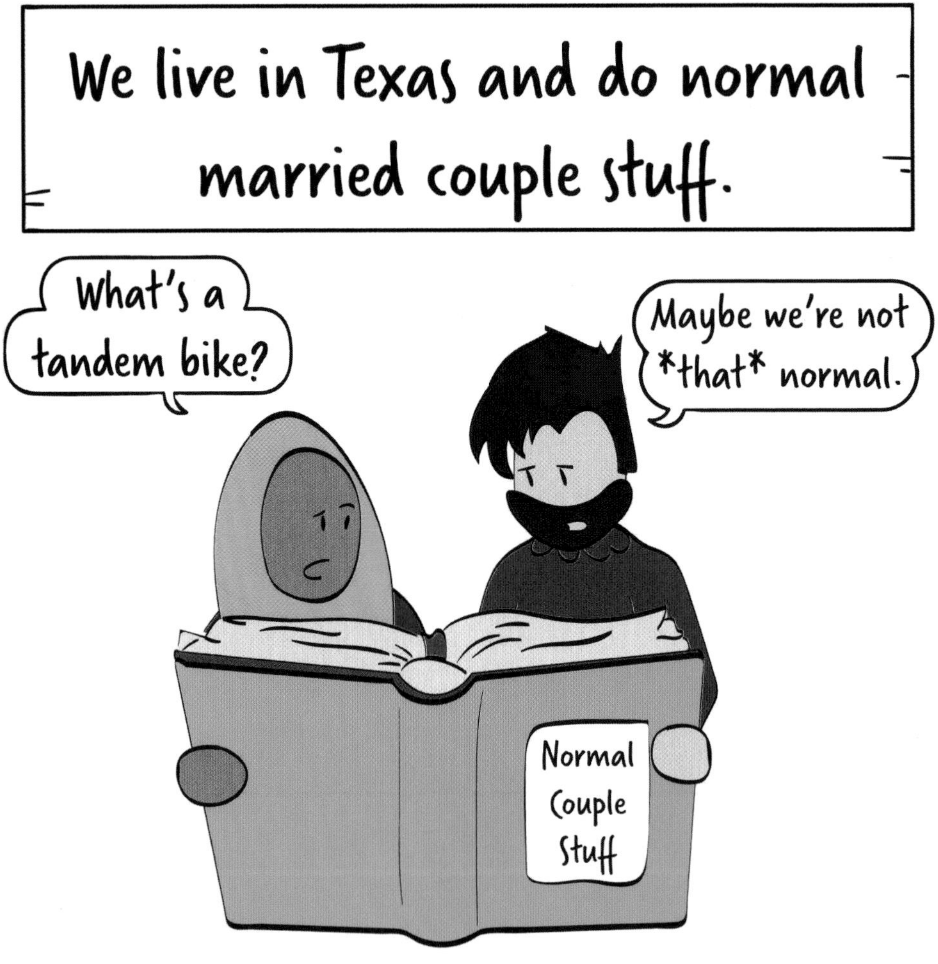
We live in Texas and do normal married couple stuff.
What's a tandem bike?
Maybe we're not *that* normal.
Normal Couple Stuff

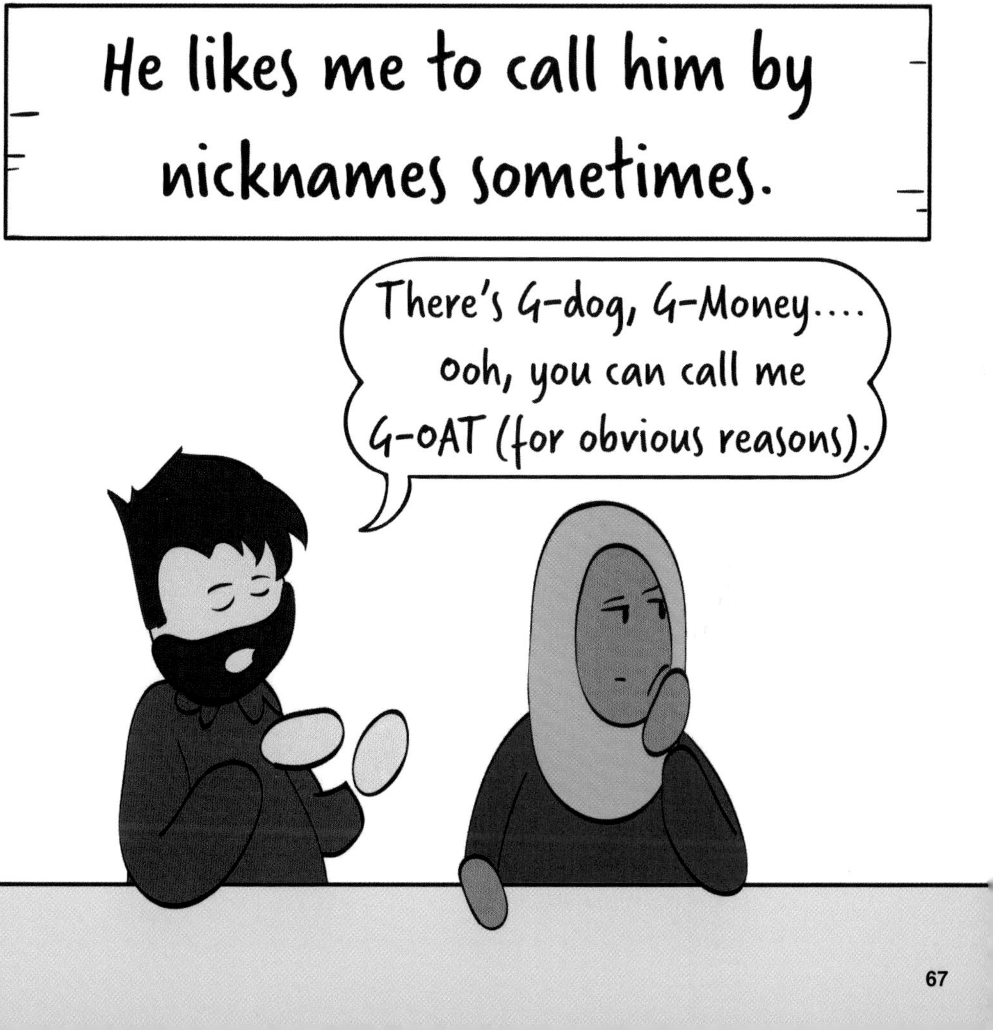
He likes me to call him by nicknames sometimes.
There's G-dog, G-Money.... Ooh, you can call me G-OAT (for obvious reasons).

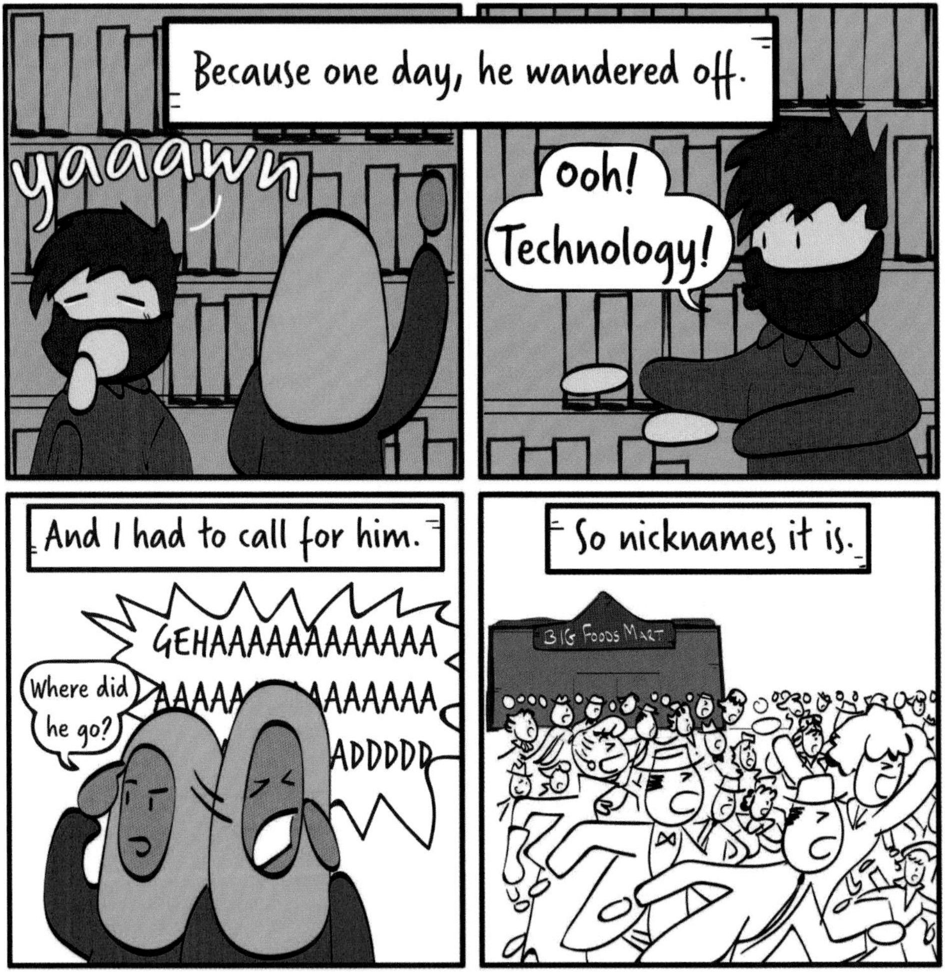

Because one day, he wandered off.
yaaawn
Ooh! Technology!
And I had to call for him.
Where did he go?
GEHAAAAAAAAAAAA
So nicknames it is.
BIG FOODS MART

How'd You Meet? (me)

How'd You Meet? (him)

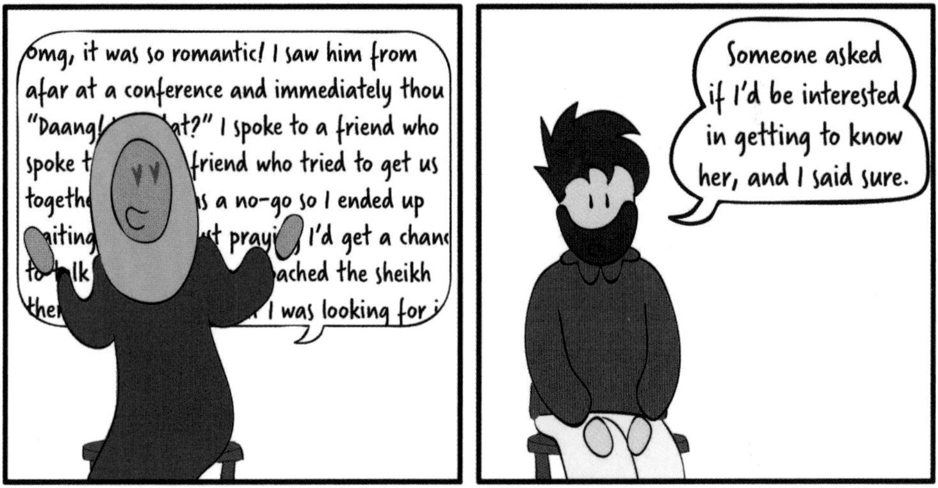
Omg, it was so romantic! I saw him from afar at a conference and immediately thou "Daang! at?" I spoke to a friend who spoke t friend who tried to get us togeth s a no-go so I ended up aiting st prayi I'd get a chanc to lk ached the sheikh ther I was looking for
Someone asked if I'd be interested in getting to know her, and I said sure.

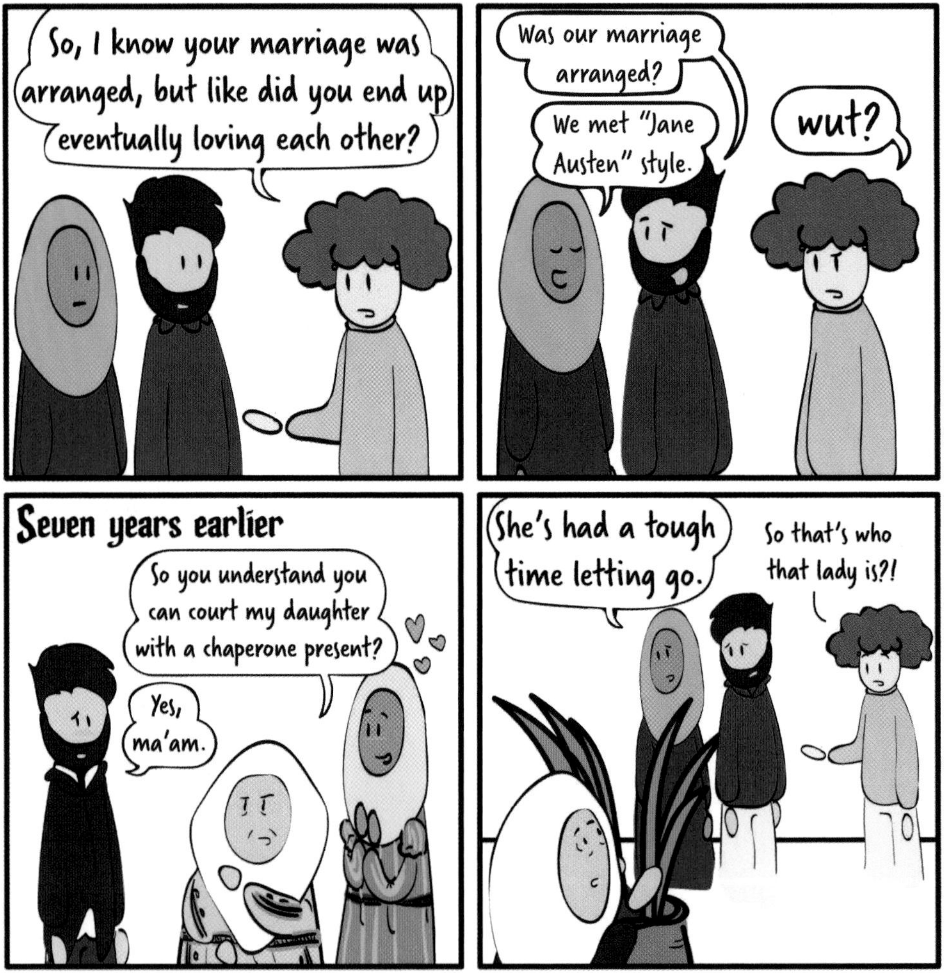
So, I know your marriage was arranged, but like did you end up eventually loving each other?
Was our marriage arranged?
We met "Jane Austen" style.
wut?
Seven years earlier
So you understand you can court my daughter with a chaperone present?
Yes, ma'am.
She's had a tough time letting go.
So that's who that lady is?!

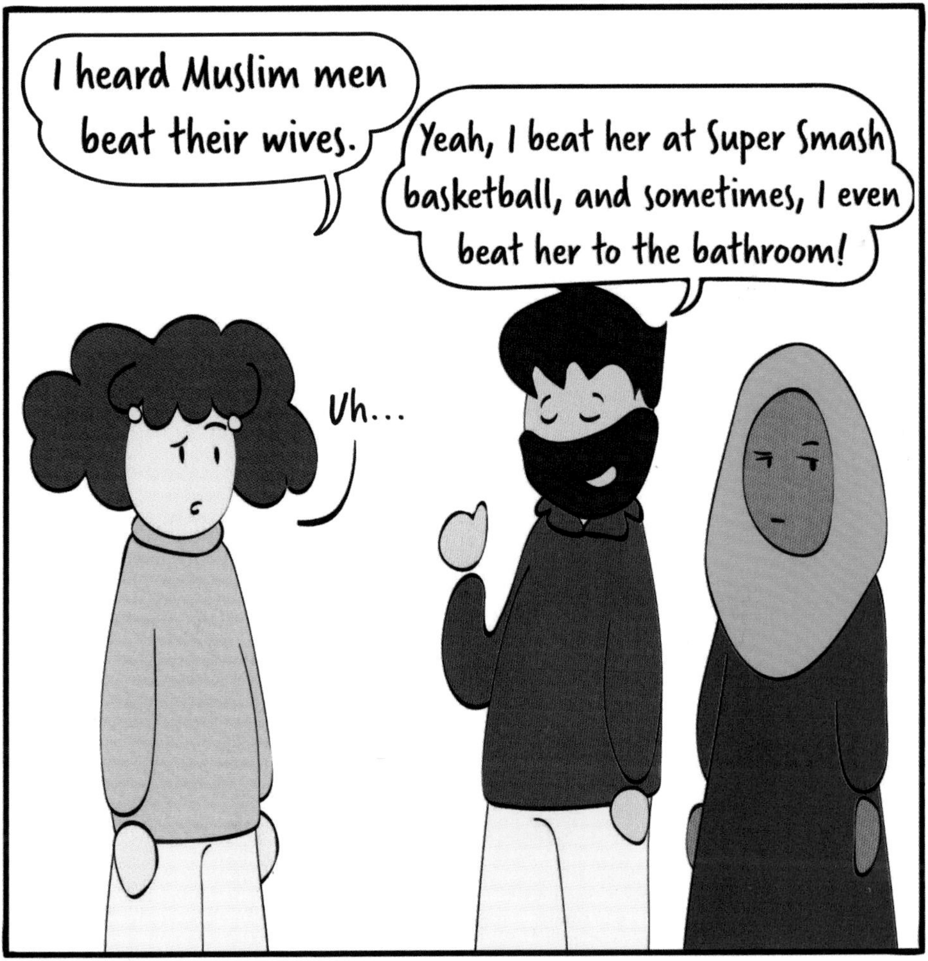
I heard Muslim men beat their wives.
Yeah, I beat her at Super Smash basketball, and sometimes, I even beat her to the bathroom!
Uh...

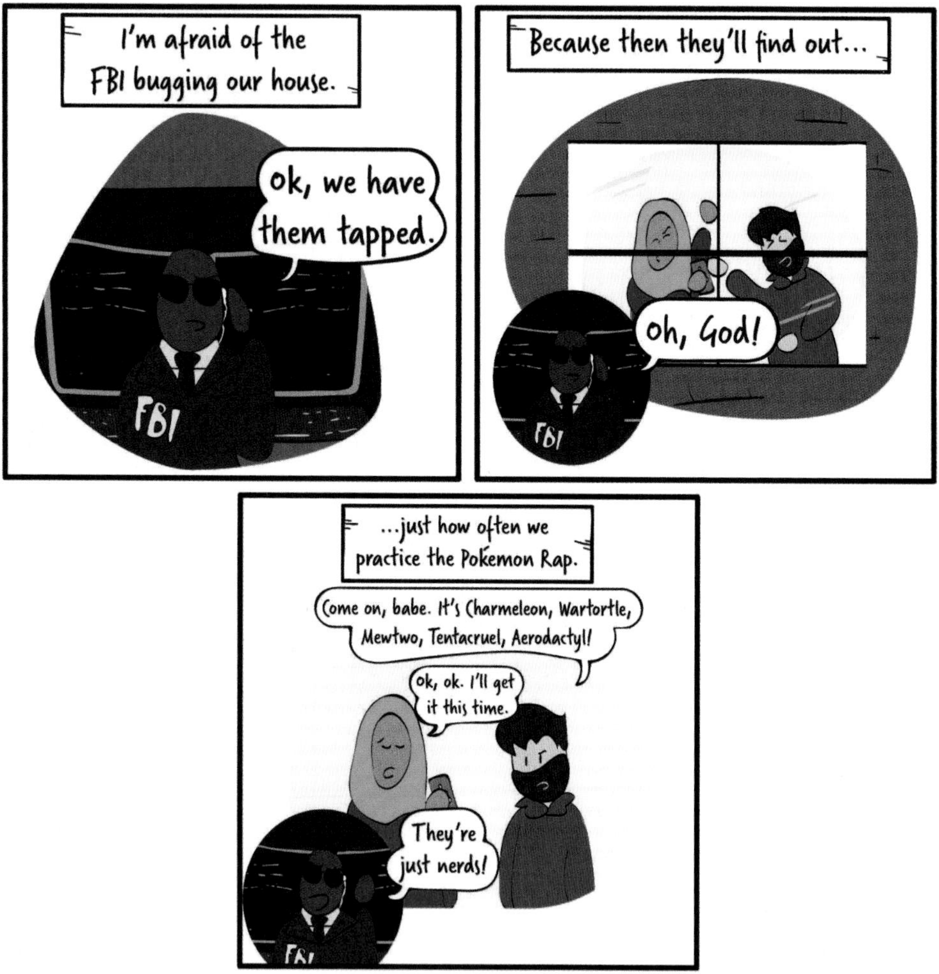

I'm afraid of the FBI bugging our house.
ok, we have them tapped.
FBI
Because then they'll find out...
Oh, God!
FBI
...just how often we practice the Pokemon Rap.
Come on, babe. It's Charmeleon, Wartortle, Mewtwo, Tentacruel, Aerodactyl!
Ok, ok. I'll get it this time.
They're just nerds!

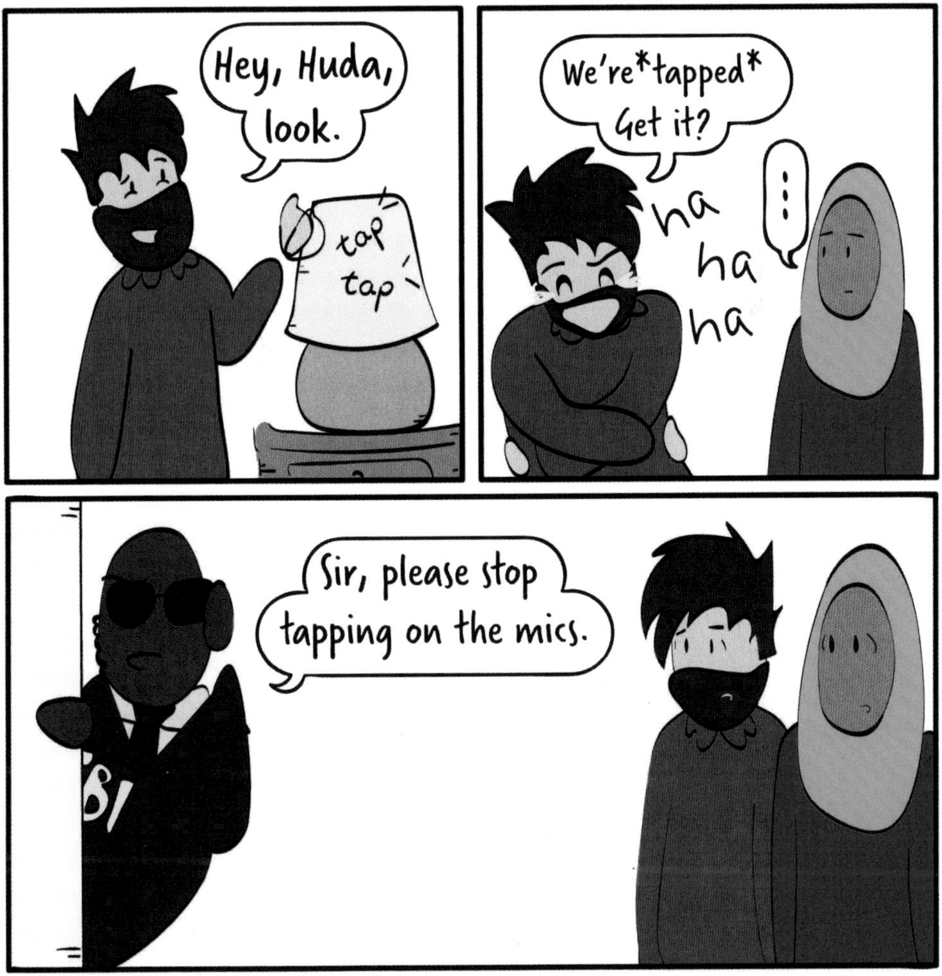
Hey, Huda, look.
tap tap
We're*tapped* Get it?
ha ha ha
...
Sir, please stop tapping on the mics.

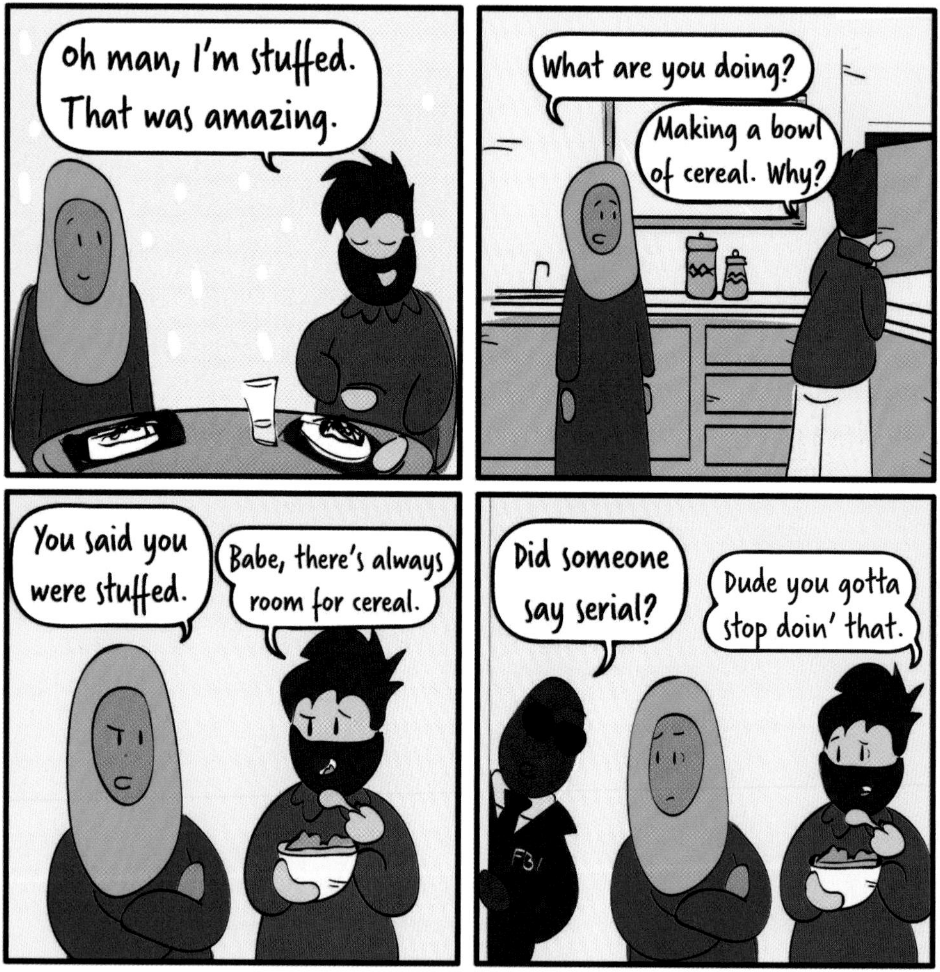
Oh man, I'm stuffed. That was amazing.
What are you doing?
Making a bowl of cereal. Why?
You said you were stuffed.
Babe, there's always room for cereal.
Did someone say serial?
Dude you gotta stop doin' that.
FBI

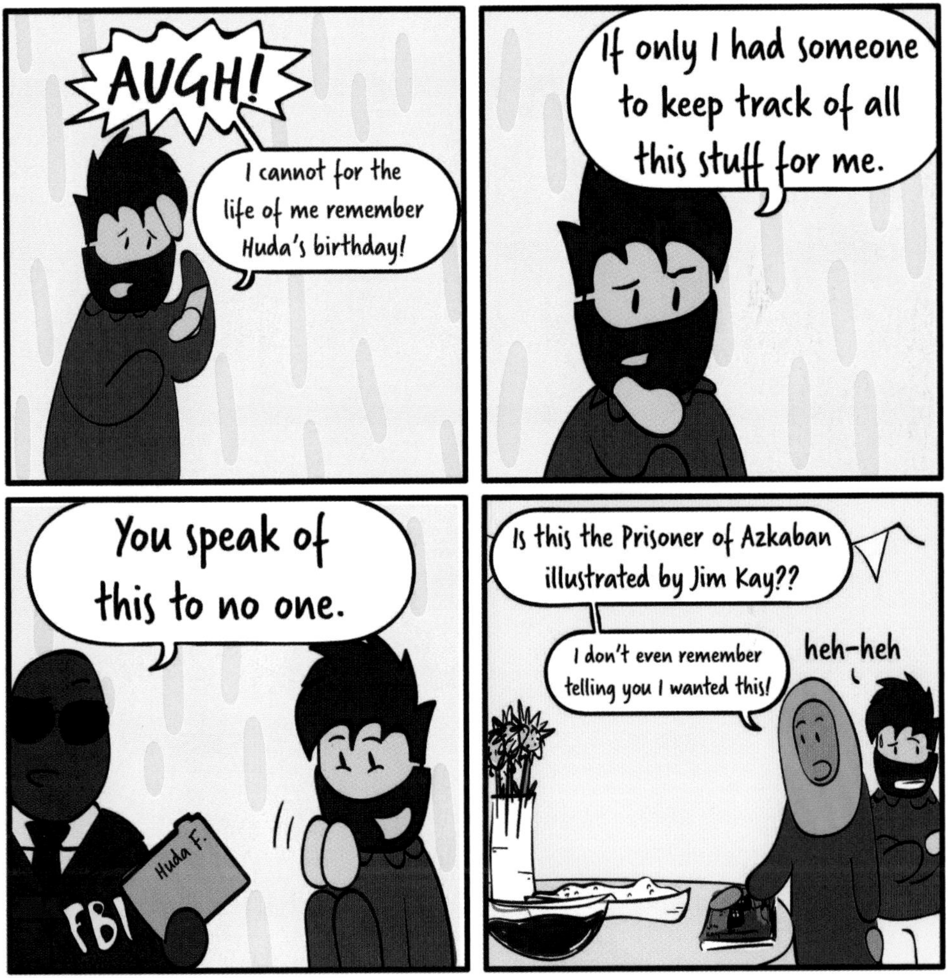
AUGH!
I cannot for the life of me remember Huda's birthday!
If only I had someone to keep track of all this stuff for me.
You speak of this to no one.
Huda F.
FBI
Is this the Prisoner of Azkaban illustrated by Jim Kay??
I don't even remember telling you I wanted this!
heh-heh

Oh no! That dude's coming over and I totally forgot his name!
Just tell him you need to add him to your phone and ask how he spells his name. Believe me, it works every time.
OK!

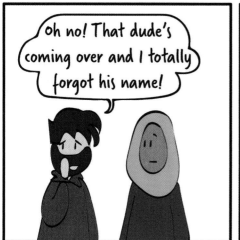

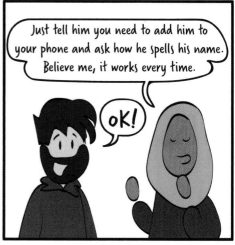

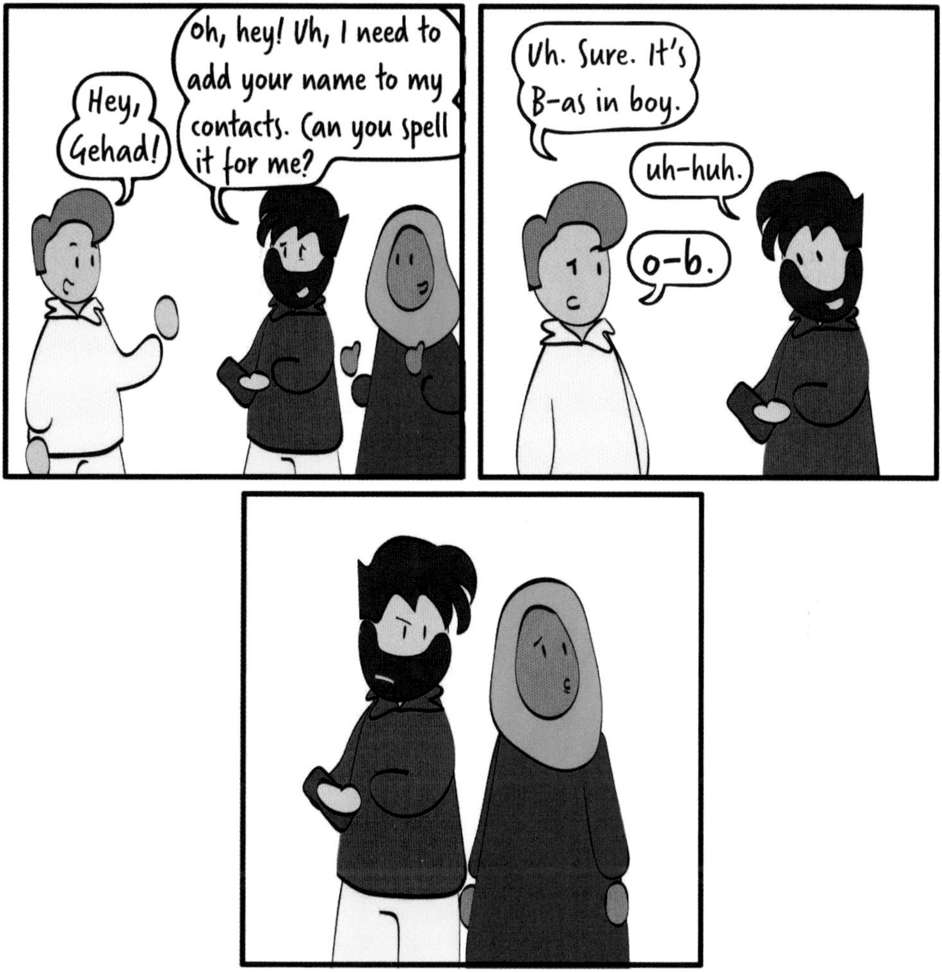
Hey, Gehad!
Oh, hey! Uh, I need to add your name to my contacts. Can you spell it for me?
Uh. Sure. It's B-as in boy.
uh-huh.
o-b.

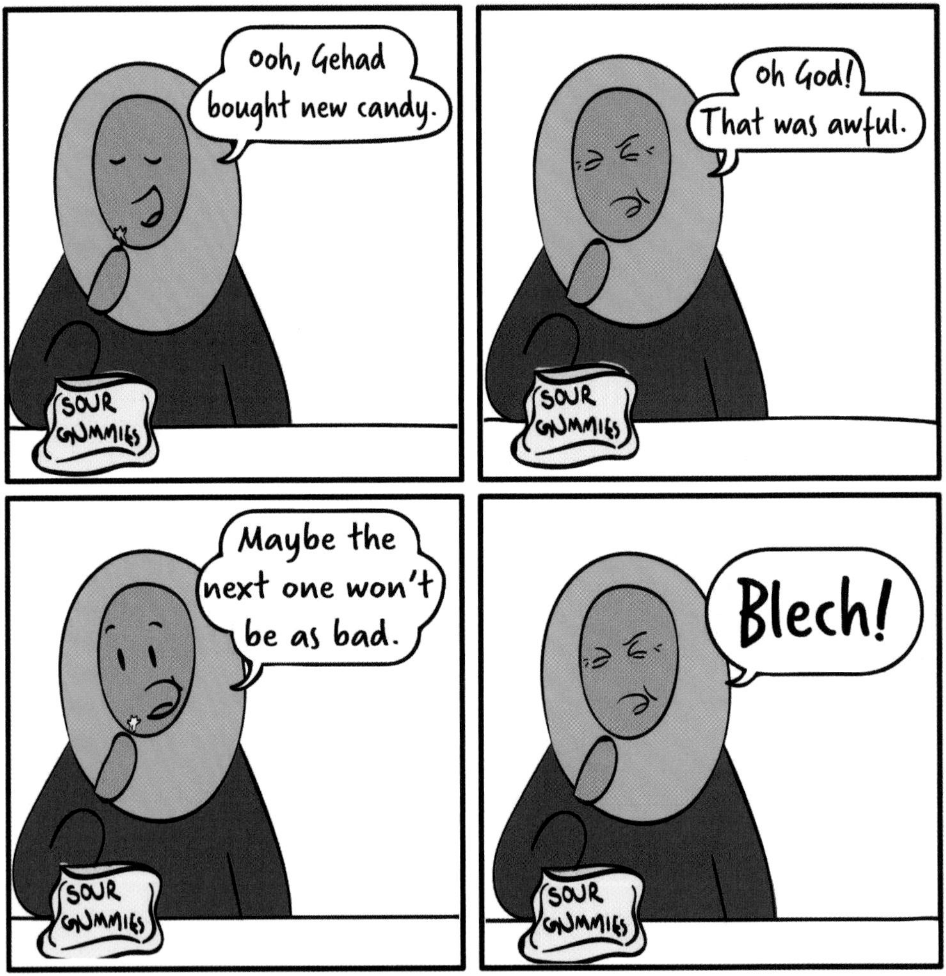
Ooh, Gehad bought new candy.
SOUR GUMMIES
Oh God! That was awful.
SOUR GUMMIES
Maybe the next one won't be as bad.
SOUR GUMMIES
Blech!
SOUR GUMMIES

SOUR GUMMIES
Did you eat all my gummies?
You should be *thanking* me. They were disgusting.

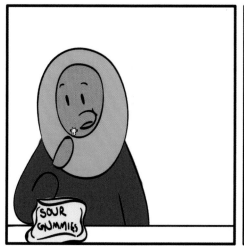

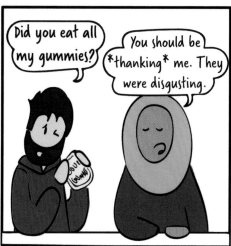

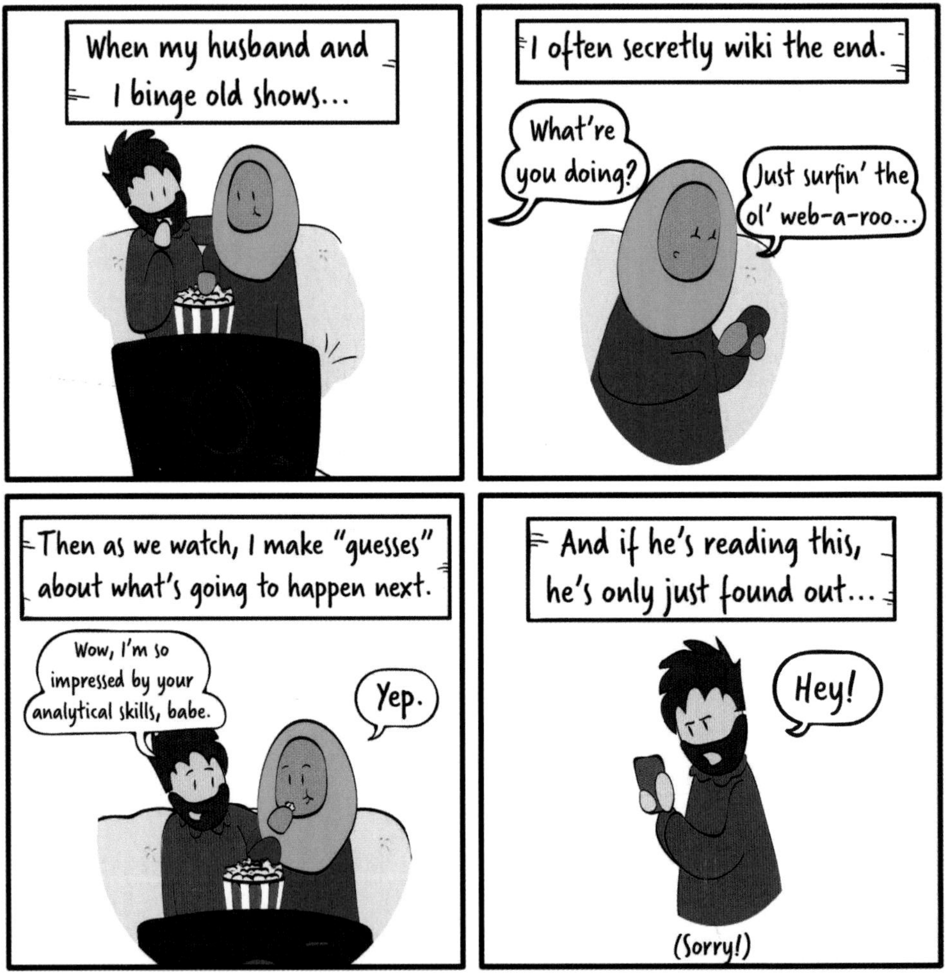

When my husband and I binge old shows...
I often secretly wiki the end.
What're you doing?
Just surfin' the ol' web-a-roo...
Then as we watch, I make "guesses" about what's going to happen next.
Wow, I'm so impressed by your analytical skills, babe.
Yep.
And if he's reading this, he's only just found out...
Hey!
(Sorry!)

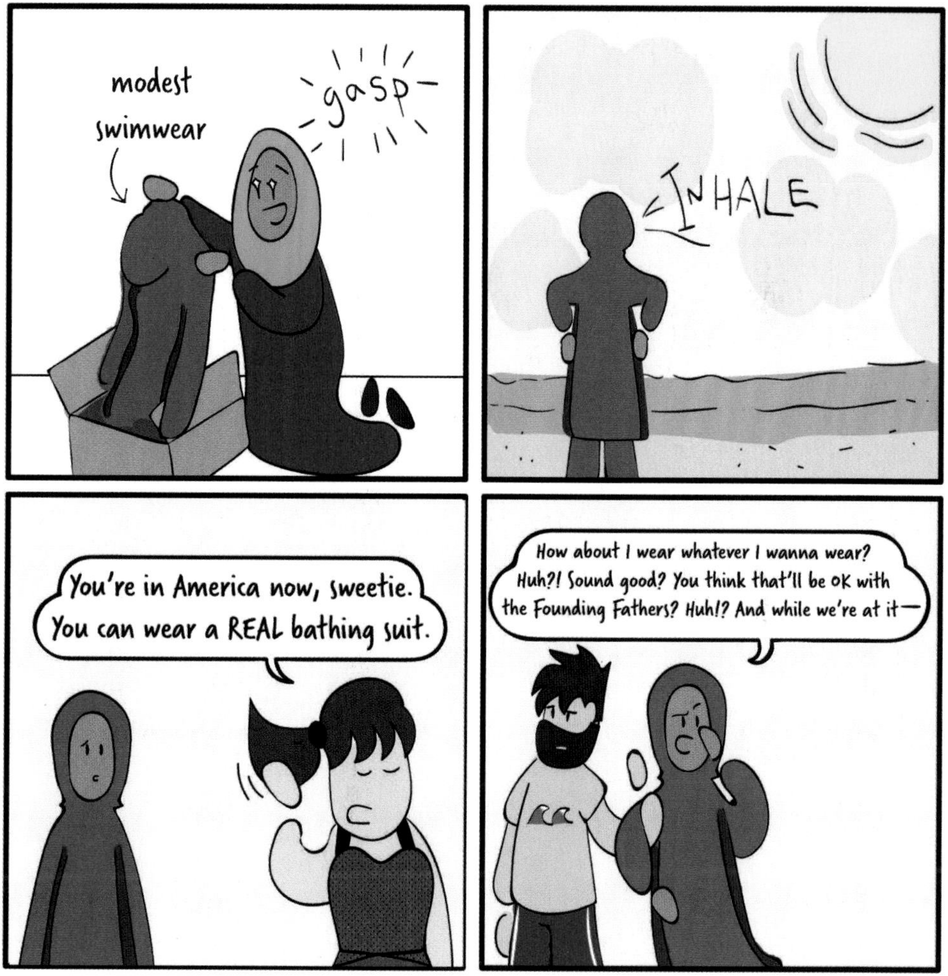
modest swimwear
gasp
INHALE
You're in America now, sweetie. You can wear a REAL bathing suit.
How about I wear whatever I wanna wear? Huh?! Sound good? You think that'll be OK with the Founding Fathers? Huh!? And while we're at it—

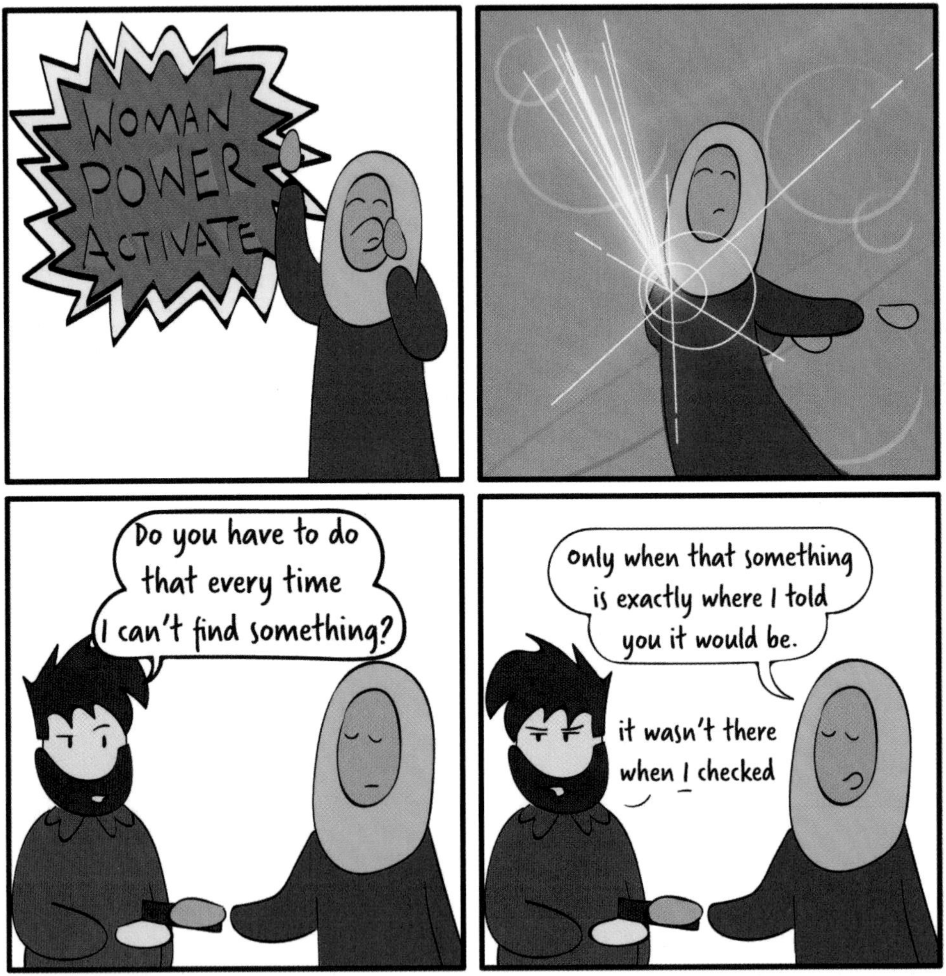
WOMAN POWER ACTIVATE
Do you have to do that every time I can't find something?
Only when that something is exactly where I told you it would be.
it wasn't there when I checked

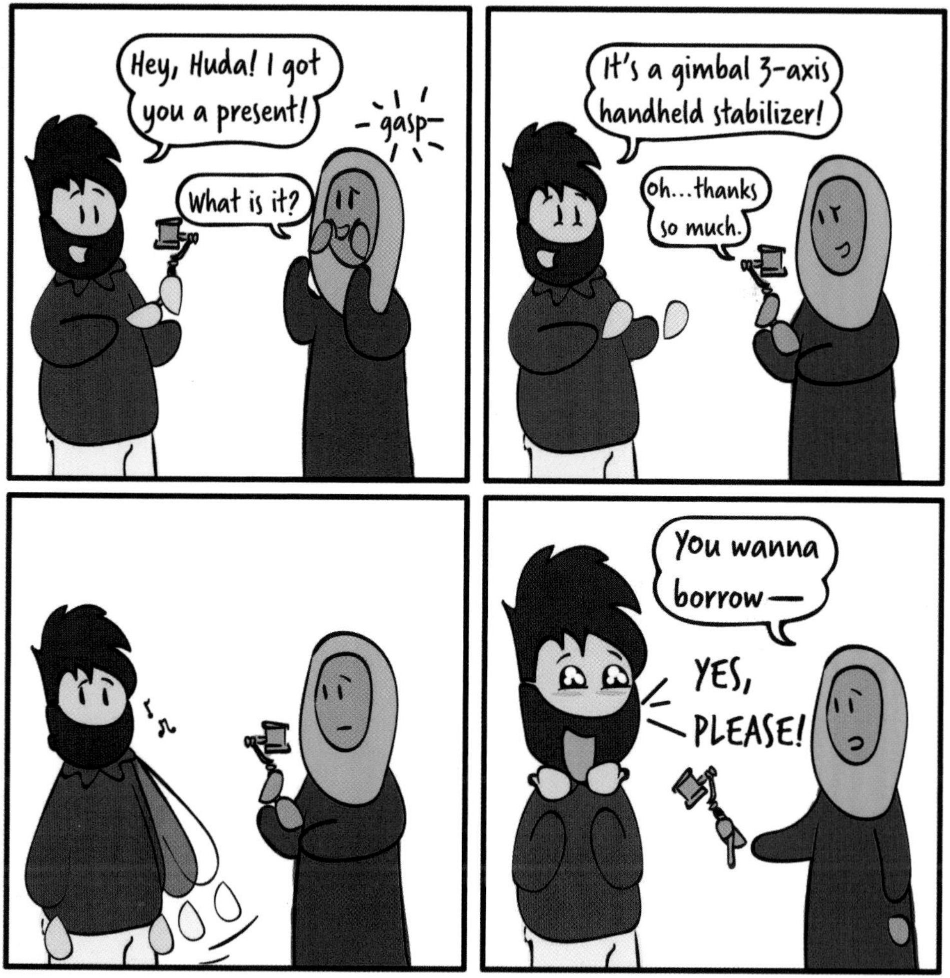
Hey, Huda! I got you a present!
-gasp-
What is it?
It's a gimbal 3-axis handheld stabilizer!
oh...thanks so much.
You wanna borrow—
YES, PLEASE!

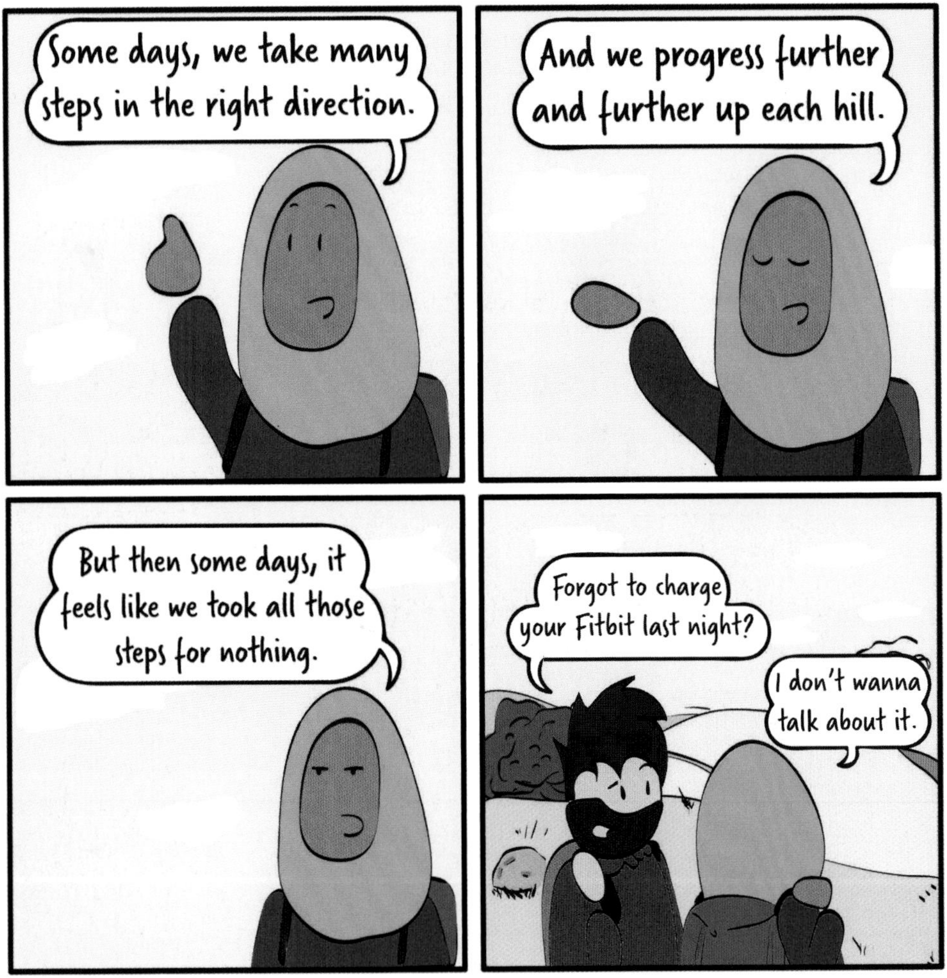
Some days, we take many steps in the right direction.
And we progress further and further up each hill.
But then some days, it feels like we took all those steps for nothing.
Forgot to charge your Fitbit last night?
I don't wanna talk about it.

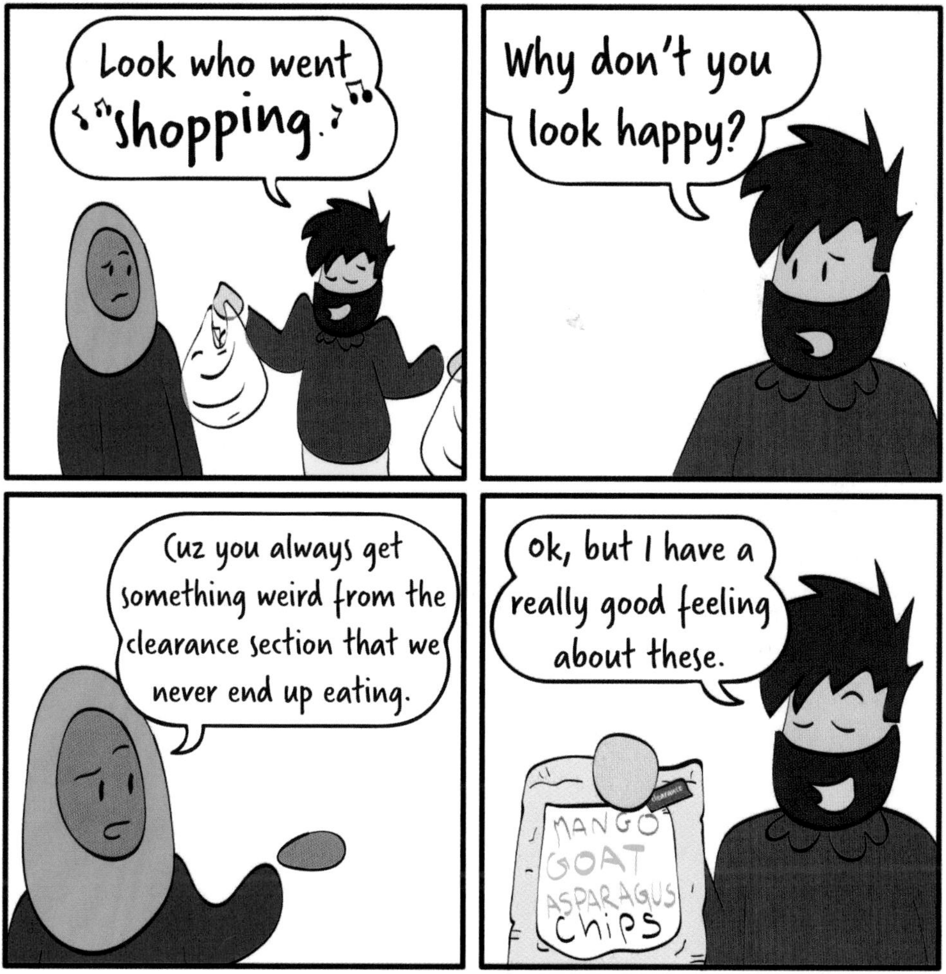
Look who went "shopping."
Why don't you look happy?
Cuz you always get something weird from the clearance section that we never end up eating.
Ok, but I have a really good feeling about these.
MANGO GOAT ASPARAGUS Chips

I feel like people care just way too much about how I live my life.
They're all up in MY business. Try'na give ME unsolicited advice.

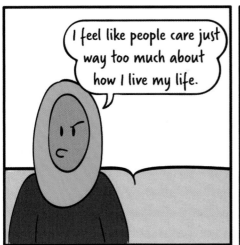

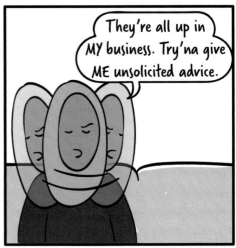

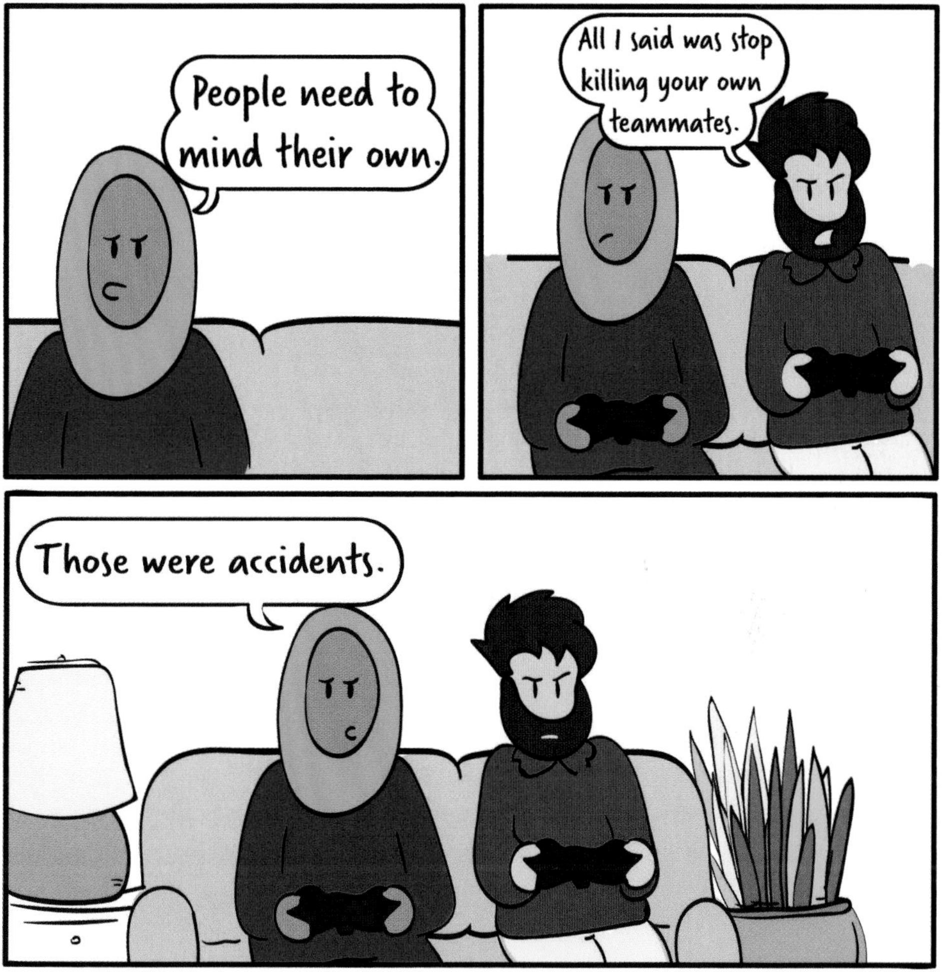
People need to mind their own.
All I said was stop killing your own teammates.
Those were accidents.

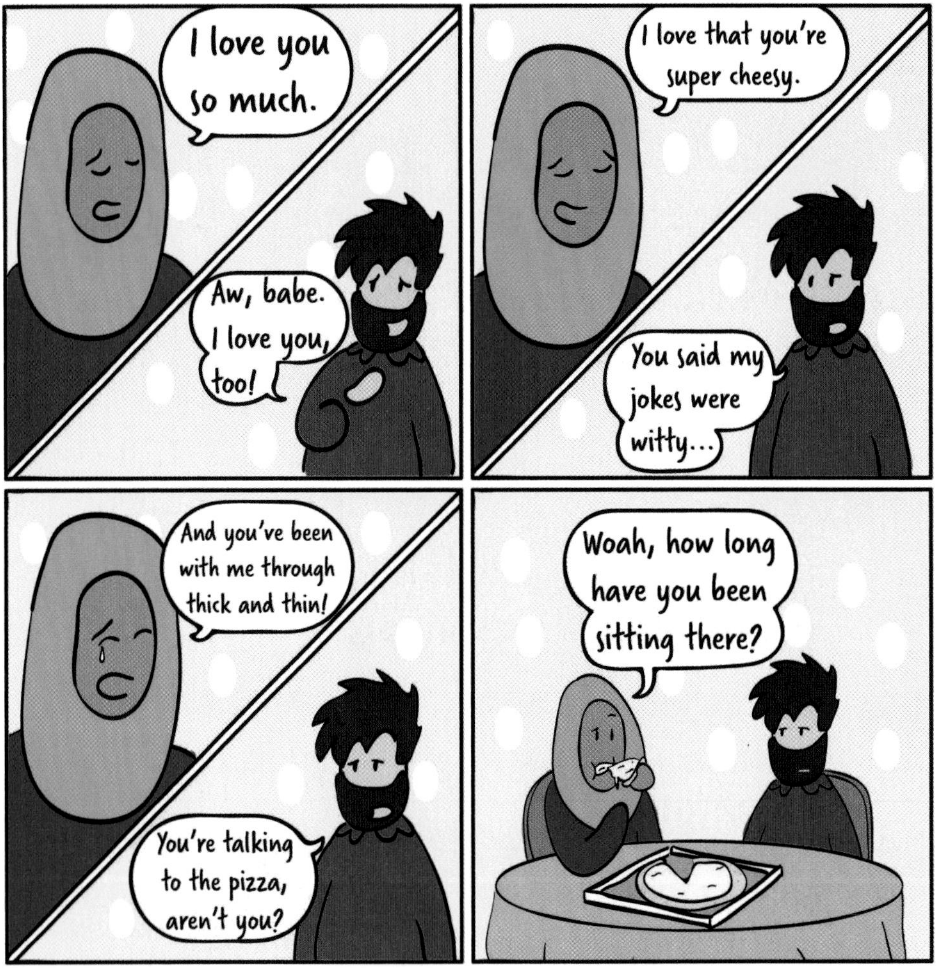
I love you so much.
Aw, babe. I love you, too!
I love that you're super cheesy.
You said my jokes were witty...
And you've been with me through thick and thin!
You're talking to the pizza, aren't you?
Woah, how long have you been sitting there?

Chapter 4: Yes, People Actually Say This Stuff to Me

Maybe I'm just really approachable.

Hey! You look like you're free to answer some personal questions!

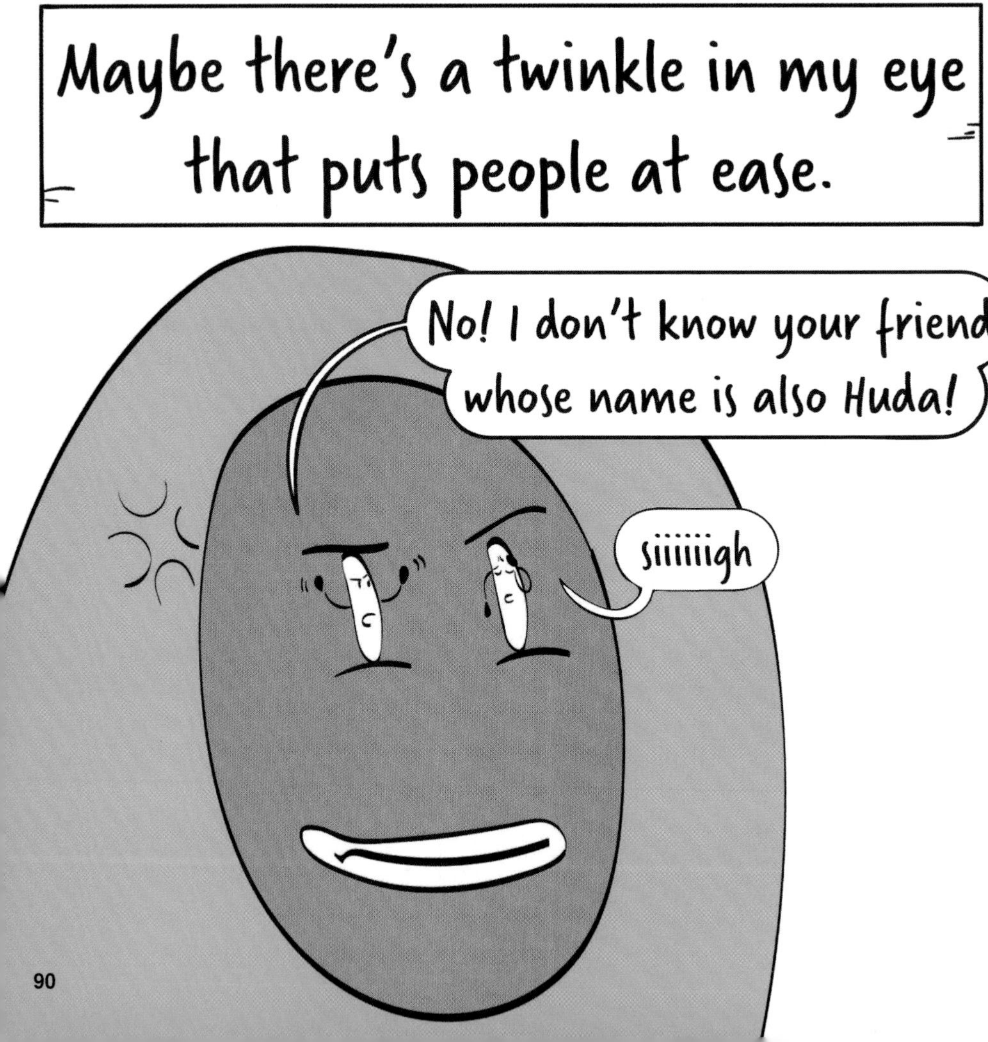
Maybe there's a twinkle in my eye that puts people at ease.
No! I don't know your friend whose name is also Huda!
siiiiiiigh

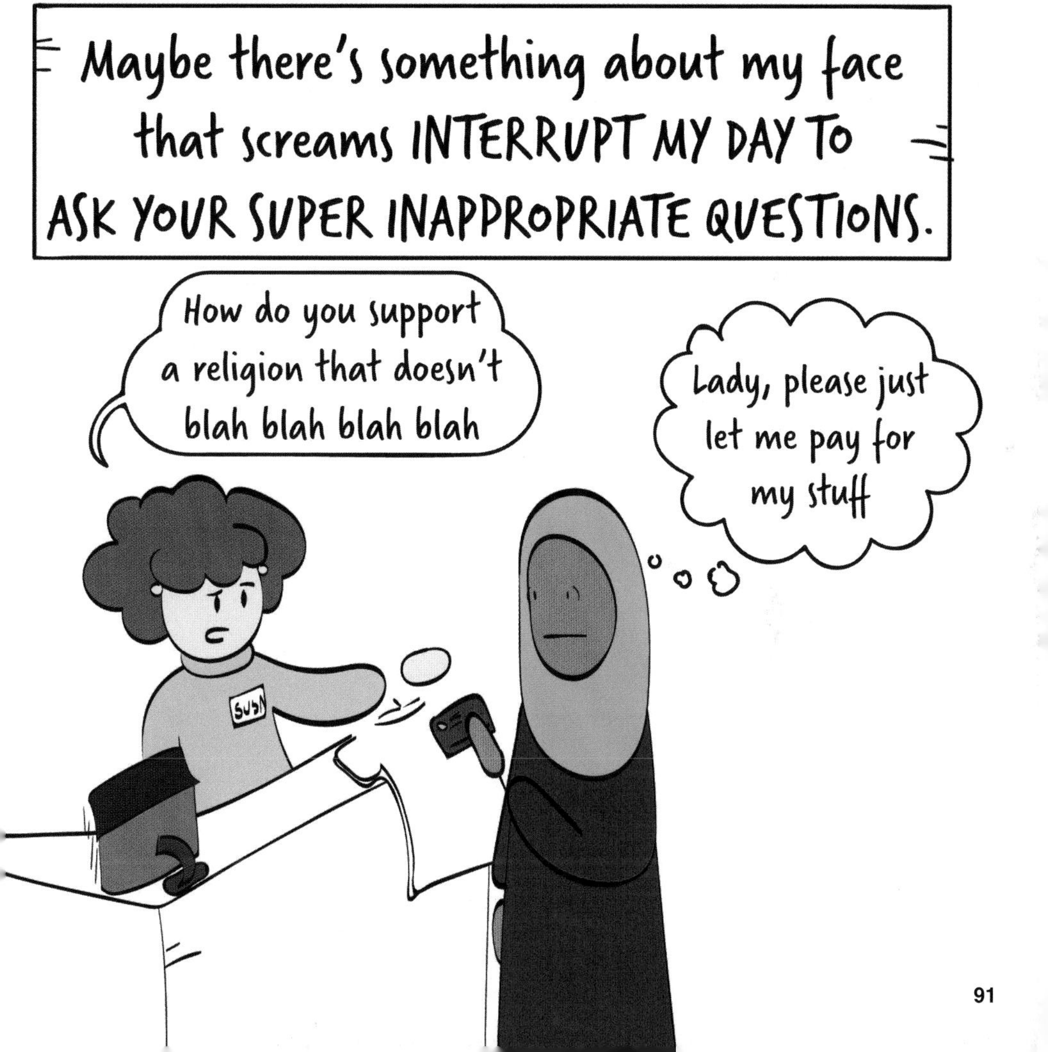
Maybe there's something about my face that screams INTERRUPT MY DAY TO ASK YOUR SUPER INAPPROPRIATE QUESTIONS.
How do you support a religion that doesn't blah blah blah blah
Lady, please just let me pay for my stuff

Maybe it's not me.

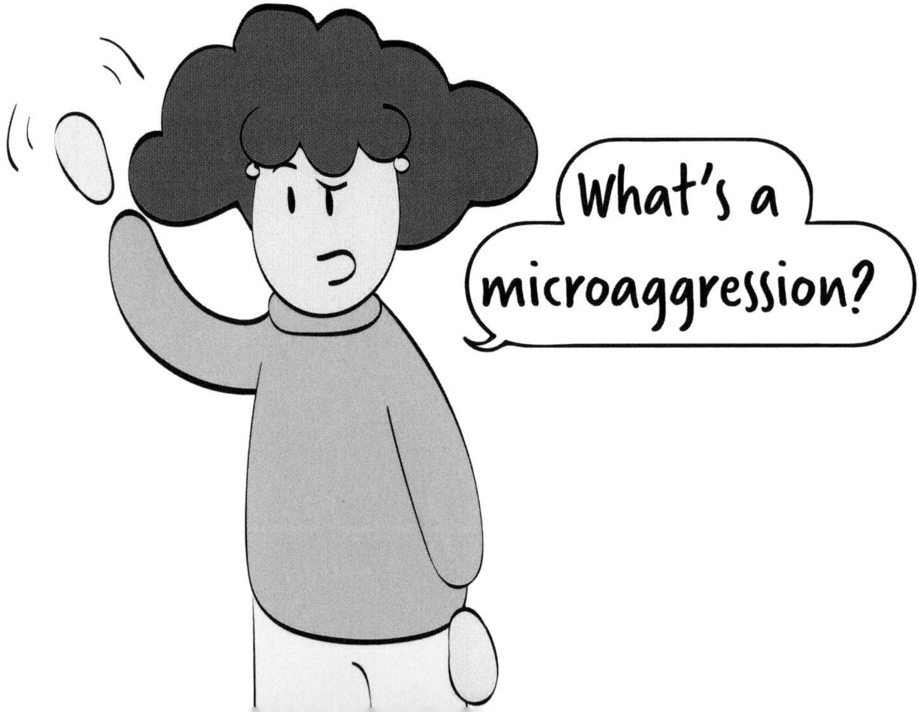
What's a microaggression?

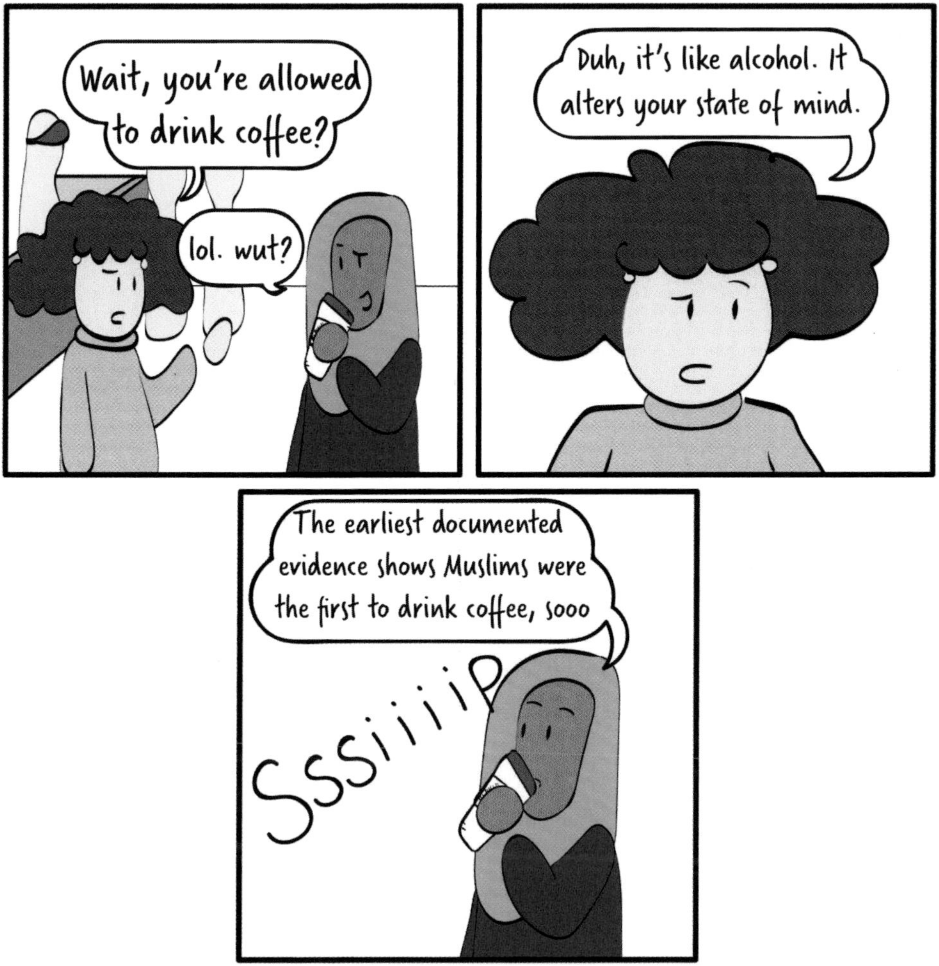
Wait, you're allowed to drink coffee?
lol. wut?
Duh, it's like alcohol. It alters your state of mind.
The earliest documented evidence shows Muslims were the first to drink coffee, sooo
SSiiiiiP

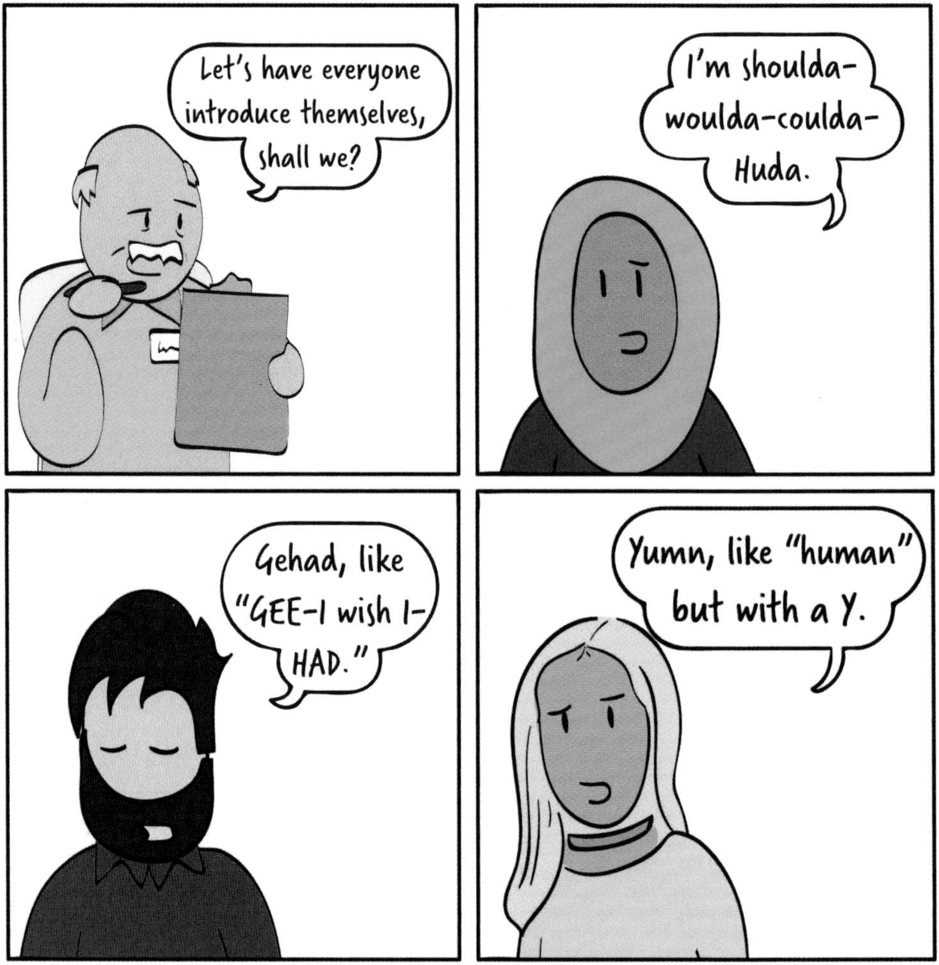
Let's have everyone introduce themselves, shall we?
I'm shoulda-woulda-coulda-Huda.
Gehad, like "GEE-I wish I-HAD."
Yumn, like "human" but with a Y.

And I'm Susan!
NAMES NO ONE CAN PRONOUNCE
What?

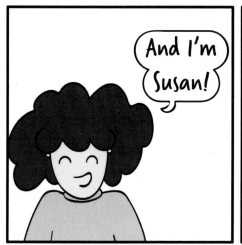

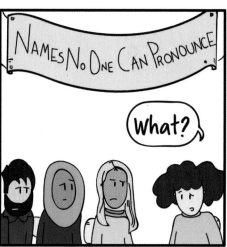

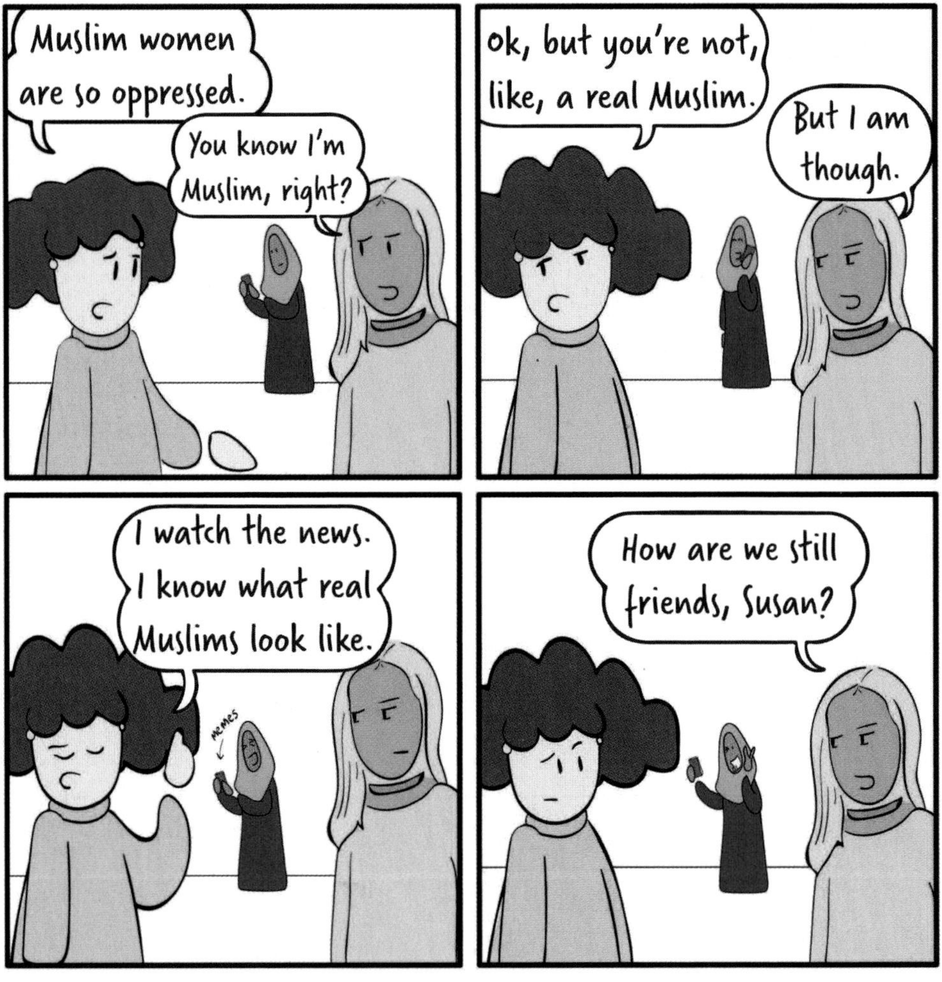
Muslim women are so oppressed.
You know I'm Muslim, right?
ok, but you're not, like, a real Muslim.
But I am though.
I watch the news. I know what real Muslims look like.
memes
How are we still friends, Susan?

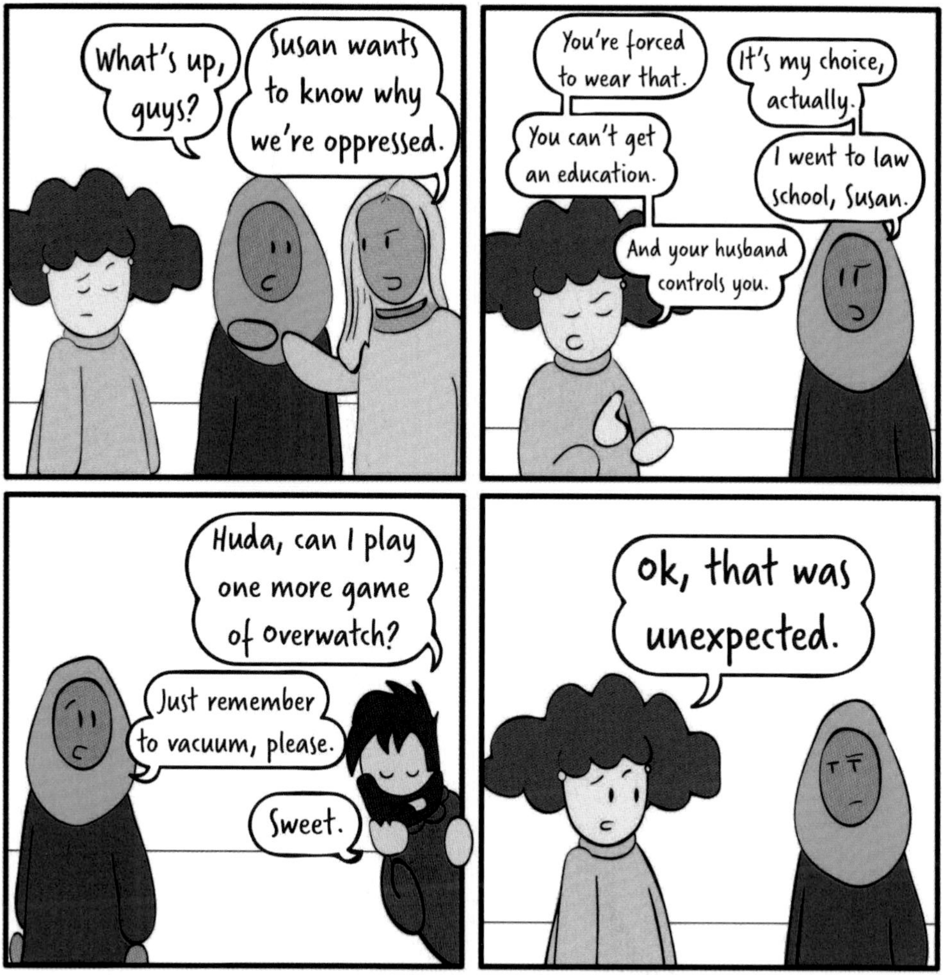
What's up, guys?
Susan wants to know why we're oppressed.
You're forced to wear that.
You can't get an education.
And your husband controls you.
It's my choice, actually.
I went to law school, Susan.
Huda, can I play one more game of Overwatch?
Just remember to vacuum, please.
Sweet.
Ok, that was unexpected.

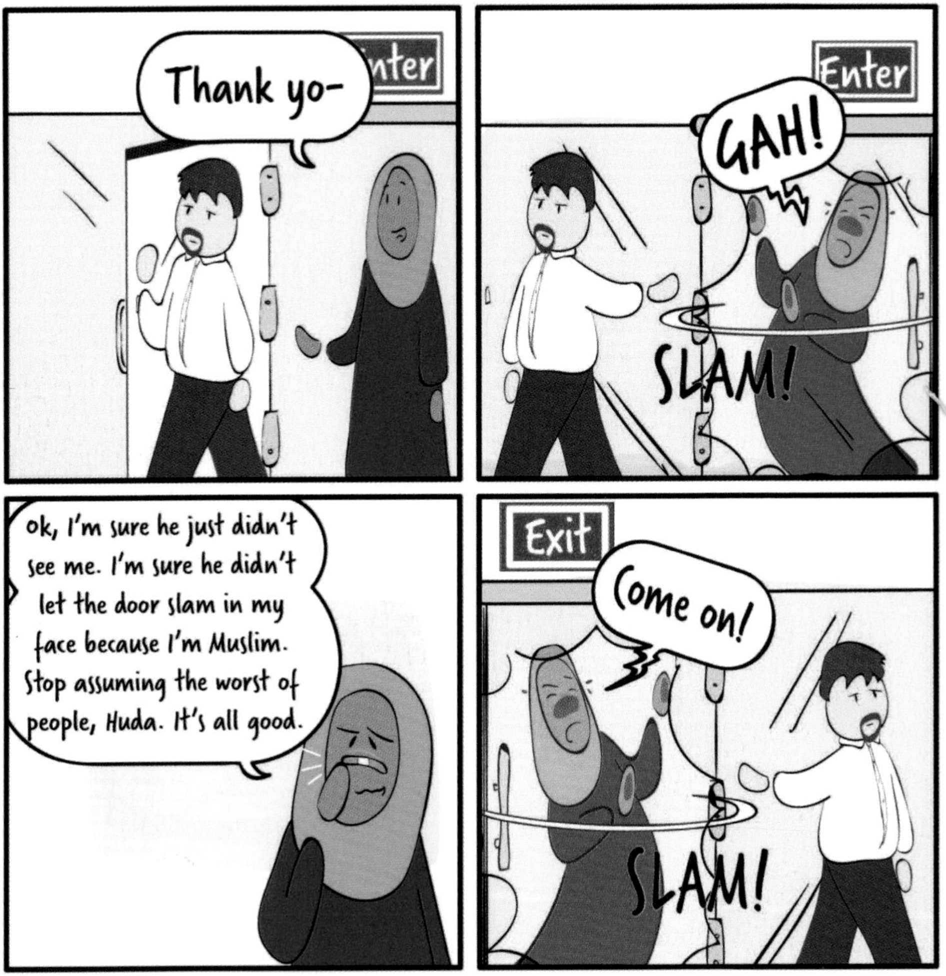
Enter
Thank yo-
Enter
GAH!
SLAM!
ok, I'm sure he just didn't see me. I'm sure he didn't let the door slam in my face because I'm Muslim. Stop assuming the worst of people, Huda. It's all good.
Exit
Come on!
SLAM!

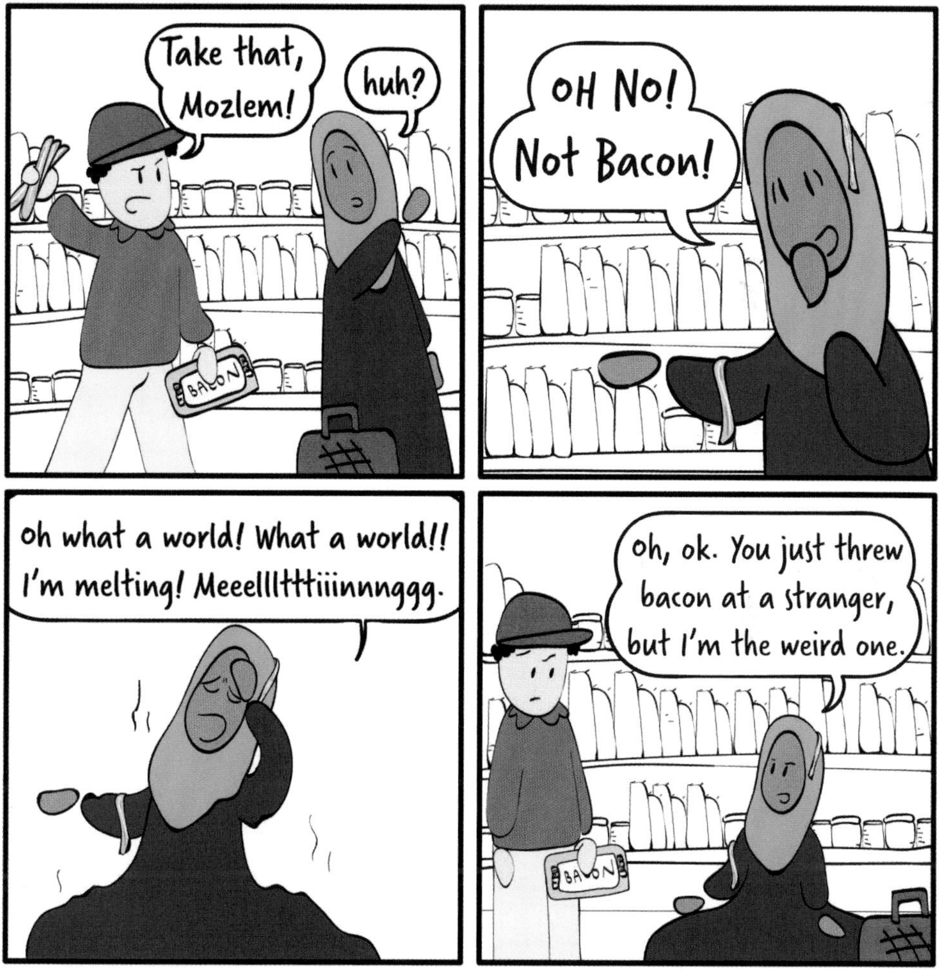
Take that, Mozlem!
huh?
BACON
OH NO! Not Bacon!
oh what a world! What a world!! I'm melting! Meeellllttttiiinnnggg.
Oh, ok. You just threw bacon at a stranger, but I'm the weird one.
BACON

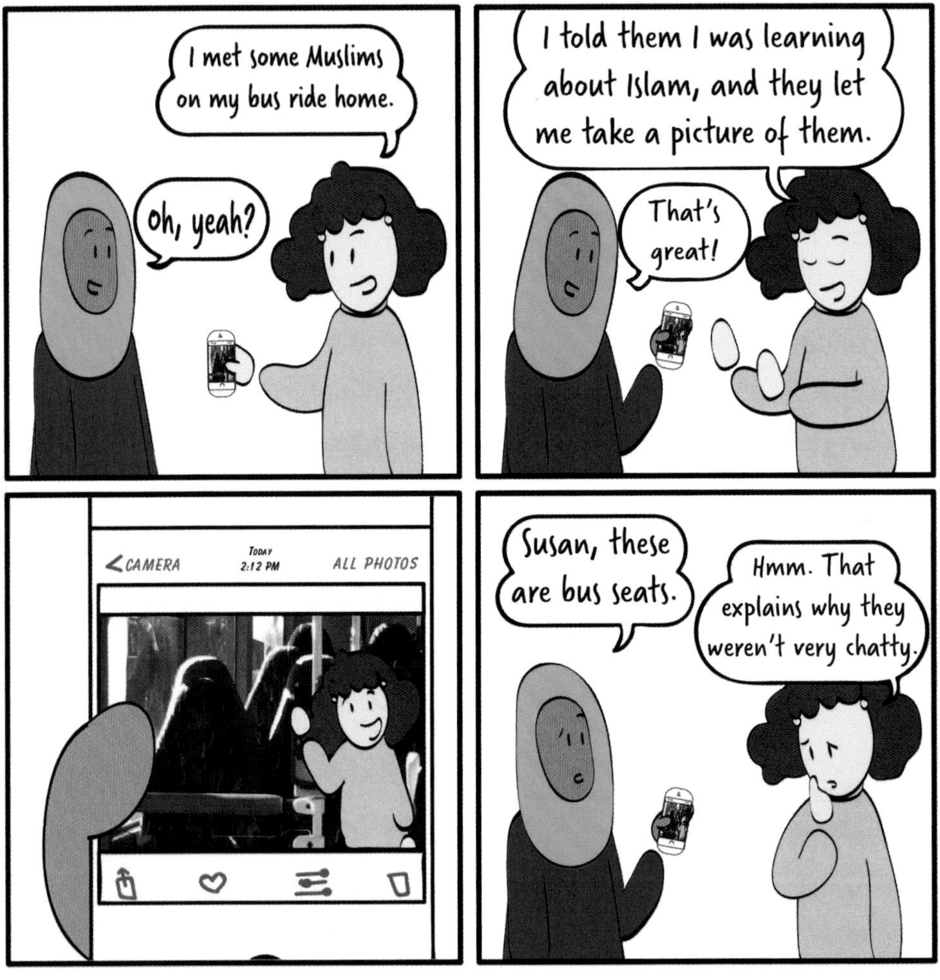
I met some Muslims on my bus ride home.
Oh, yeah?
I told them I was learning about Islam, and they let me take a picture of them.
That's great!
< CAMERA
TODAY 2:12 PM
ALL PHOTOS
Susan, these are bus seats.
Hmm. That explains why they weren't very chatty.

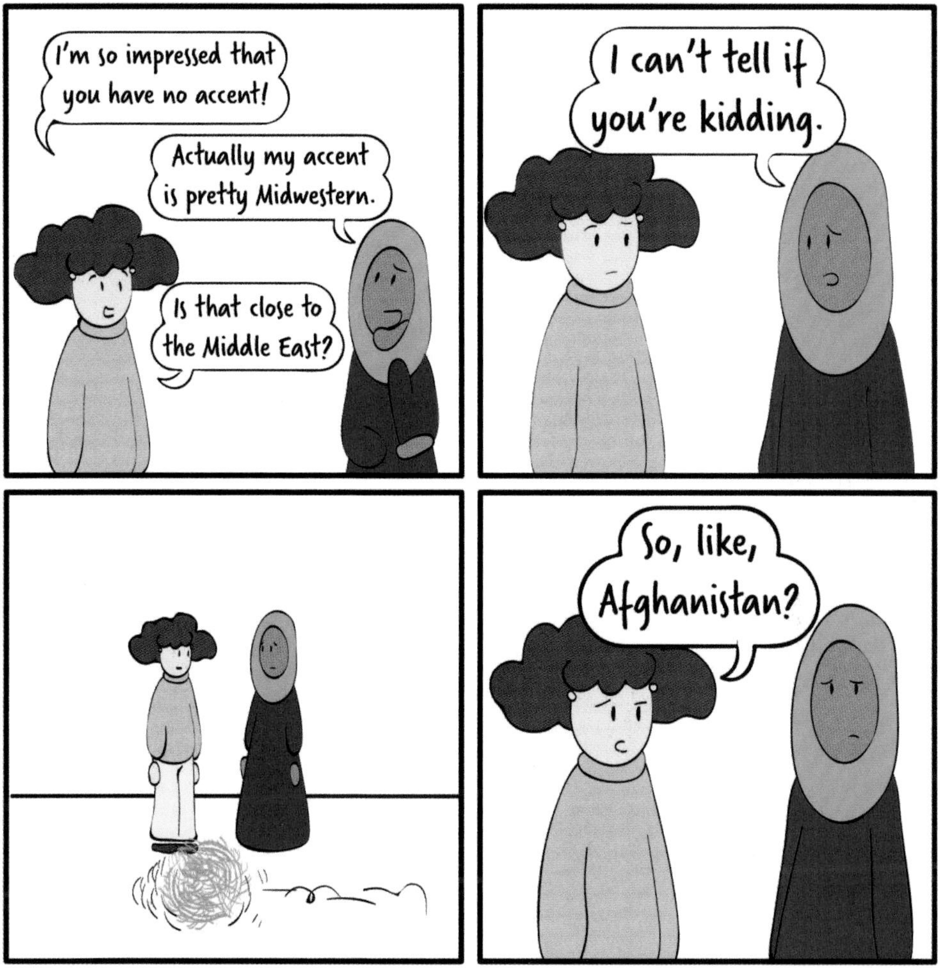
I'm so impressed that you have no accent!
Actually my accent is pretty Midwestern.
Is that close to the Middle East?
I can't tell if you're kidding.
So, like, Afghanistan?

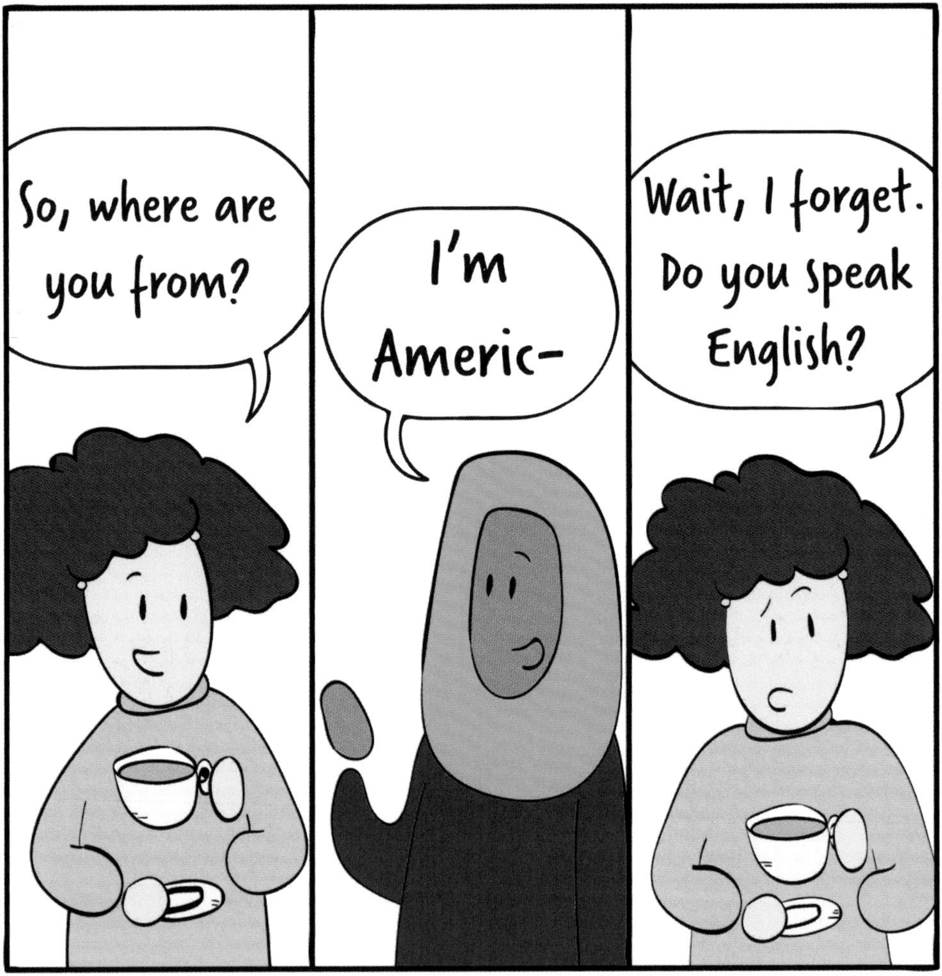
So, where are you from?
I'm Americ-
Wait, I forget. Do you speak English?

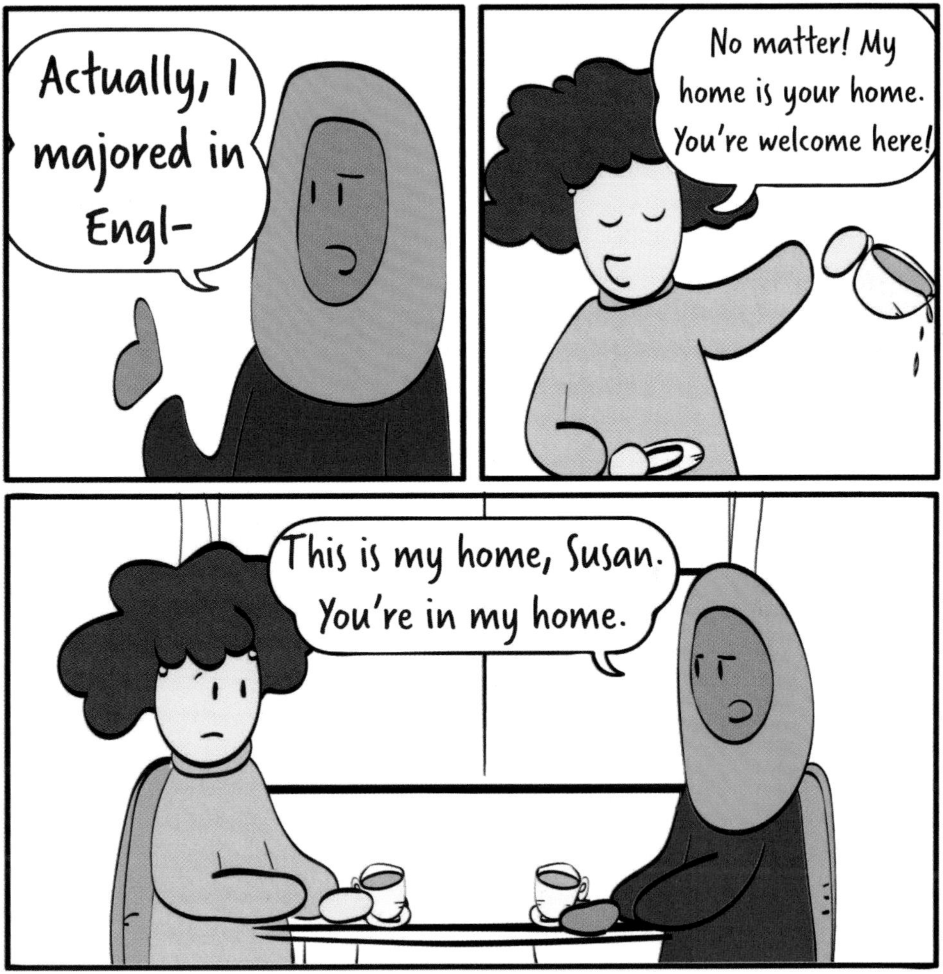
Actually, I majored in Engl-
No matter! My home is your home. You're welcome here!
This is my home, Susan. You're in my home.

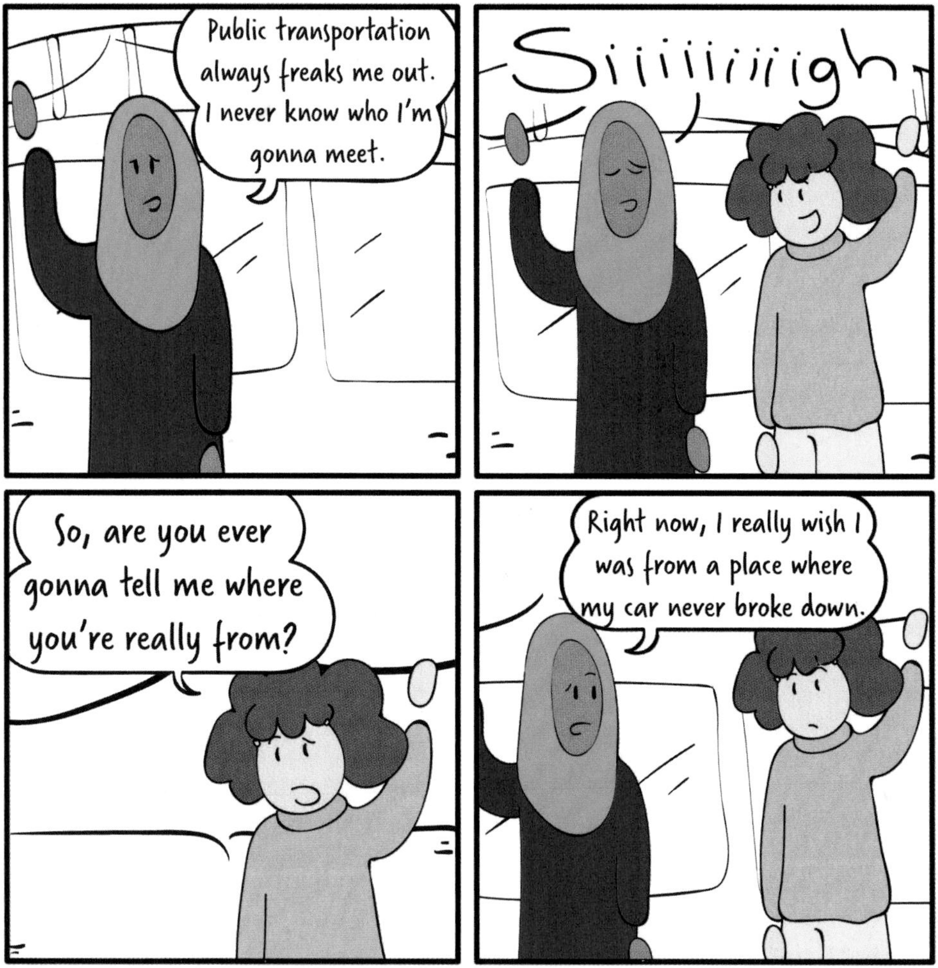
Public transportation always freaks me out. I never know who I'm gonna meet.
Siiiiiiiigh
So, are you ever gonna tell me where you're really from?
Right now, I really wish I was from a place where my car never broke down.

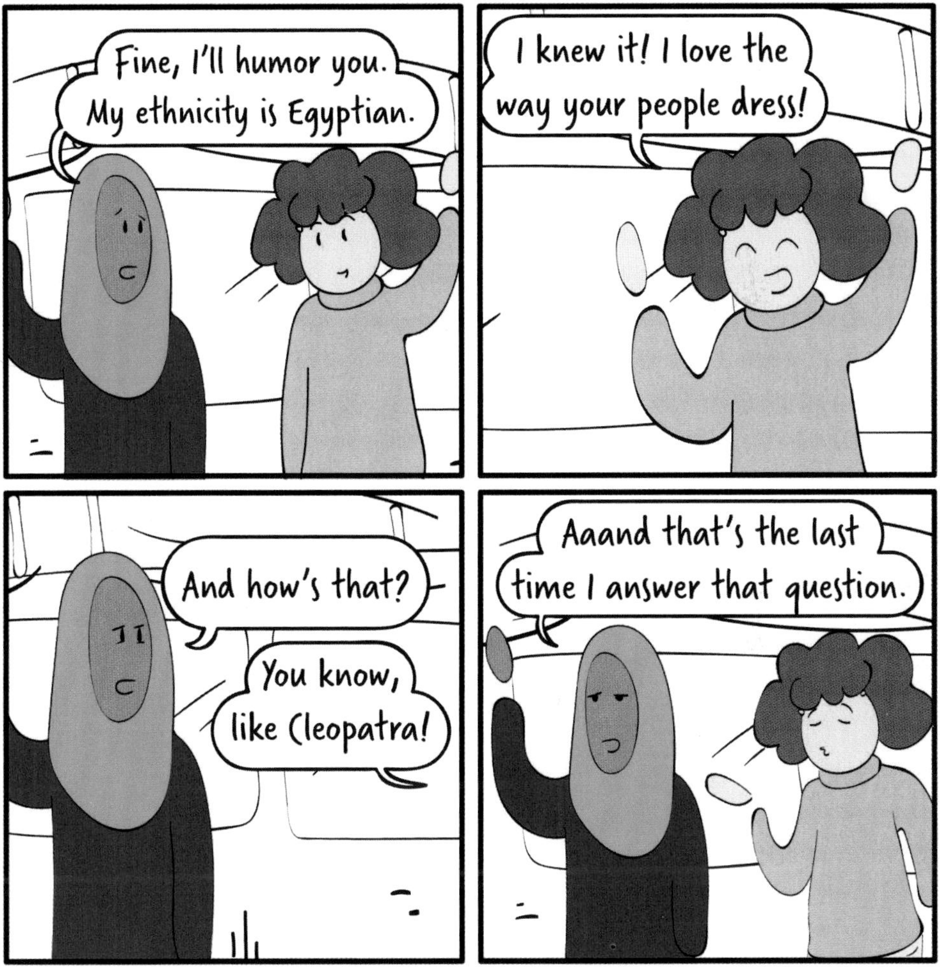
Fine, I'll humor you. My ethnicity is Egyptian.
I knew it! I love the way your people dress!
And how's that?
You know, like Cleopatra!
Aaand that's the last time I answer that question.

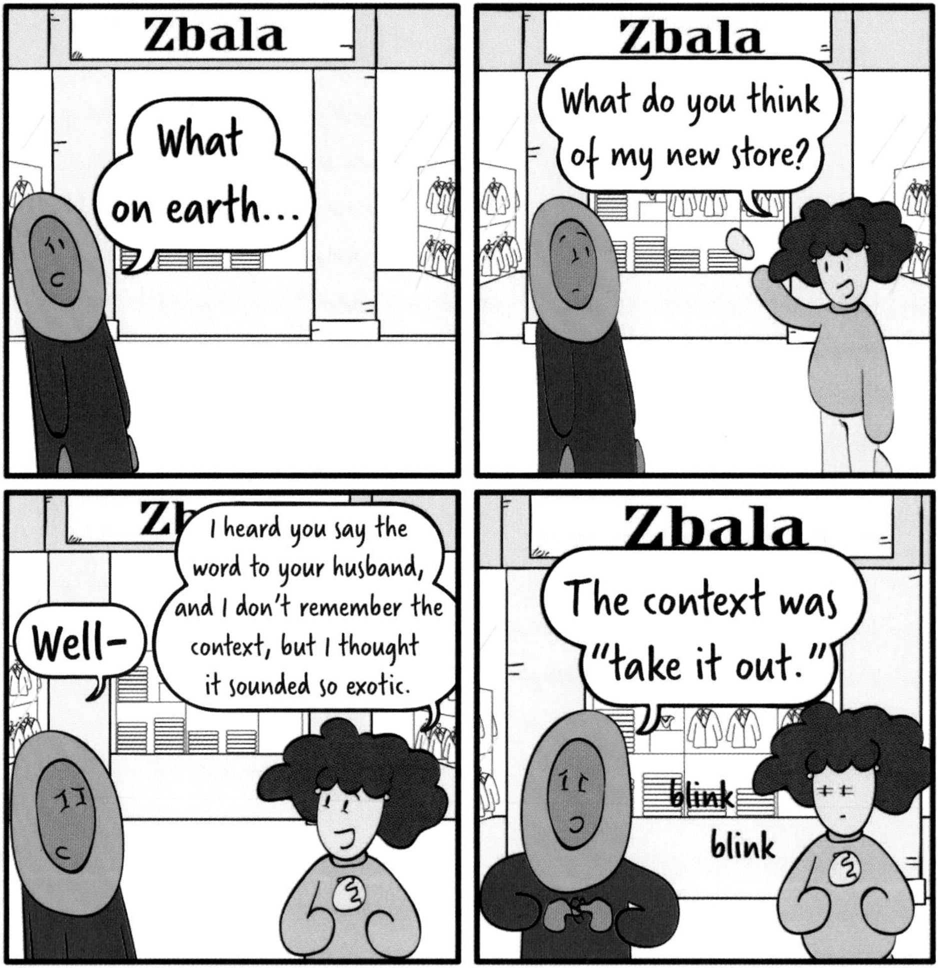
Zbala
What on earth...
Zbala
What do you think of my new store?
I heard you say the word to your husband, and I don't remember the context, but I thought it sounded so exotic.
Well-
Zbala
The context was "take it out."
blink
blink

As in "take out the trash."
blink
blink
blink
It means trash, Susan.

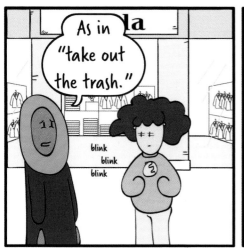

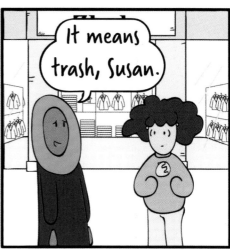

I hope Susan doesn't realize I only need the fitting room to pray.
This one, please!
SALE!
Um, that's a men's shirt...
She suspects! Think fast!
SUSAN

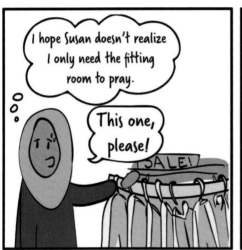

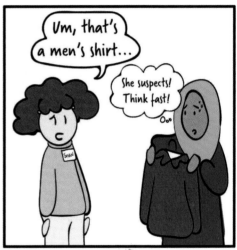

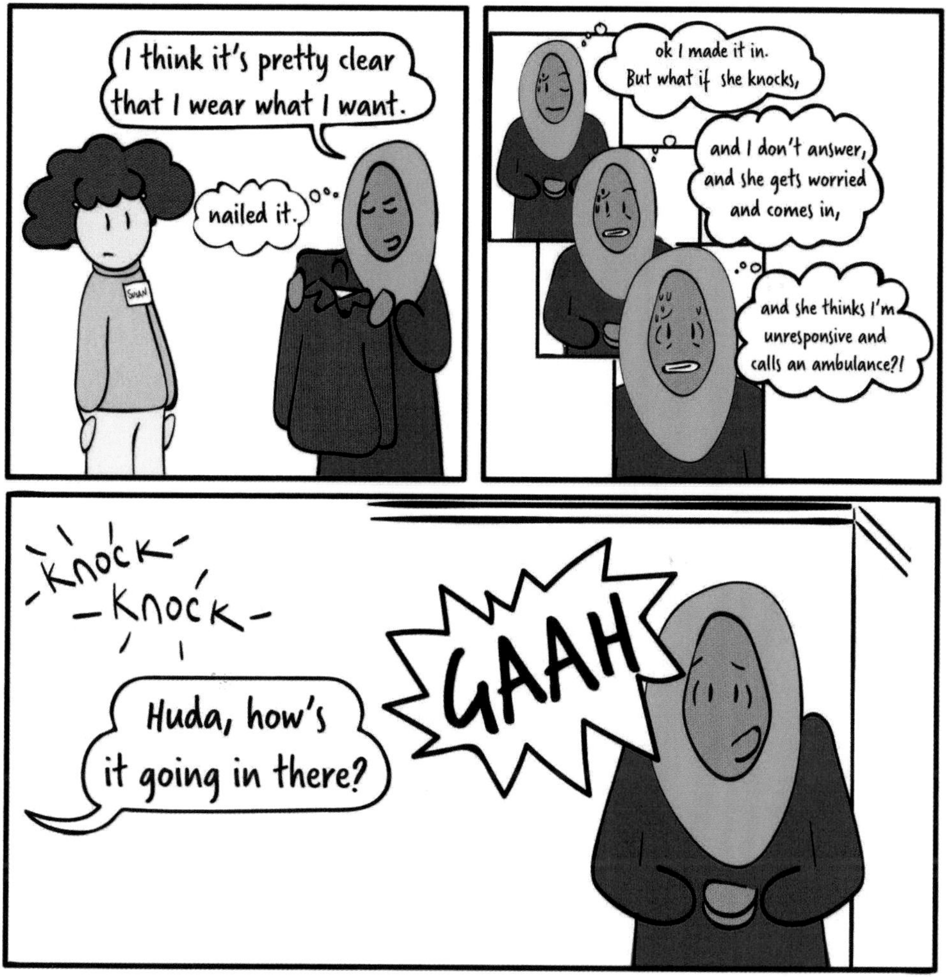
I think it's pretty clear that I wear what I want.
nailed it.
SUSAN
ok I made it in. But what if she knocks,
and I don't answer, and she gets worried and comes in,
and she thinks I'm unresponsive and calls an ambulance?!
KNOCK KNOCK
Huda, how's it going in there?
GAAH

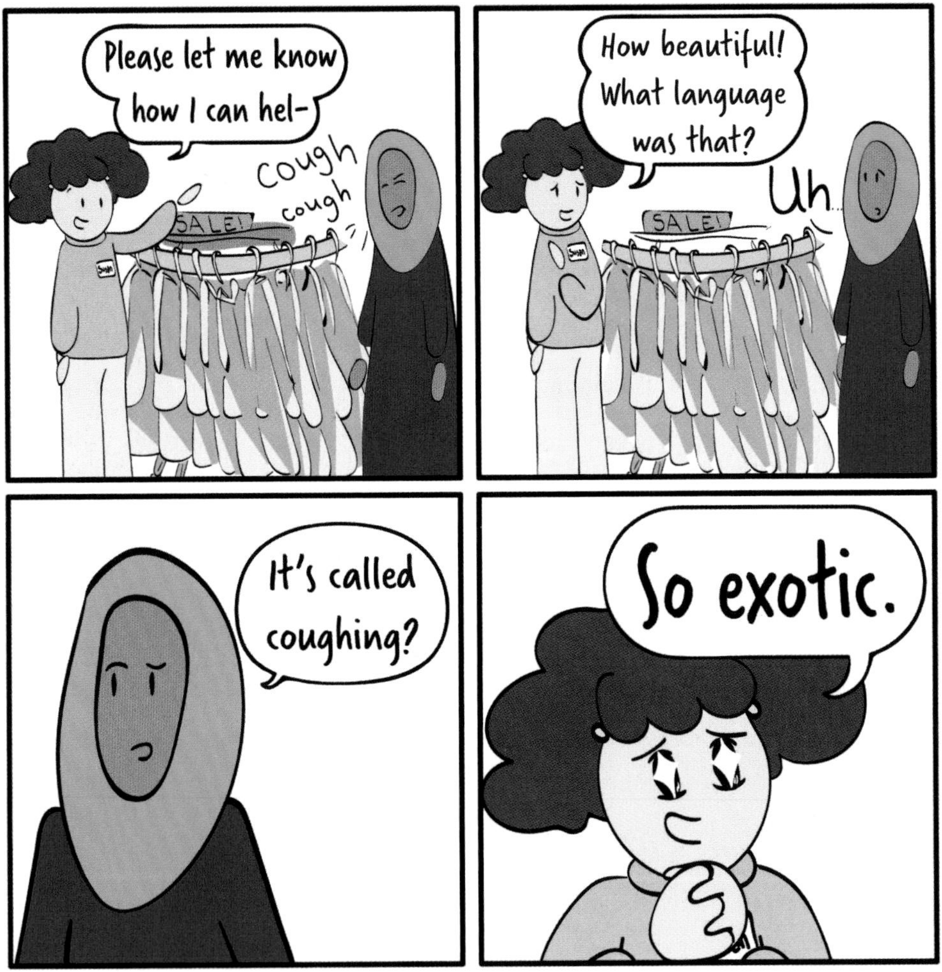
Please let me know how I can hel-
cough
cough
How beautiful! What language was that?
Uh...
It's called coughing?
So exotic.

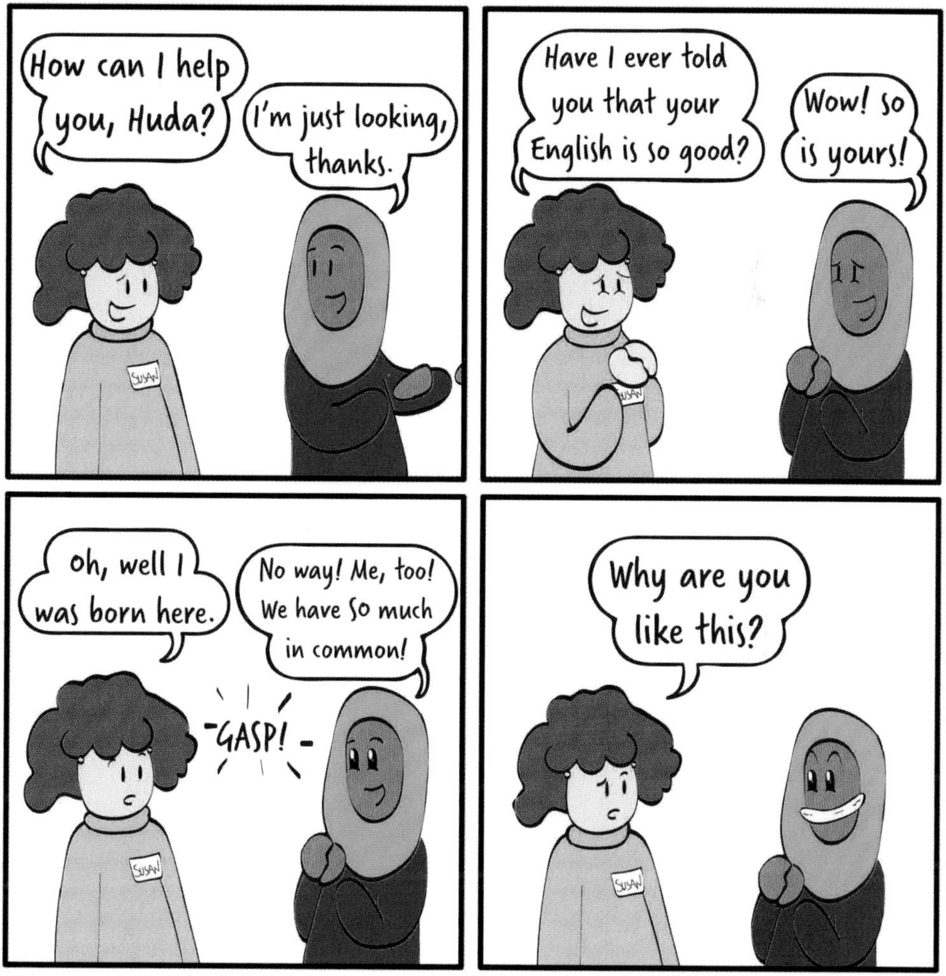
How can I help you, Huda?
I'm just looking, thanks.
SUSAN
Have I ever told you that your English is so good?
Wow! so is yours!
SUSAN
oh, well I was born here.
No way! Me, too! We have So much in common!
-GASP! -
SUSAN
Why are you like this?
SUSAN

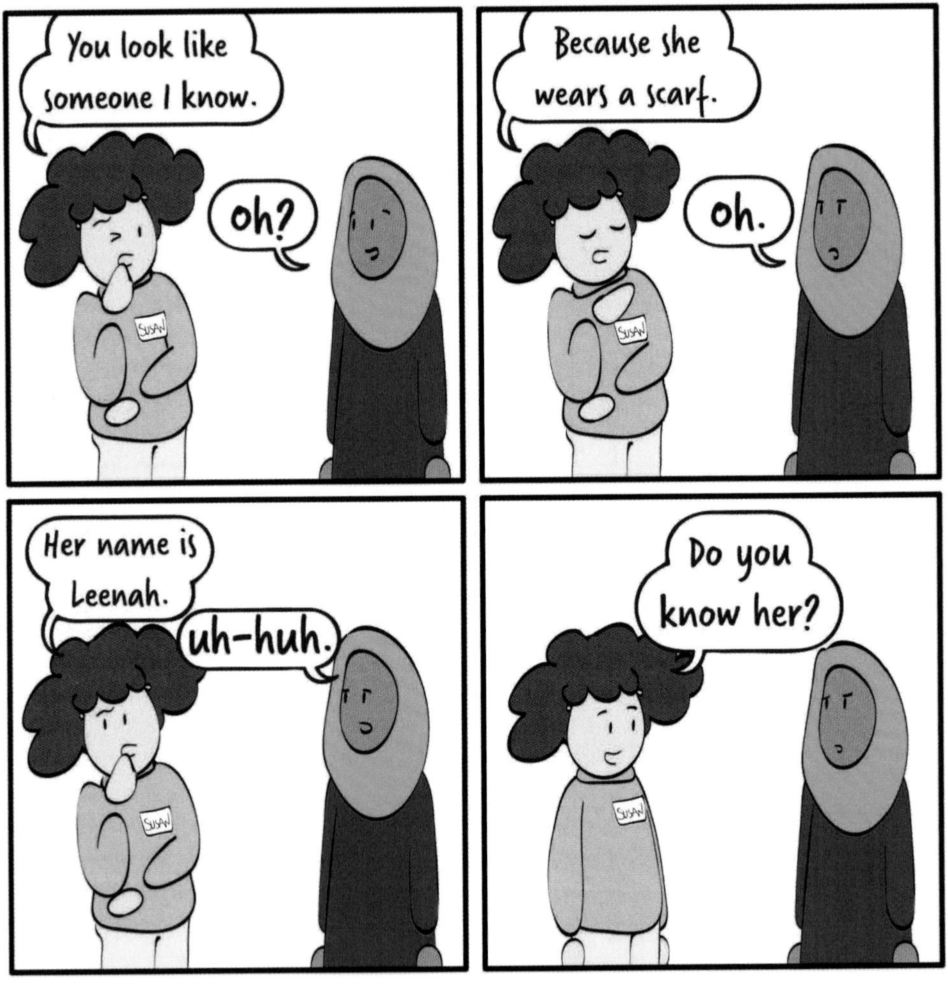
You look like someone I know.
Oh?
Because she wears a scarf.
Oh.
Her name is Leenah.
uh-huh.
Do you know her?

Why would you think I'd know her?
SUSAN
Her scarf was also blue.
SUSAN

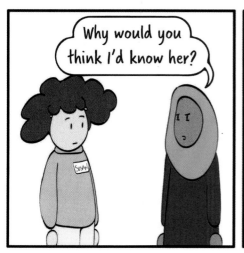

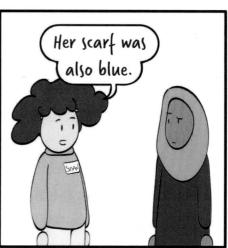

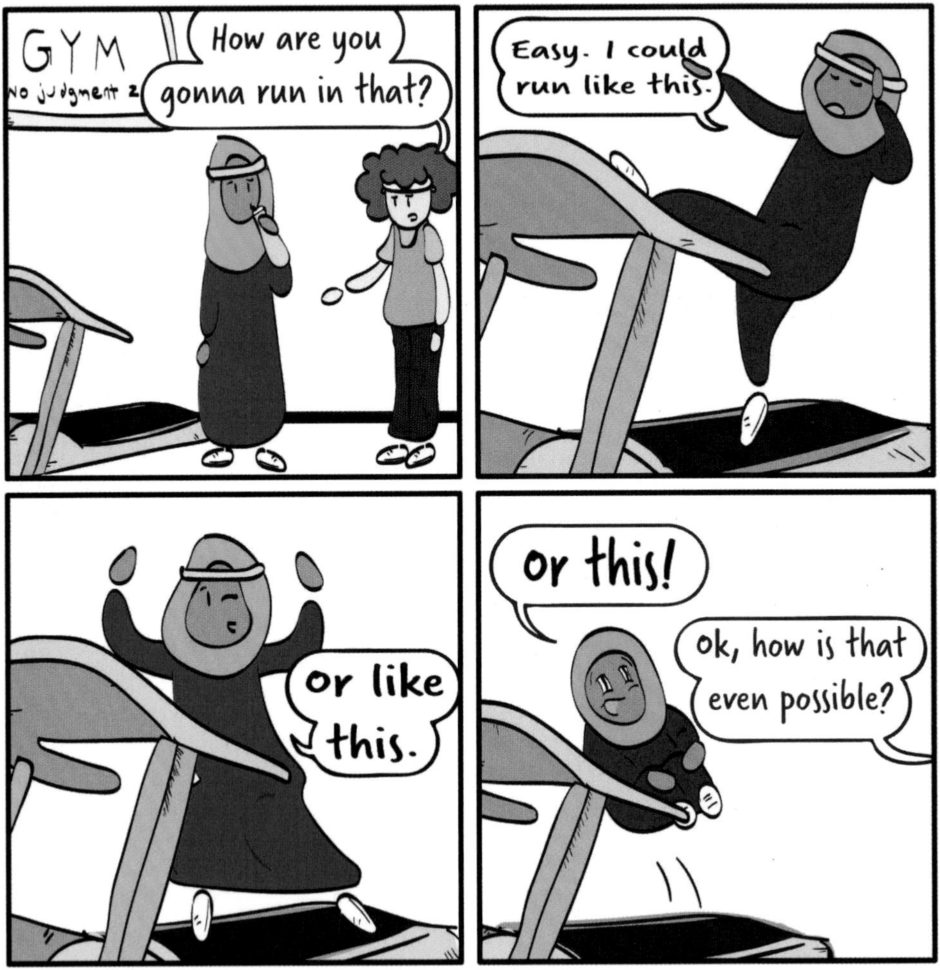
GYM
No judgment z
How are you gonna run in that?
Easy. I could run like this.
Or like this.
Or this!
Ok, how is that even possible?

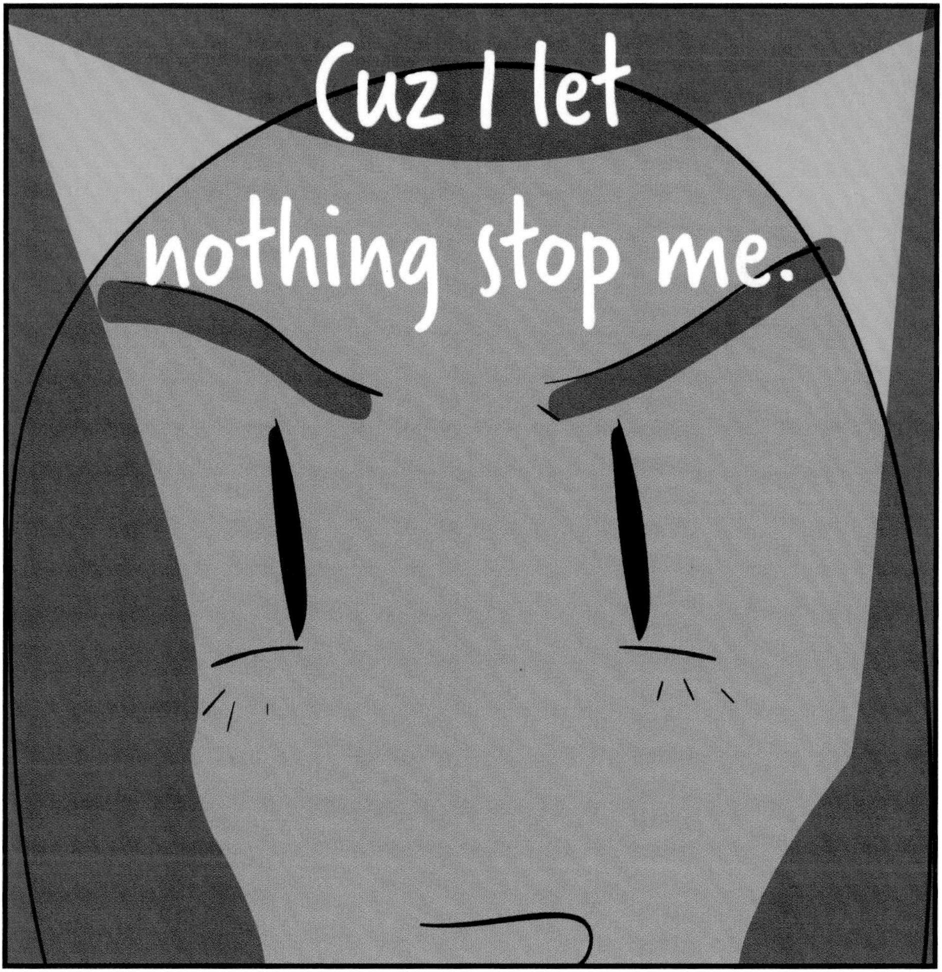
Cuz I let nothing stop me.

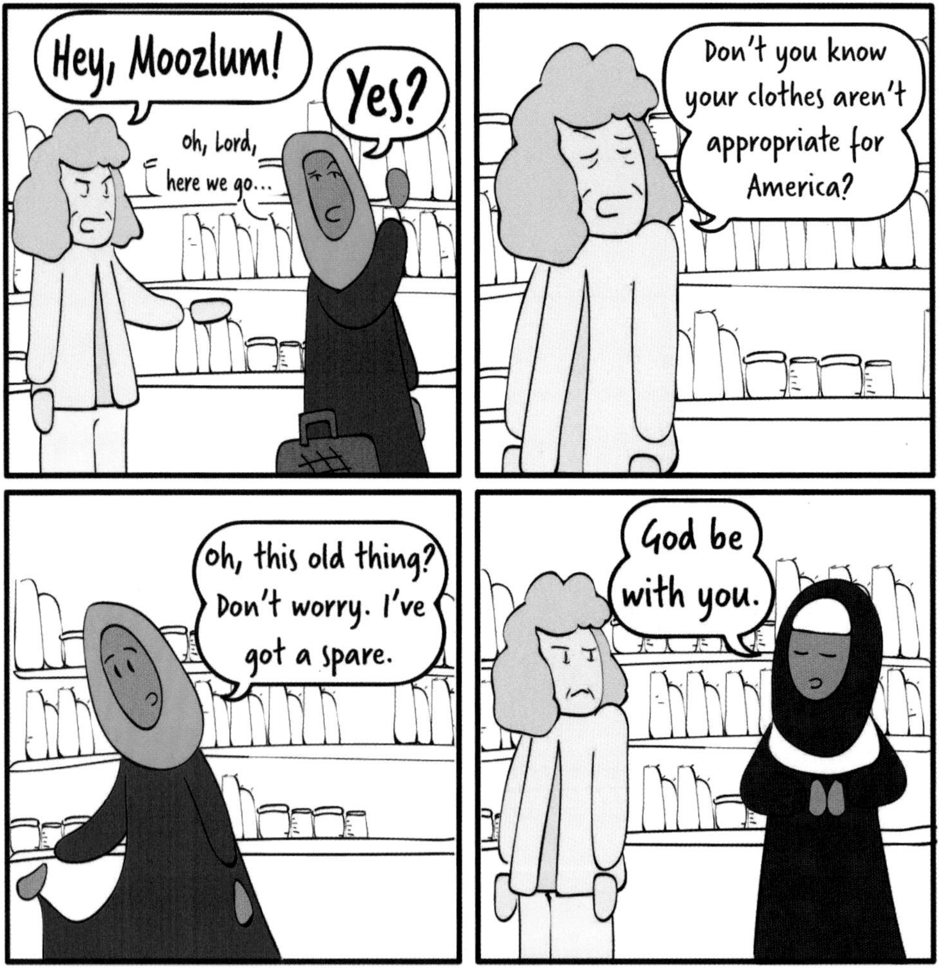
Hey, Moozlum!
Yes?
Oh, Lord, here we go...
Don't you know your clothes aren't appropriate for America?
Oh, this old thing? Don't worry. I've got a spare.
God be with you.

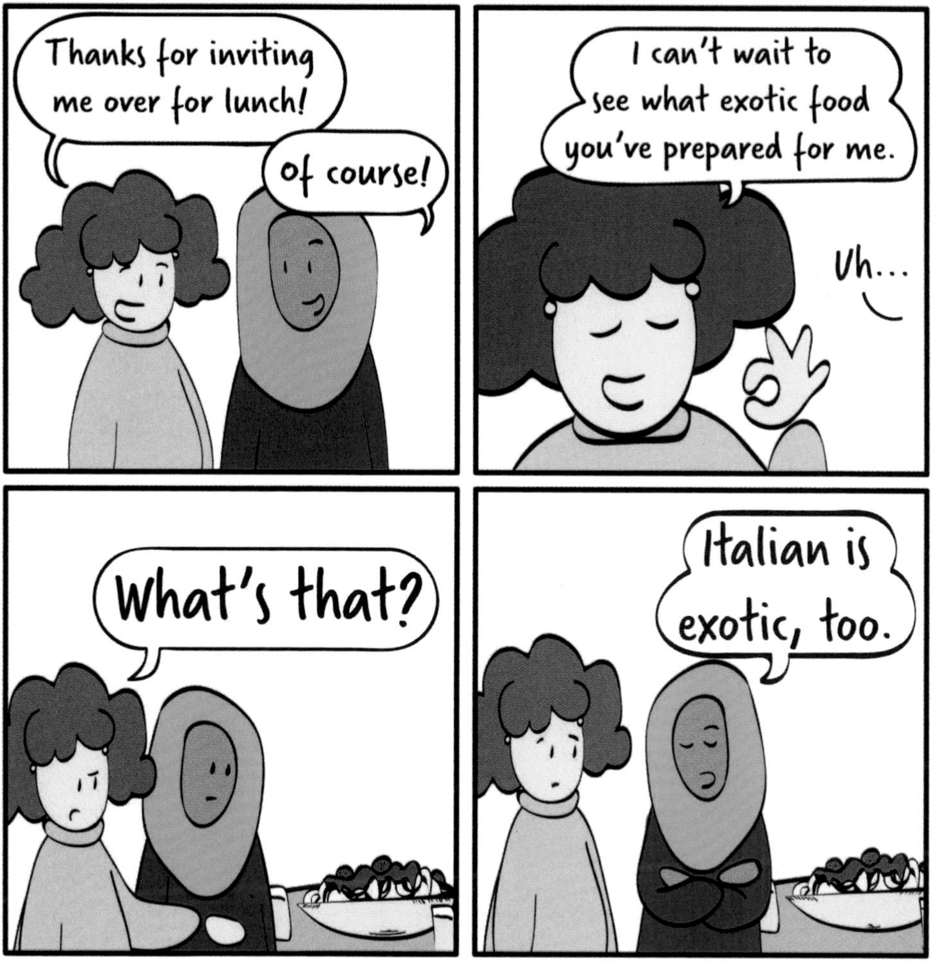
Thanks for inviting me over for lunch!
Of course!
I can't wait to see what exotic food you've prepared for me.
Uh...
What's that?
Italian is exotic, too.

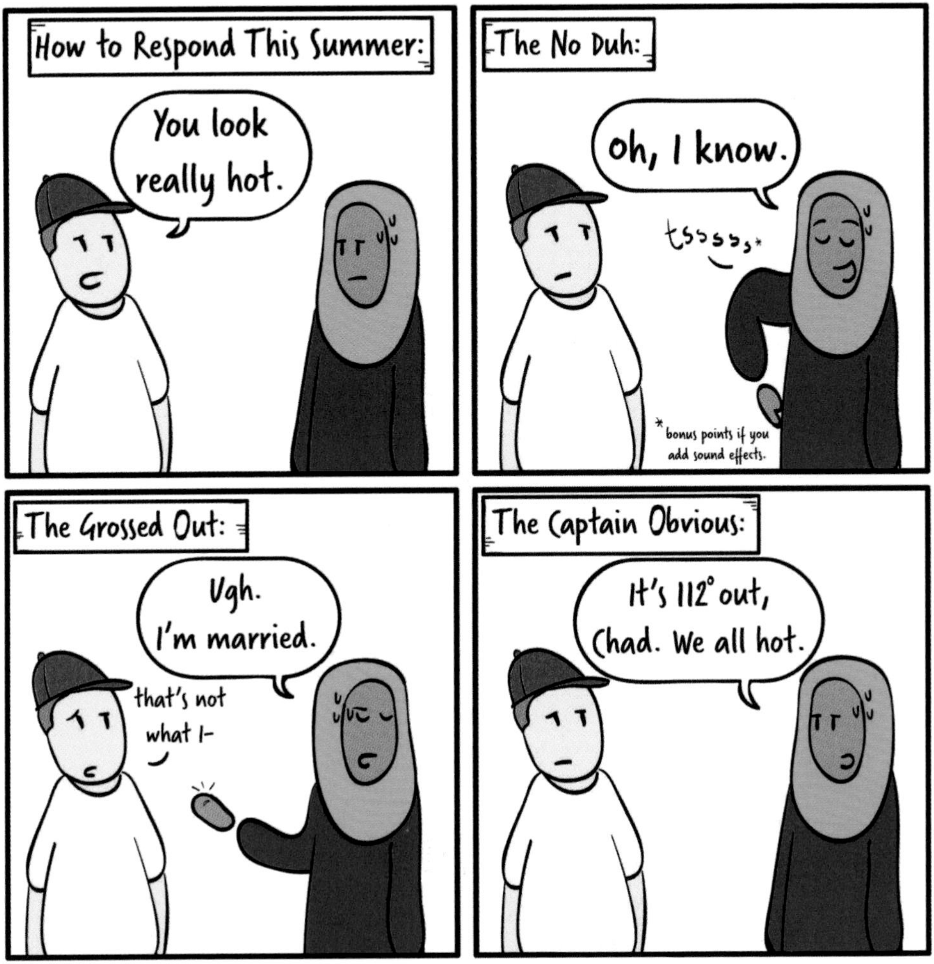
How to Respond This Summer:
You look really hot.
The No Duh:
oh, I know.
tsssss,*
* bonus points if you add sound effects.
The Grossed Out:
Ugh. I'm married.
that's not what I-
The Captain Obvious:
It's 112° out, Chad. We all hot.

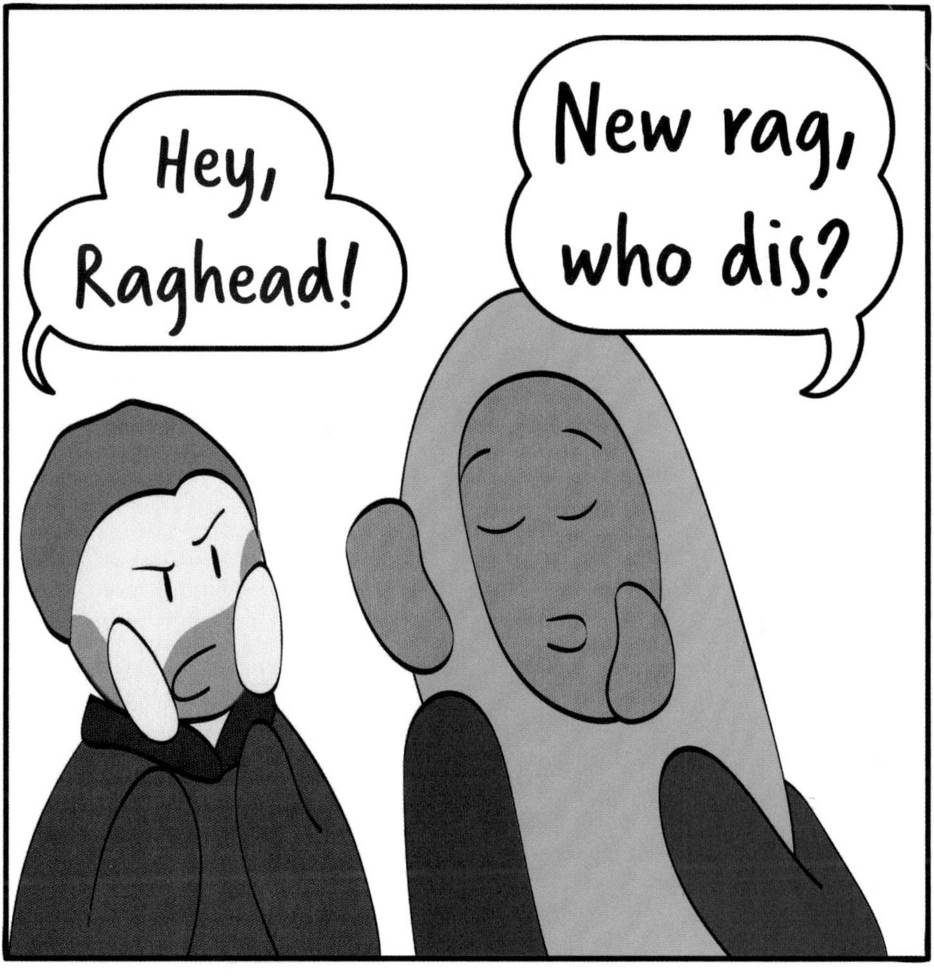
Hey, Raghead!
New rag, who dis?

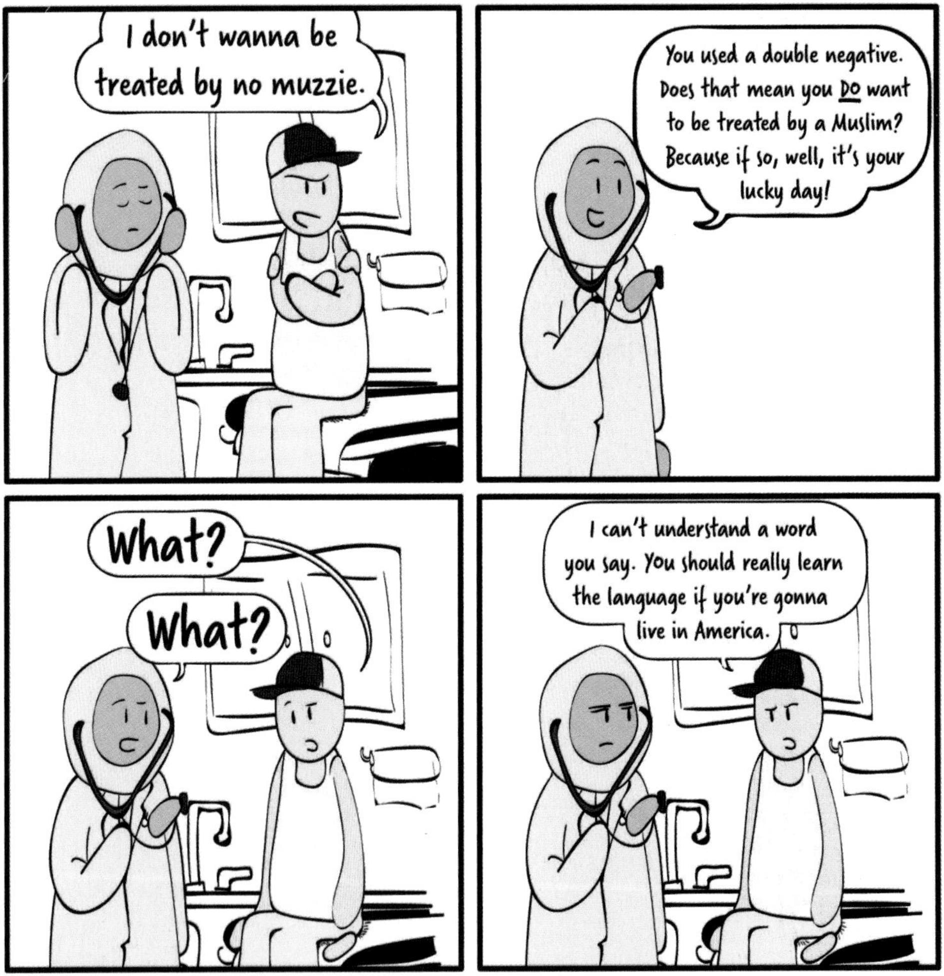
I don't wanna be treated by no muzzie.
You used a double negative. Does that mean you DO want to be treated by a Muslim? Because if so, well, it's your lucky day!
What?
What?
I can't understand a word you say. You should really learn the language if you're gonna live in America.

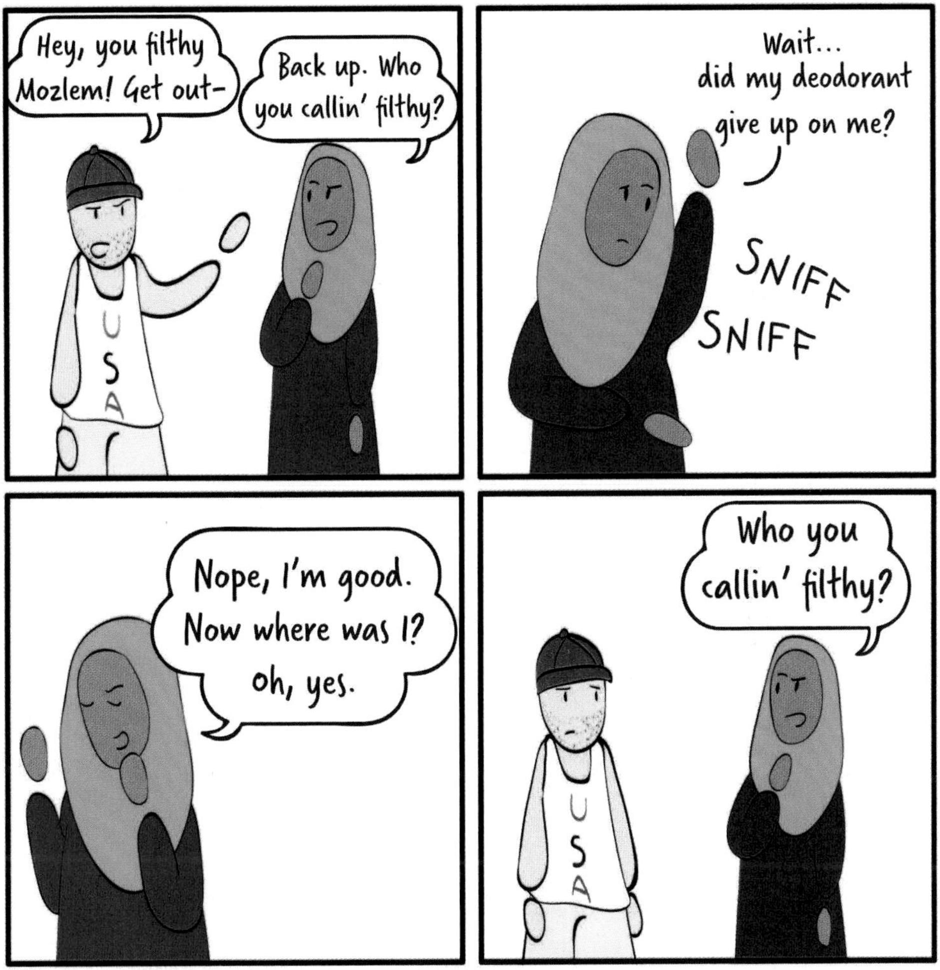
Hey, you filthy Mozlem! Get out-
Back up. Who you callin' filthy?
USA
Wait... did my deodorant give up on me?
SNIFF
SNIFF
Nope, I'm good. Now where was I? Oh, yes.
Who you callin' filthy?
USA

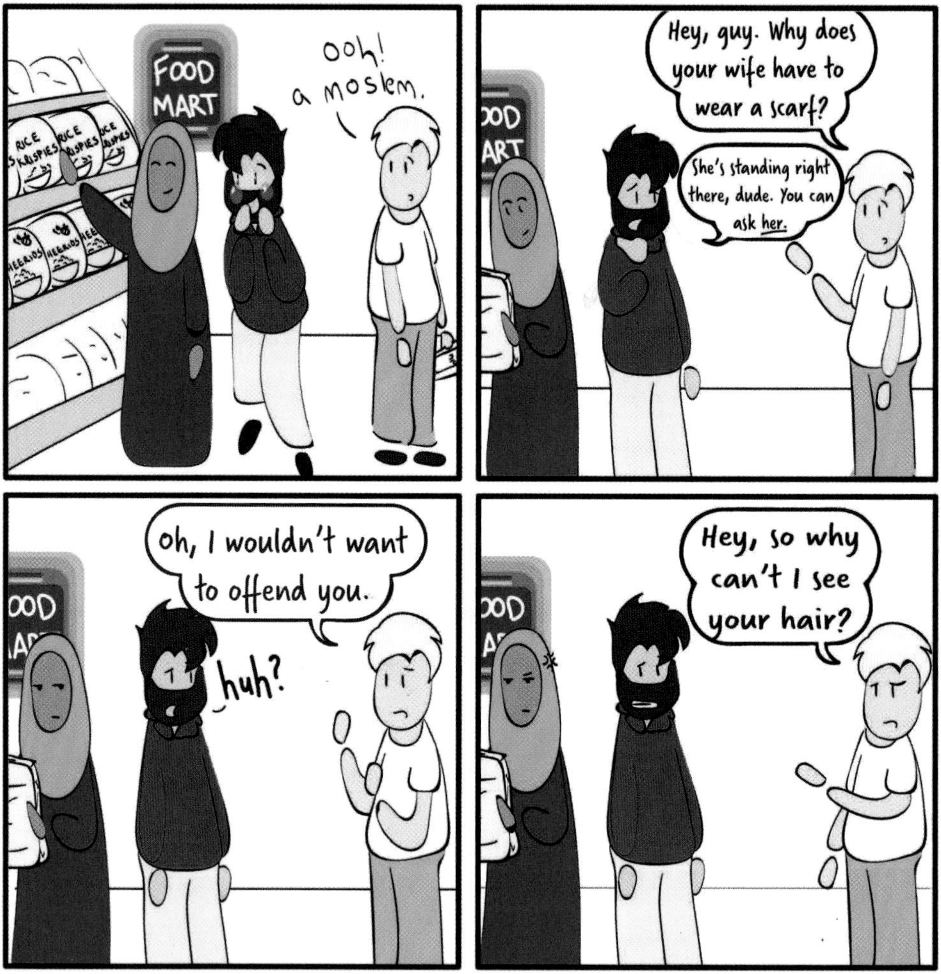
FOOD MART
RICE KRISPIES
CHEERIOS
ooh! a moslem.
Hey, guy. Why does your wife have to wear a scarf?
She's standing right there, dude. You can ask her.
oh, I wouldn't want to offend you.
huh?
Hey, so why can't I see your hair?

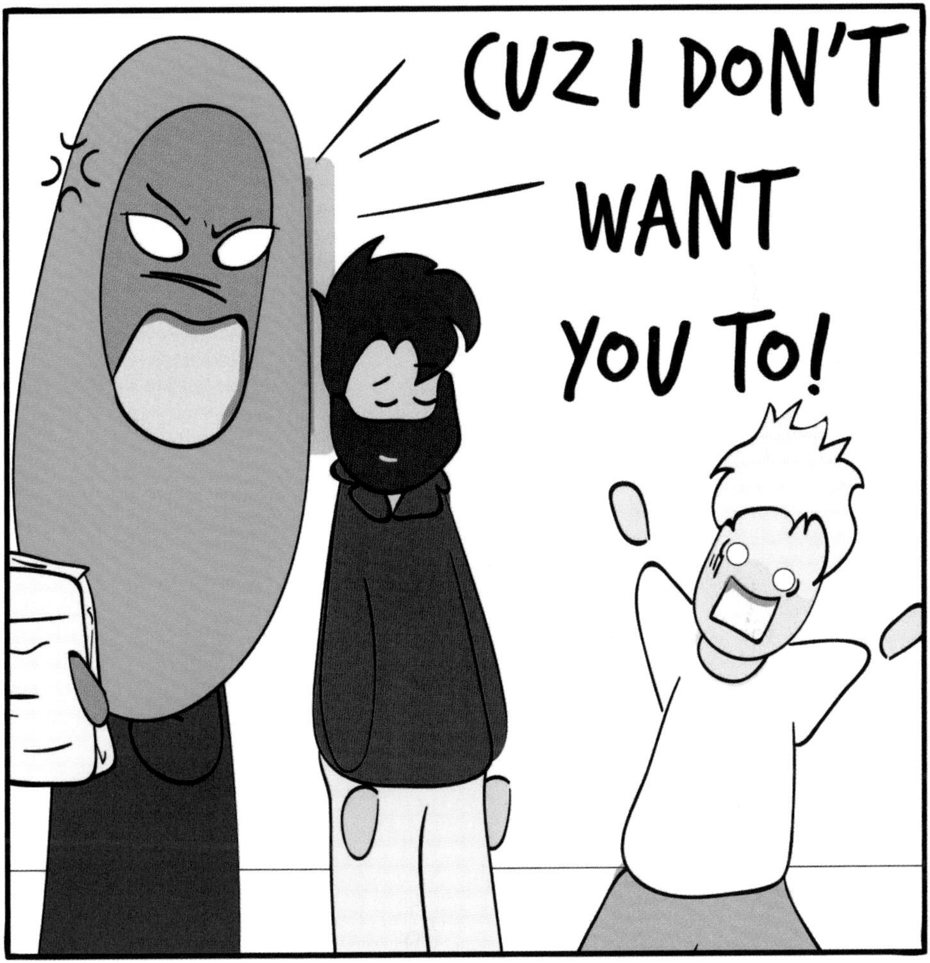
CUZ I DON'T WANT YOU TO!

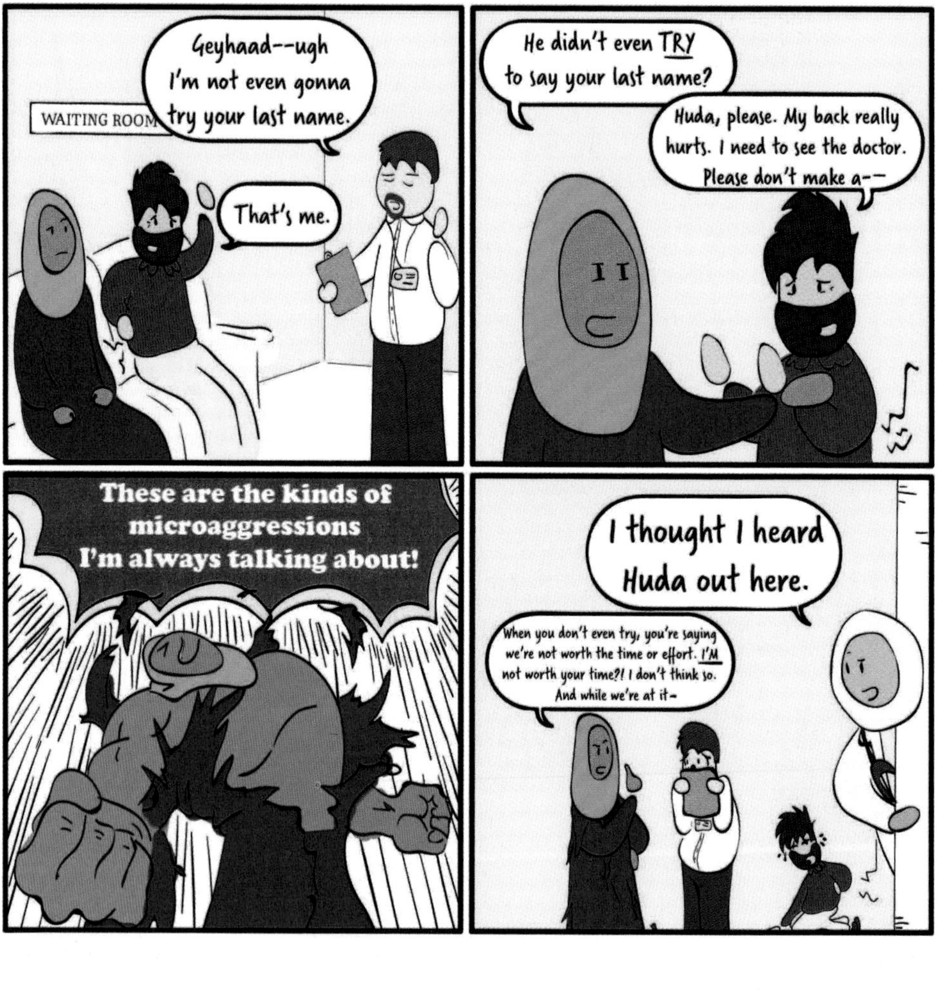
WAITING ROOM
Geyhaad--ugh I'm not even gonna try your last name.
That's me.
He didn't even TRY to say your last name?
Huda, please. My back really hurts. I need to see the doctor. Please don't make a--
These are the kinds of microaggressions I'm always talking about!
I thought I heard Huda out here.
When you don't even try, you're saying we're not worth the time or effort. I'M not worth your time?! I don't think so. And while we're at it-

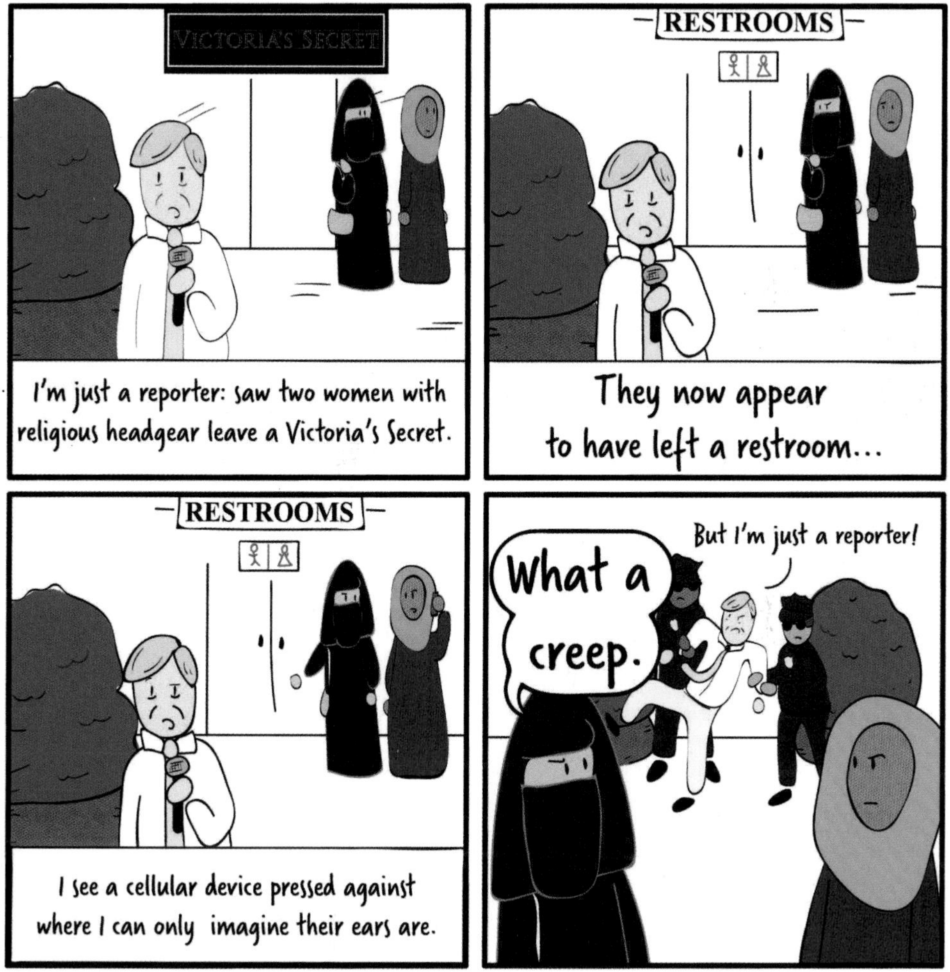
VICTORIA'S SECRET
I'm just a reporter: saw two women with religious headgear leave a Victoria's Secret.
RESTROOMS
They now appear to have left a restroom...
RESTROOMS
I see a cellular device pressed against where I can only imagine their ears are.
What a creep.
But I'm just a reporter!

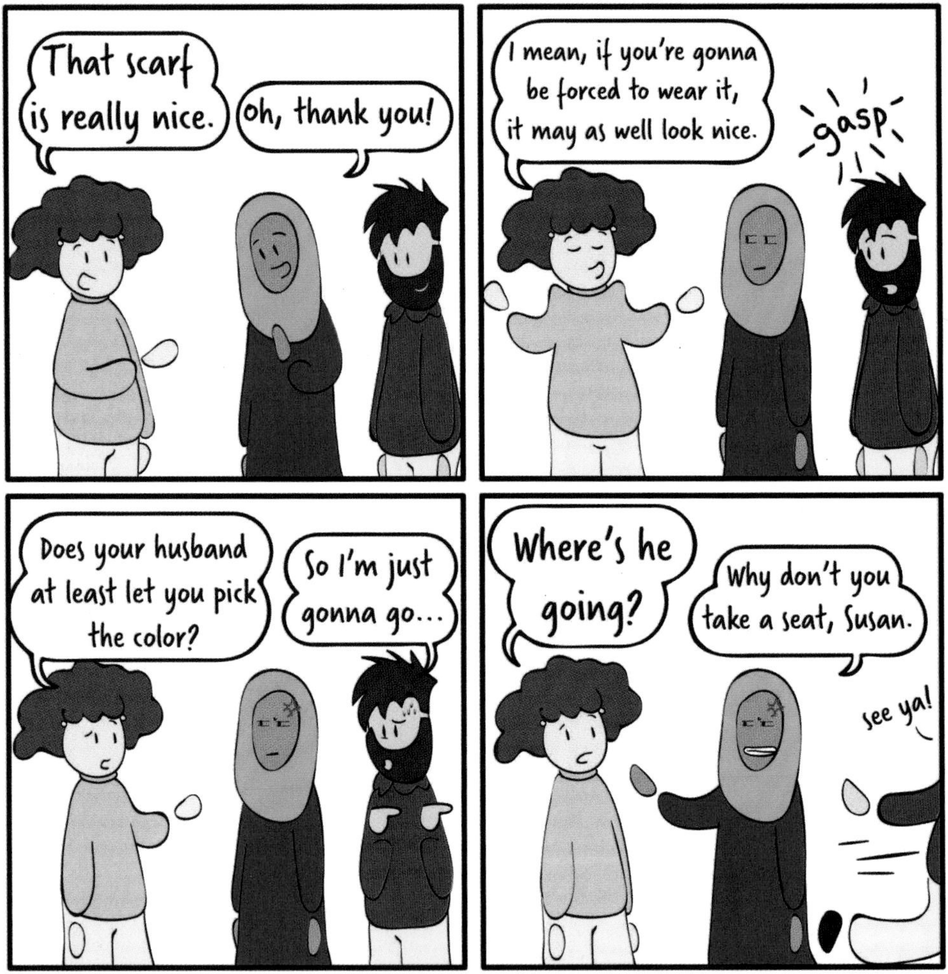
That scarf is really nice.
Oh, thank you!
I mean, if you're gonna be forced to wear it, it may as well look nice.
gasp
Does your husband at least let you pick the color?
So I'm just gonna go...
Where's he going?
Why don't you take a seat, Susan.
see ya!

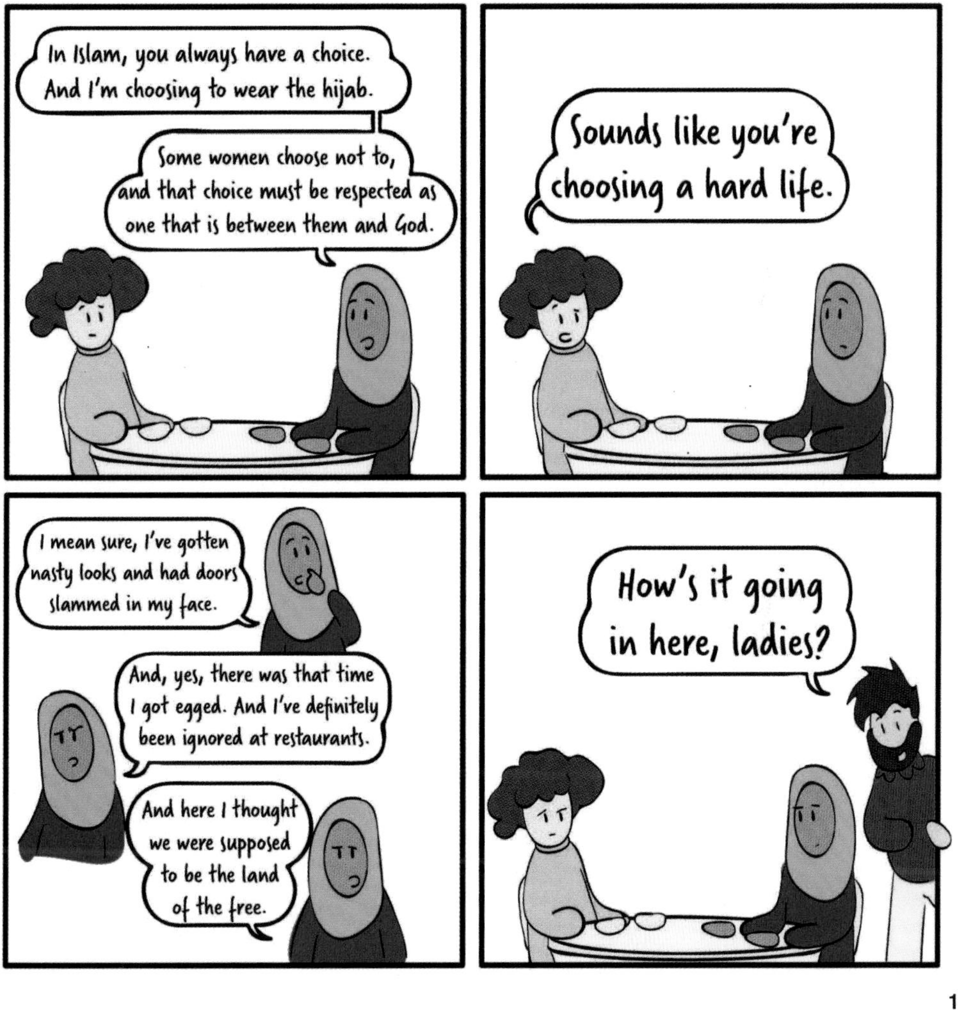
In Islam, you always have a choice. And I'm choosing to wear the hijab.
Some women choose not to, and that choice must be respected as one that is between them and God.
Sounds like you're choosing a hard life.
I mean sure, I've gotten nasty looks and had doors slammed in my face.
And, yes, there was that time I got egged. And I've definitely been ignored at restaurants.
And here I thought we were supposed to be the land of the free.
How's it going in here, ladies?

Sounds like your wife hates America.
Aaaaaand I'm gone.

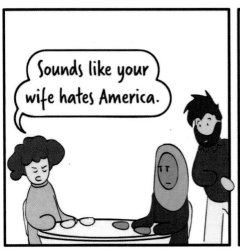

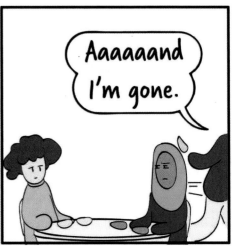

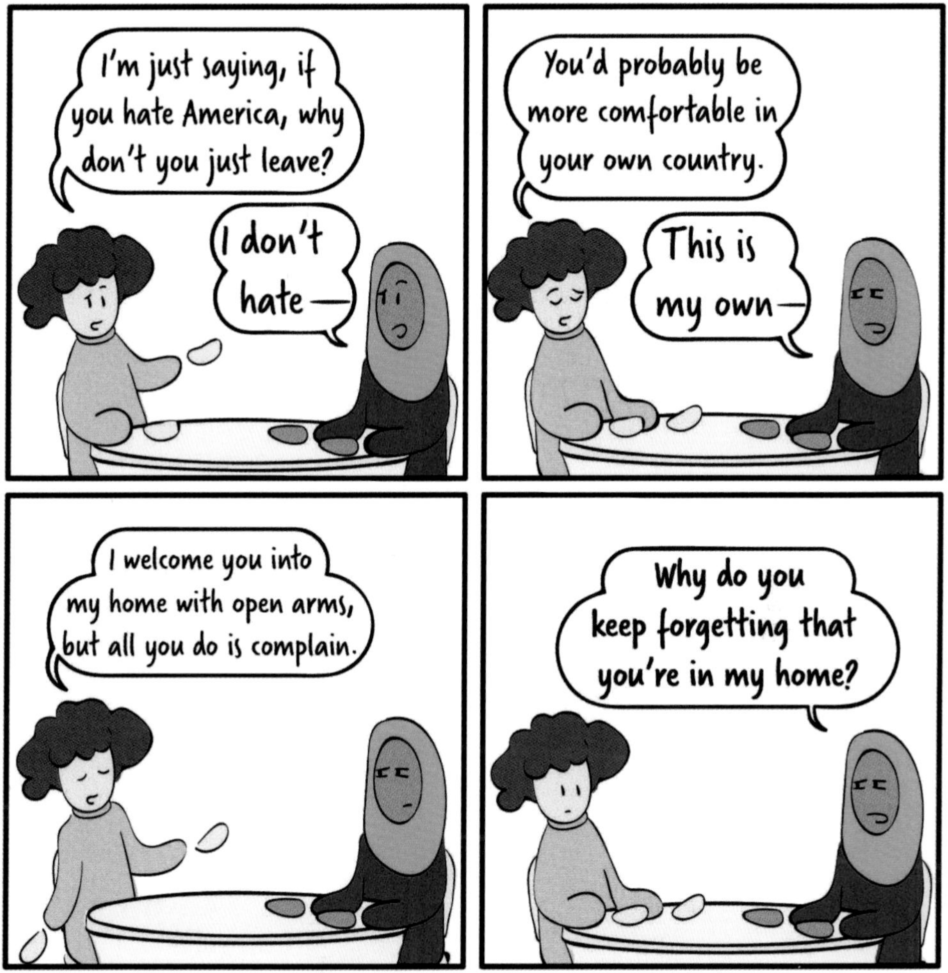
I'm just saying, if you hate America, why don't you just leave?
I don't hate—
You'd probably be more comfortable in your own country.
This is my own—
I welcome you into my home with open arms, but all you do is complain.
Why do you keep forgetting that you're in my home?

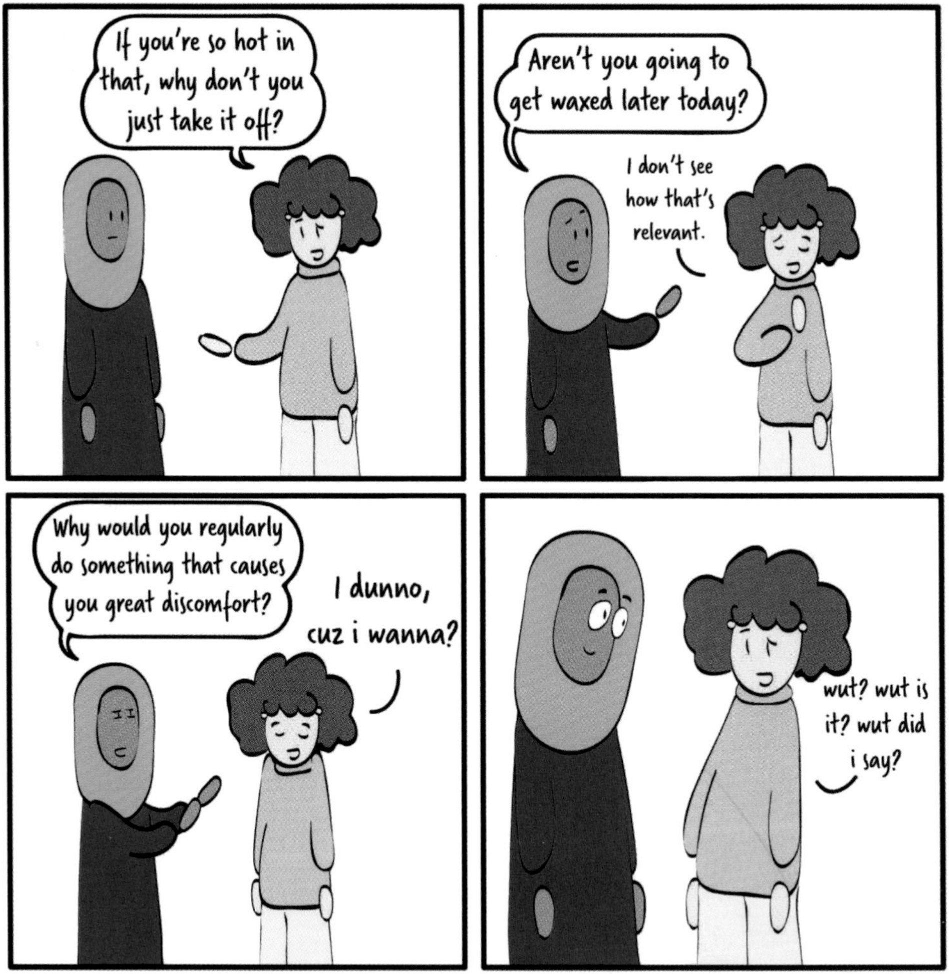
If you're so hot in that, why don't you just take it off?
Aren't you going to get waxed later today?
I don't see how that's relevant.
Why would you regularly do something that causes you great discomfort?
I dunno, cuz i wanna?
wut? wut is it? wut did i say?

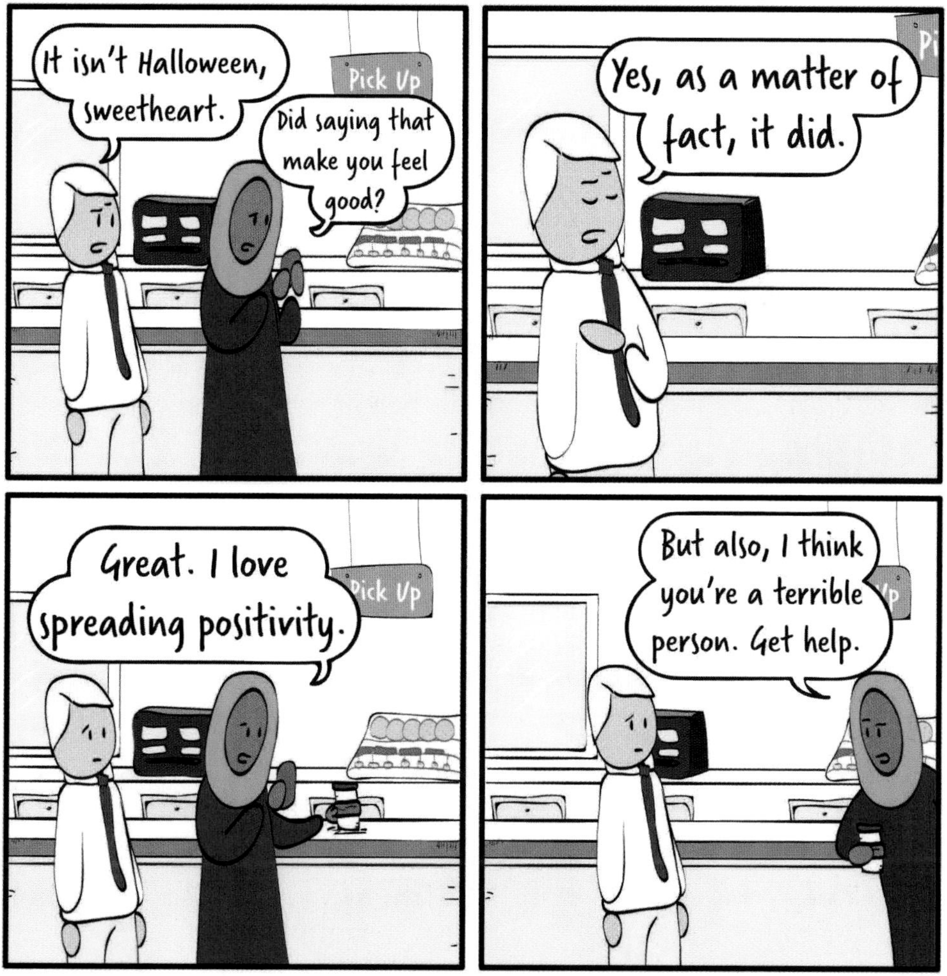
It isn't Halloween, sweetheart.
Did saying that make you feel good?
Pick Up
Yes, as a matter of fact, it did.
Great. I love spreading positivity.
Pick Up
But also, I think you're a terrible person. Get help.

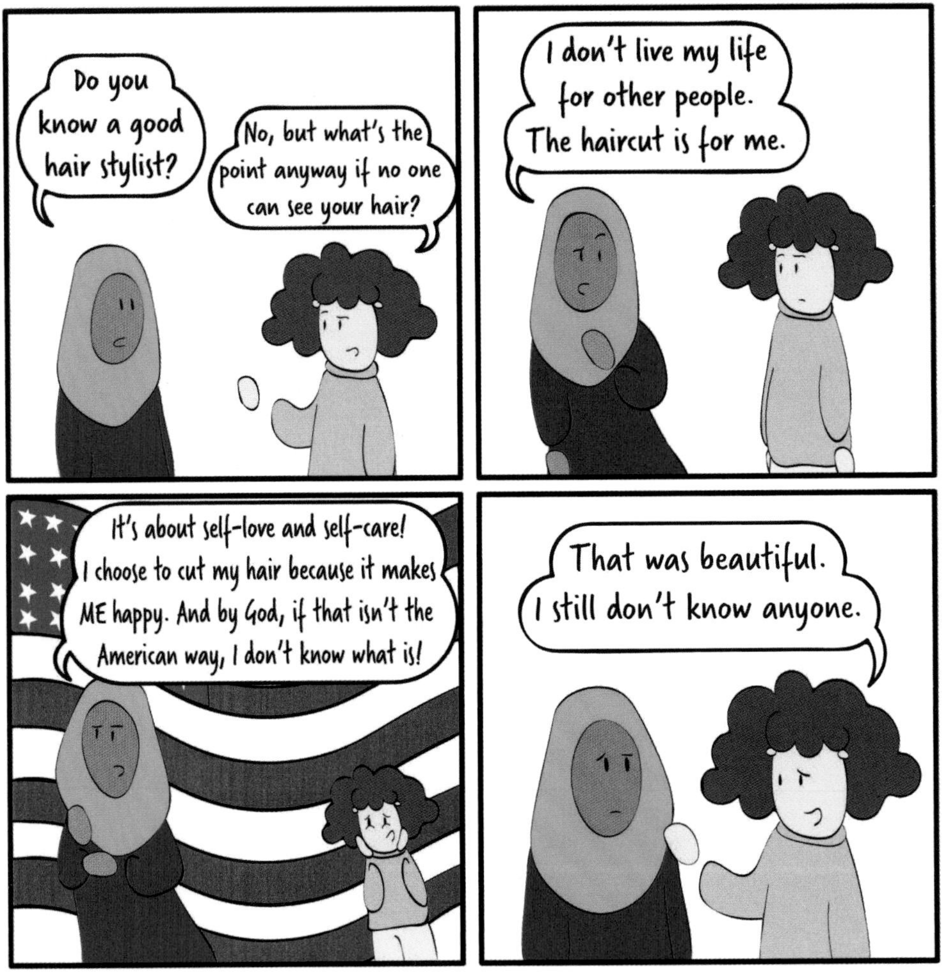
Do you know a good hair stylist?
No, but what's the point anyway if no one can see your hair?
I don't live my life for other people. The haircut is for me.
It's about self-love and self-care! I choose to cut my hair because it makes ME happy. And by God, if that isn't the American way, I don't know what is!
That was beautiful. I still don't know anyone.

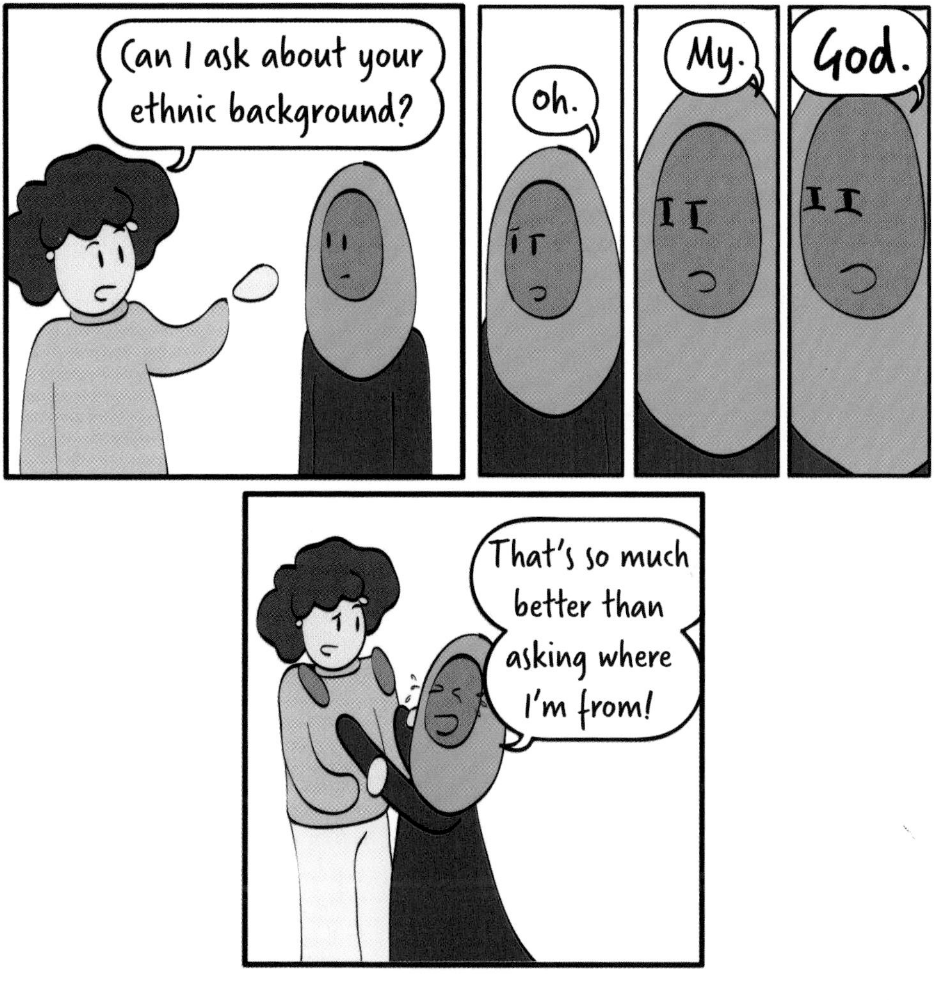

Can I ask about your ethnic background?
Oh.
My.
God.
That's so much better than asking where I'm from!

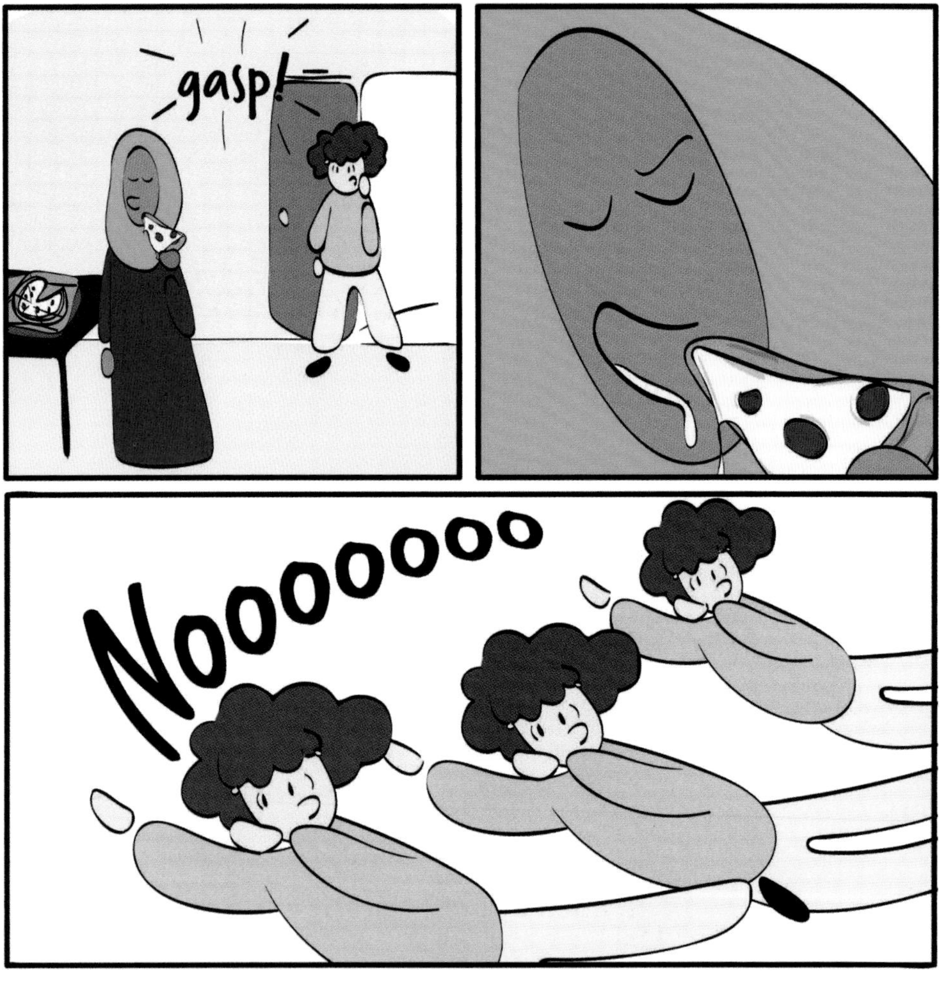
gasp!
Nooooooo

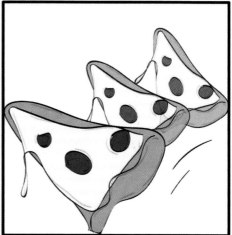

I'm gonna take a wild guess and say you've never heard of halal pepperoni.

my bad.

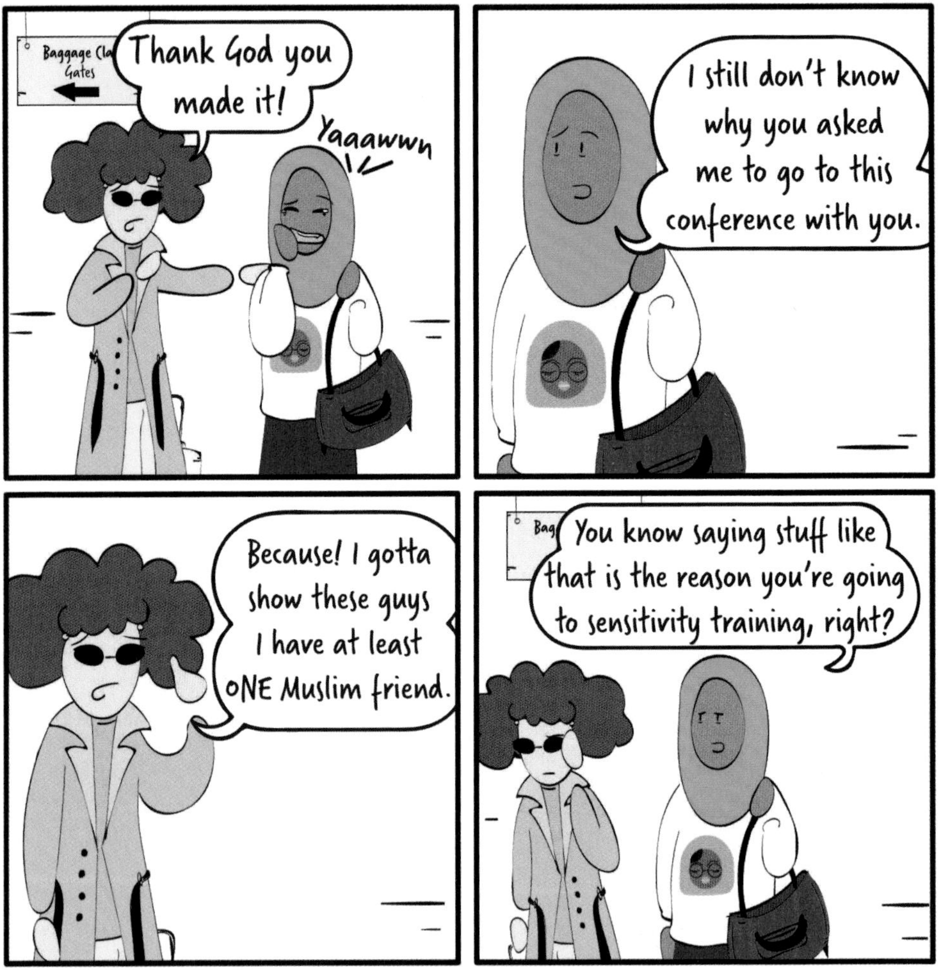
Baggage Cla
Gates
Thank God you made it!
Yaaawwn
I still don't know why you asked me to go to this conference with you.
Because! I gotta show these guys I have at least ONE Muslim friend.
You know saying stuff like that is the reason you're going to sensitivity training, right?

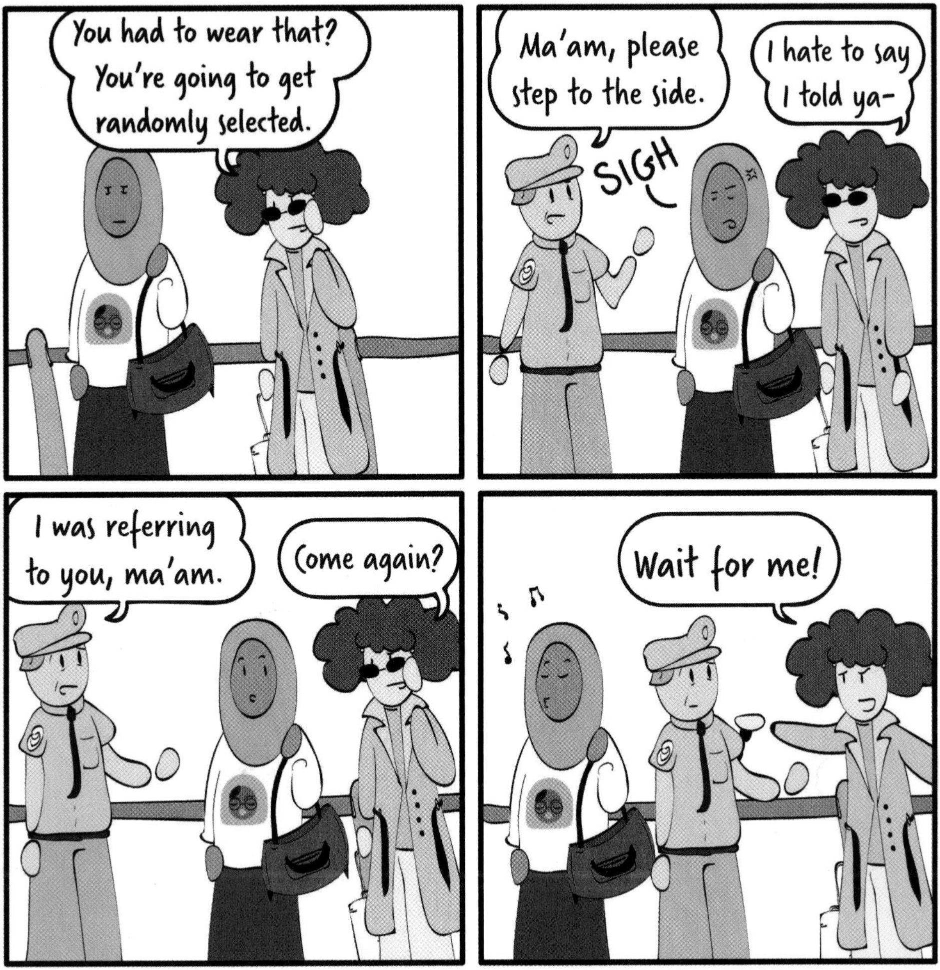
You had to wear that? You're going to get randomly selected.
Ma'am, please step to the side.
I hate to say I told ya-
SIGH
I was referring to you, ma'am.
Come again?
Wait for me!

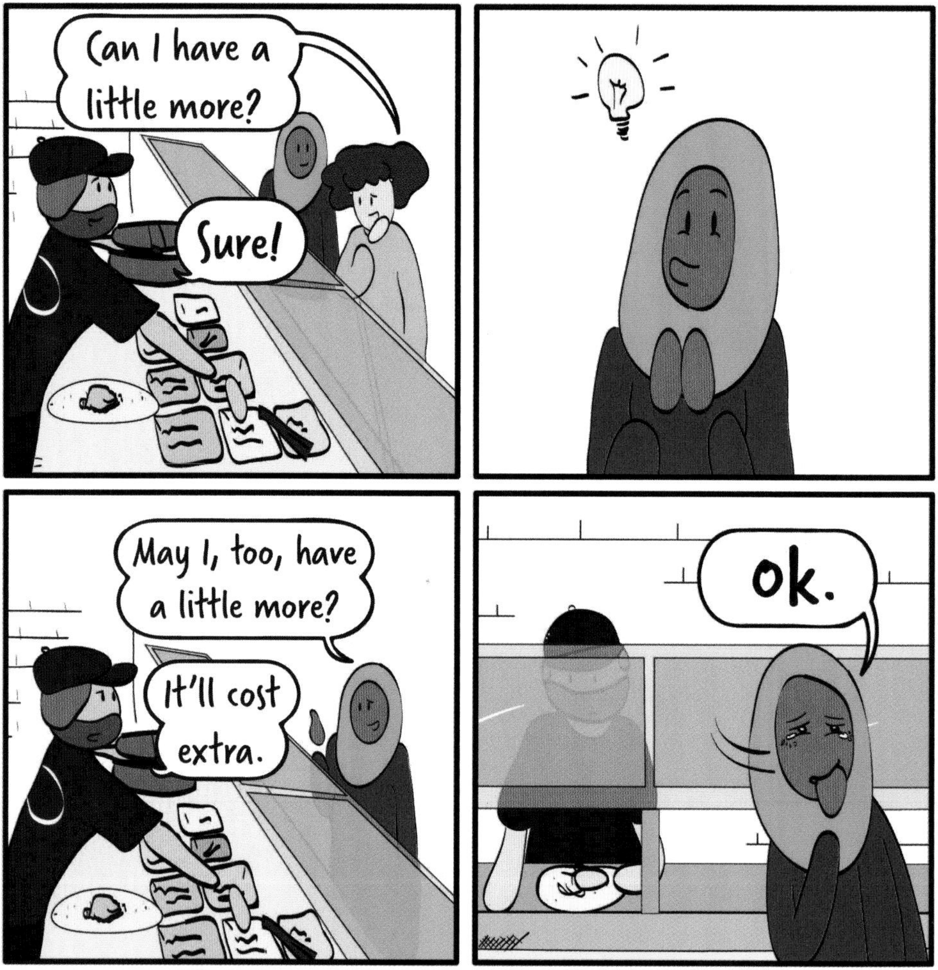
Can I have a little more?
Sure!
May I, too, have a little more?
It'll cost extra.
Ok.

ME
Also Me
Go back to where ya came from!
Ay! You first!
o-oh yeah? Well-um…uh…
freezes up

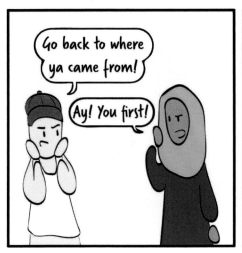

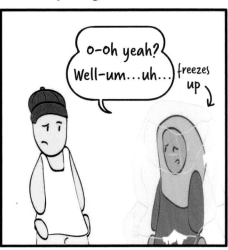

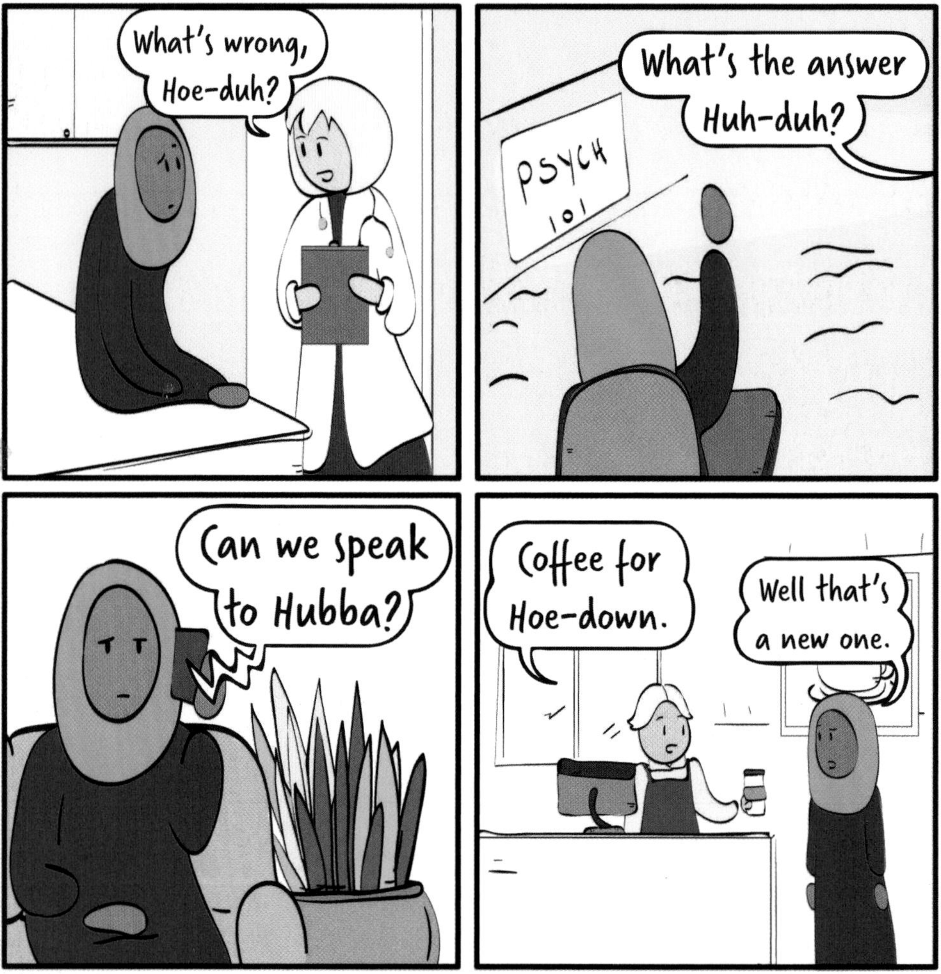
What's wrong, Hoe-duh?
PSYCH 101
What's the answer Huh-duh?
Can we speak to Hubba?
Coffee for Hoe-down.
Well that's a new one.

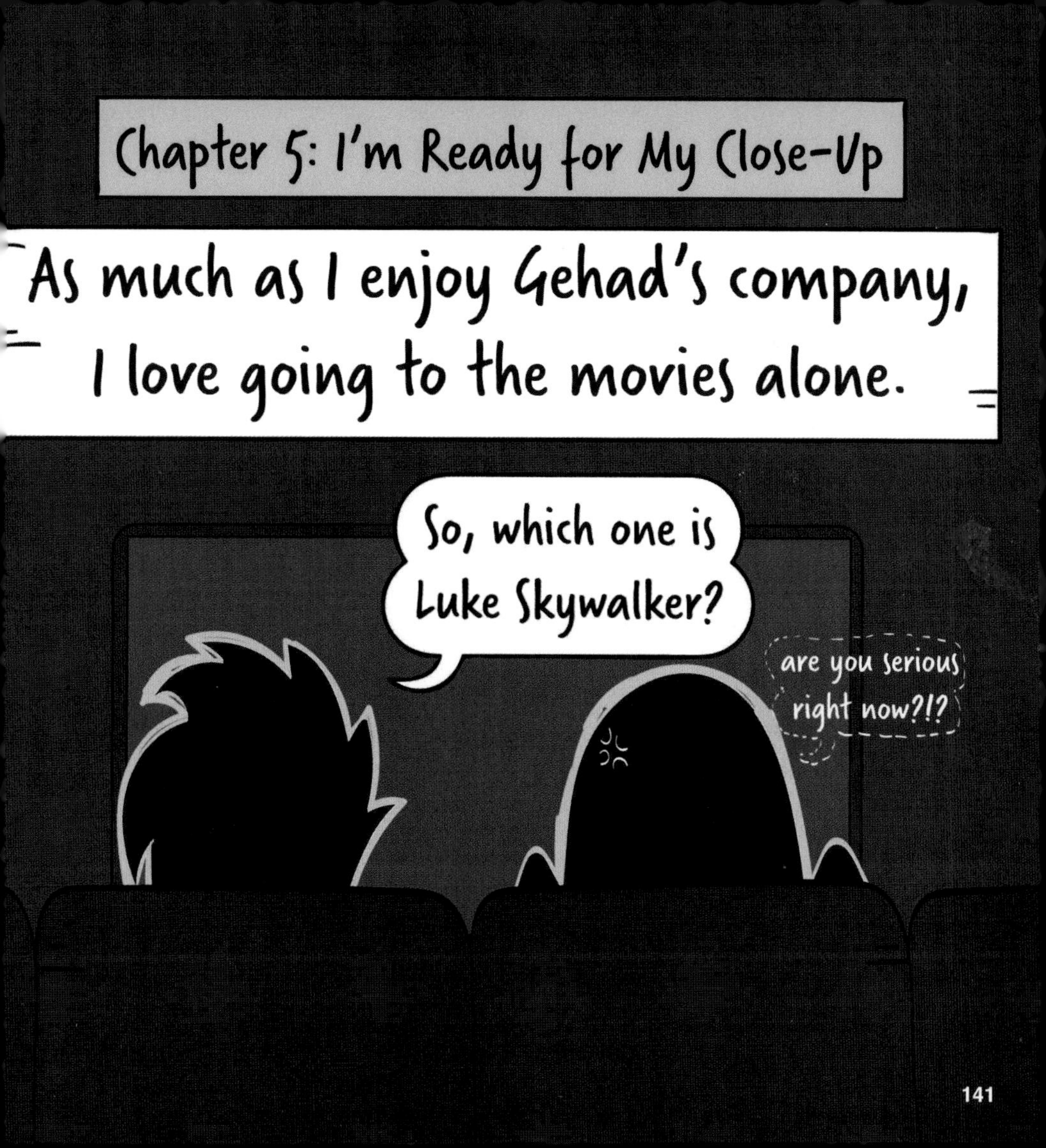
Chapter 5: I'm Ready for My Close-Up
As much as I enjoy Gehad's company, I love going to the movies alone.
So, which one is Luke Skywalker?
are you serious right now?!?

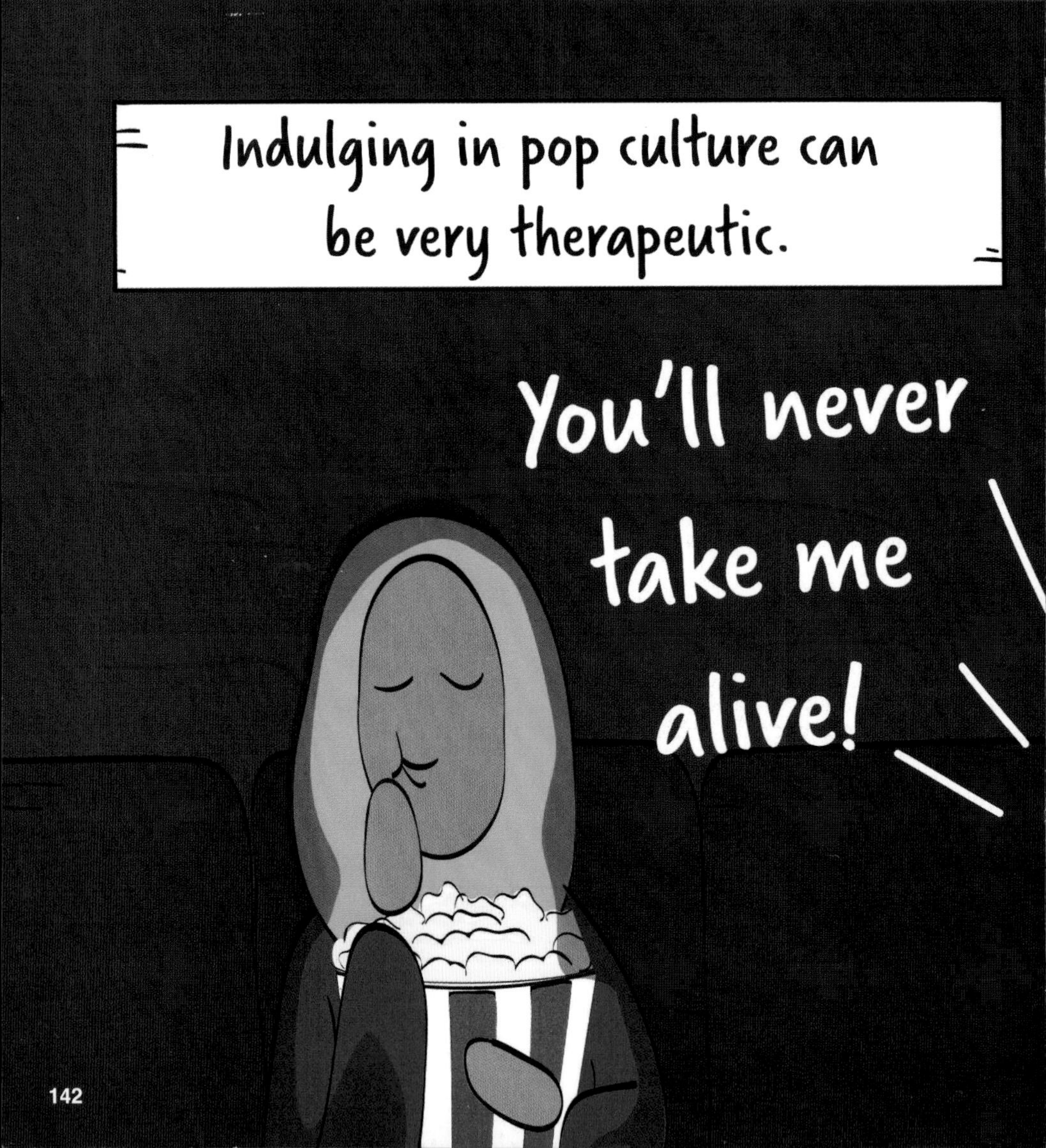
Indulging in pop culture can be very therapeutic.
You'll never take me alive!

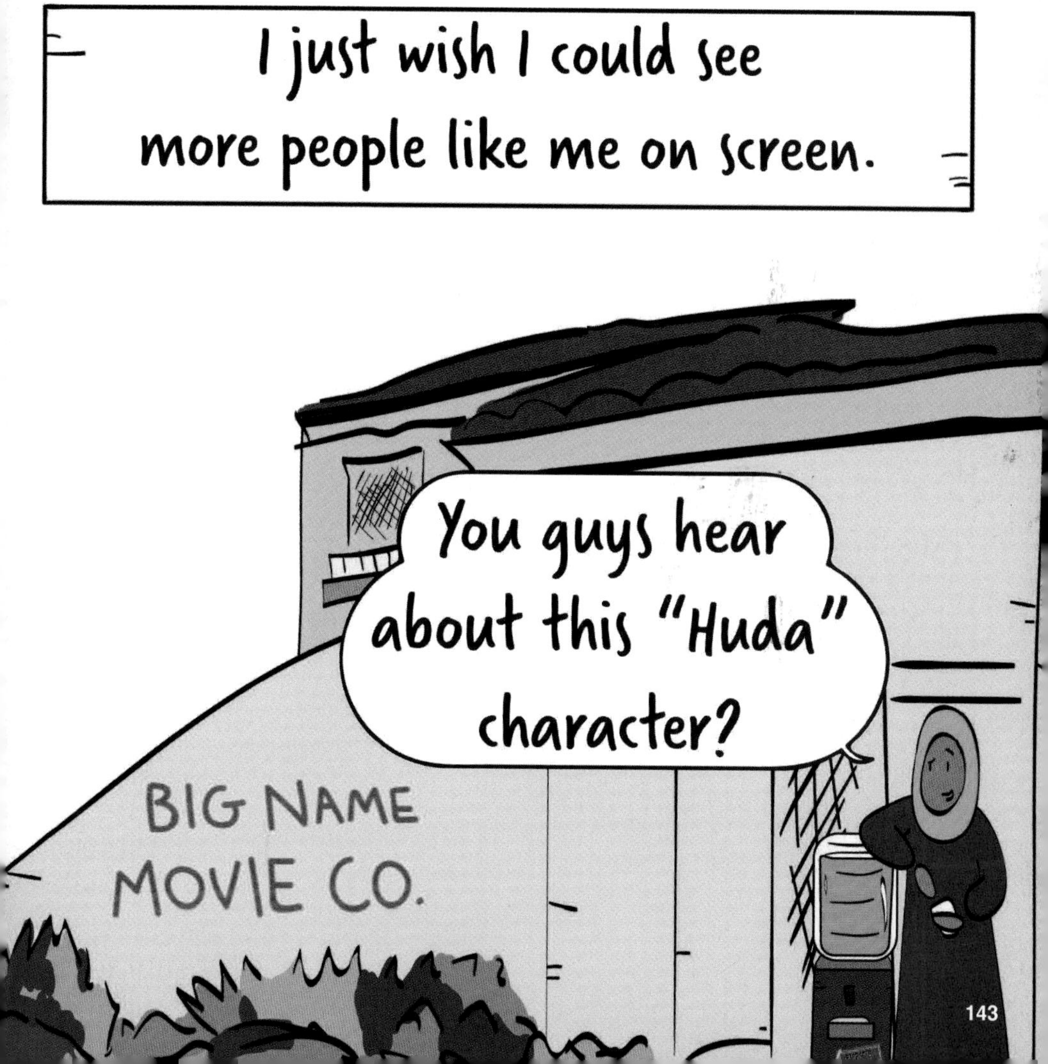
I just wish I could see more people like me on screen.
You guys hear about this "Huda" character?
BIG NAME MOVIE CO.

Because if there's anything Hollywood is lacking, it's hot women.

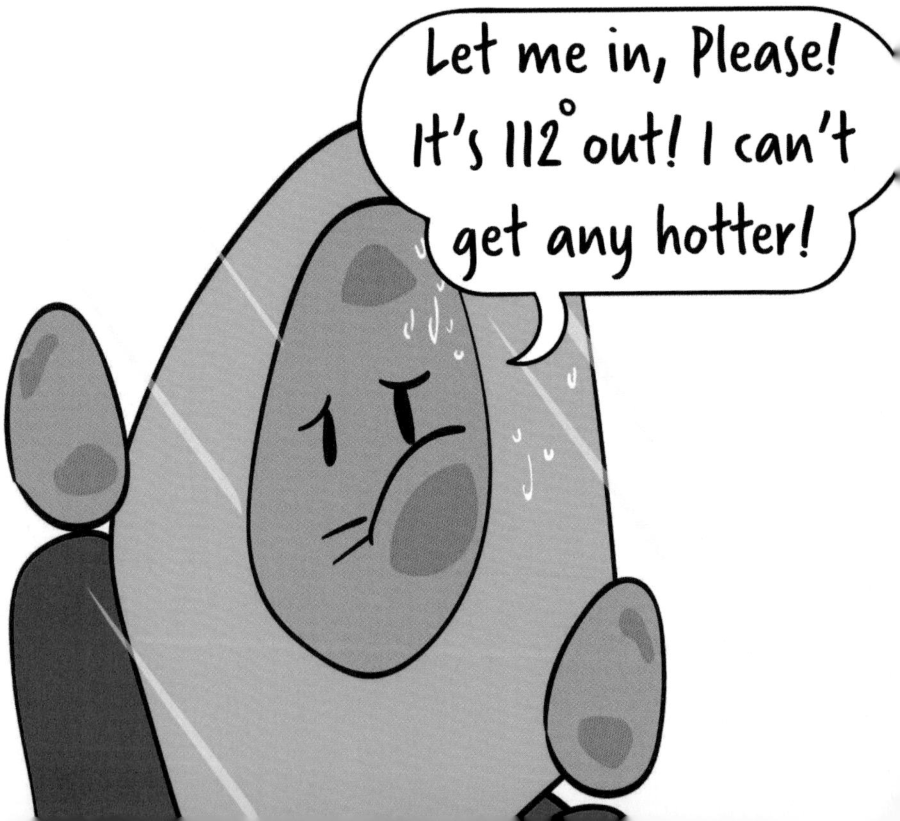
Let me in, Please! It's 112° out! I can't get any hotter!

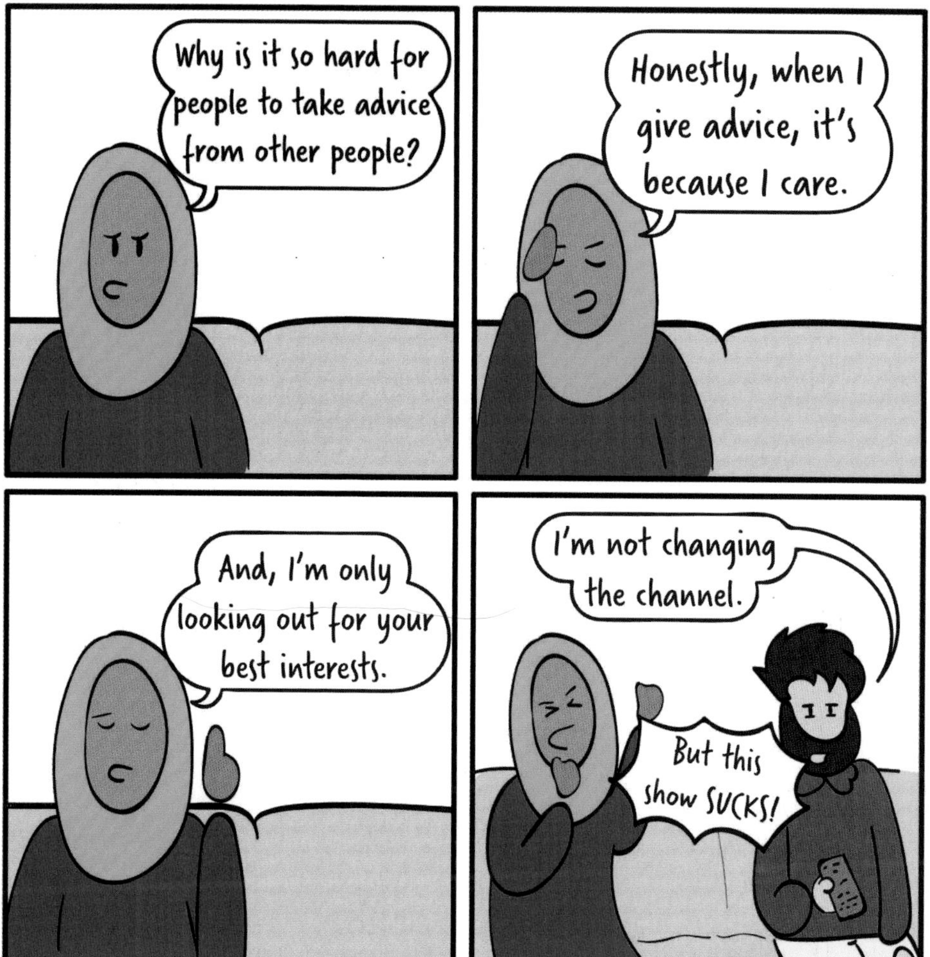
Why is it so hard for people to take advice from other people?
Honestly, when I give advice, it's because I care.
And, I'm only looking out for your best interests.
I'm not changing the channel.
But this show SUCKS!

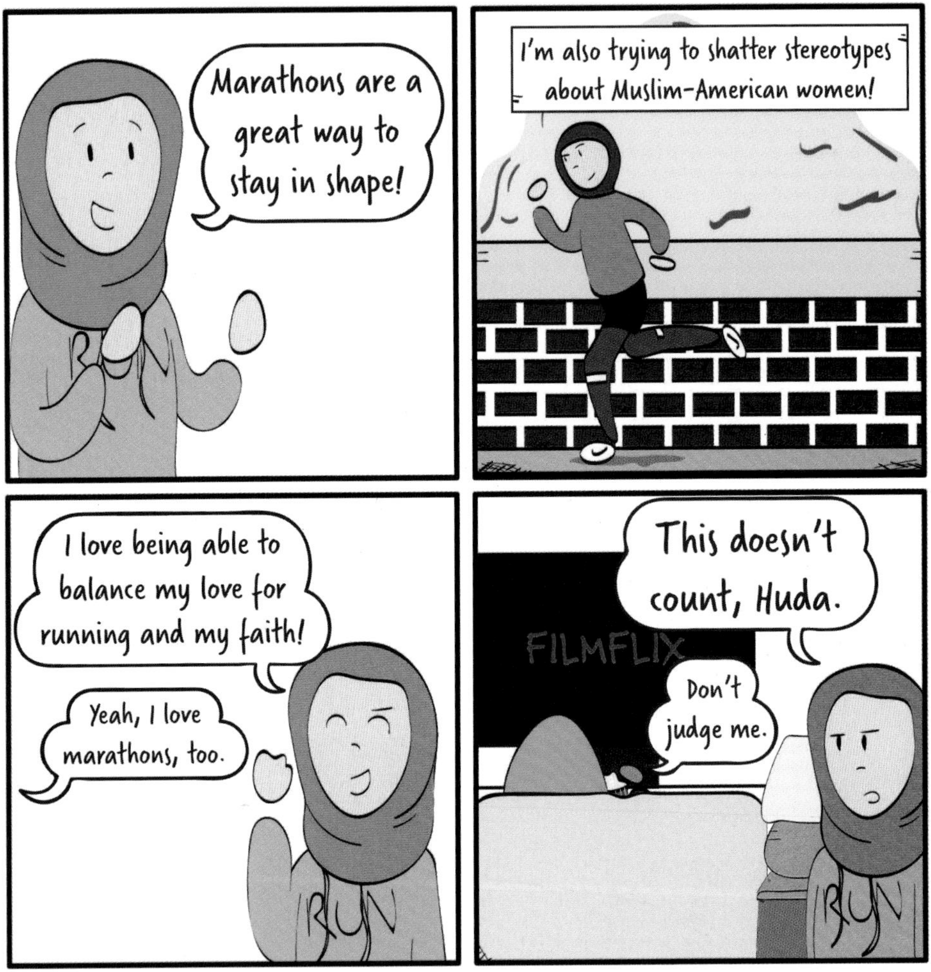
Marathons are a great way to stay in shape!
I'm also trying to shatter stereotypes about Muslim-American women!
I love being able to balance my love for running and my faith!
Yeah, I love marathons, too.
This doesn't count, Huda.
FILMFLIX
Don't judge me.

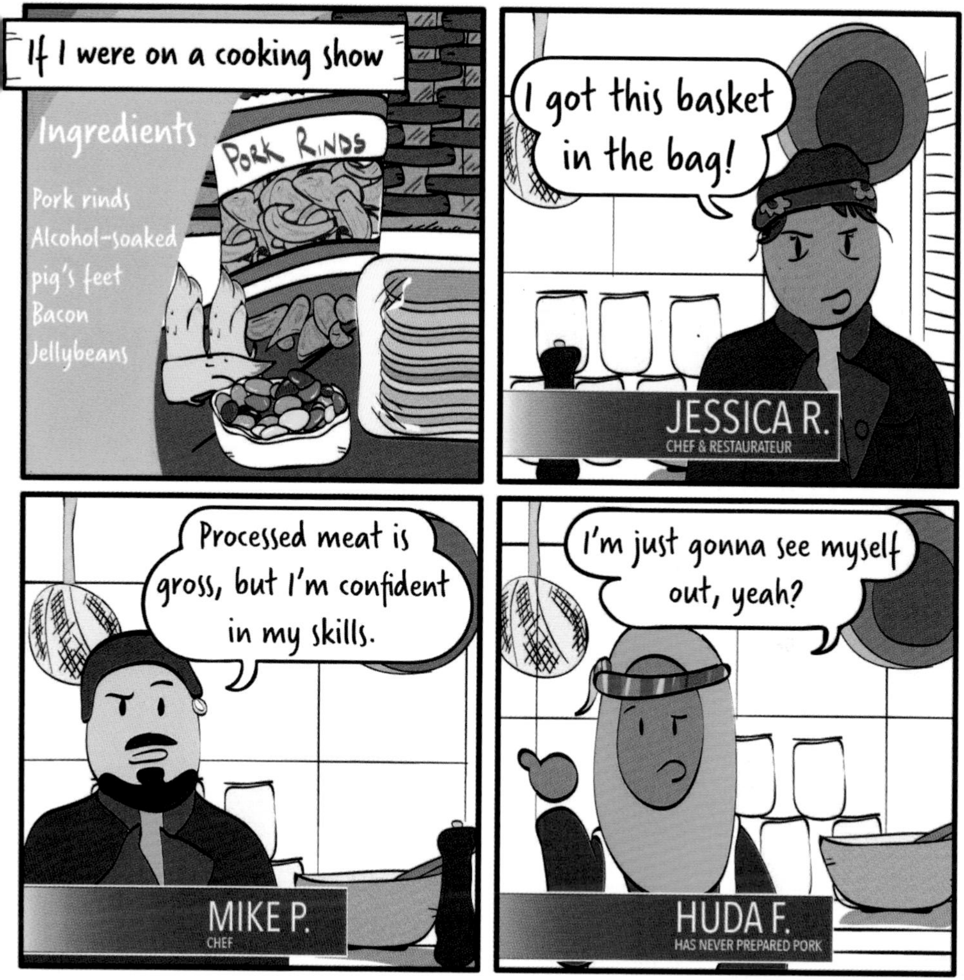
If I were on a cooking show
Ingredients
Pork rinds
Alcohol-soaked pig's feet
Bacon
Jellybeans
PORK RINDS
I got this basket in the bag!
JESSICA R.
CHEF & RESTAURATEUR
Processed meat is gross, but I'm confident in my skills.
MIKE P.
CHEF
I'm just gonna see myself out, yeah?
HUDA F.
HAS NEVER PREPARED PORK

Why do you look so disappointed? I thought you were craving this stuff?
I was. There just never seems to be enough.
Representation for Women of Color

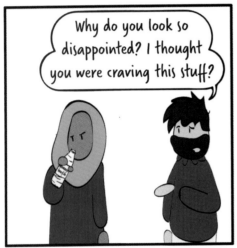

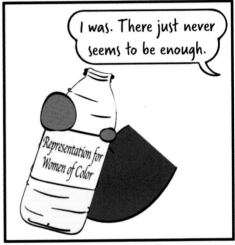

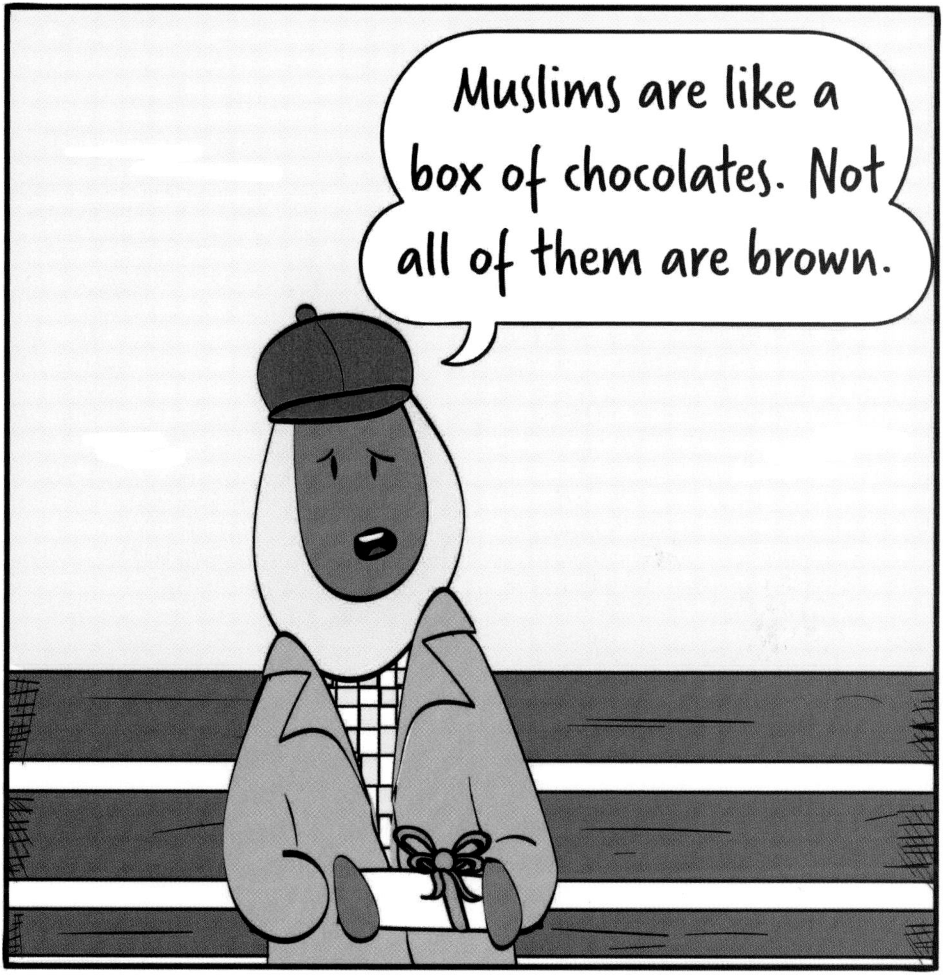
Muslims are like a box of chocolates. Not all of them are brown.

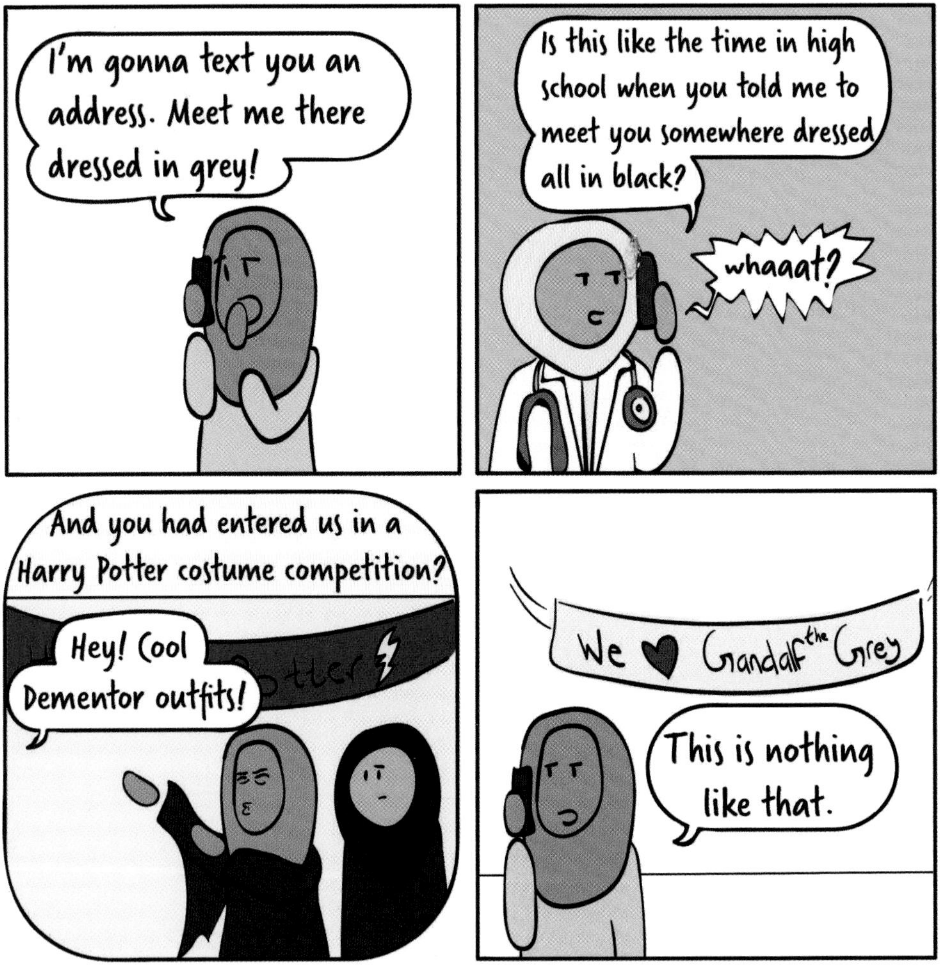
I'm gonna text you an address. Meet me there dressed in grey!
Is this like the time in high school when you told me to meet you somewhere dressed all in black?
whaaat?
And you had entered us in a Harry Potter costume competition?
Hey! Cool Dementor outfits!
otter
We ♥ Gandalf the Grey
This is nothing like that.

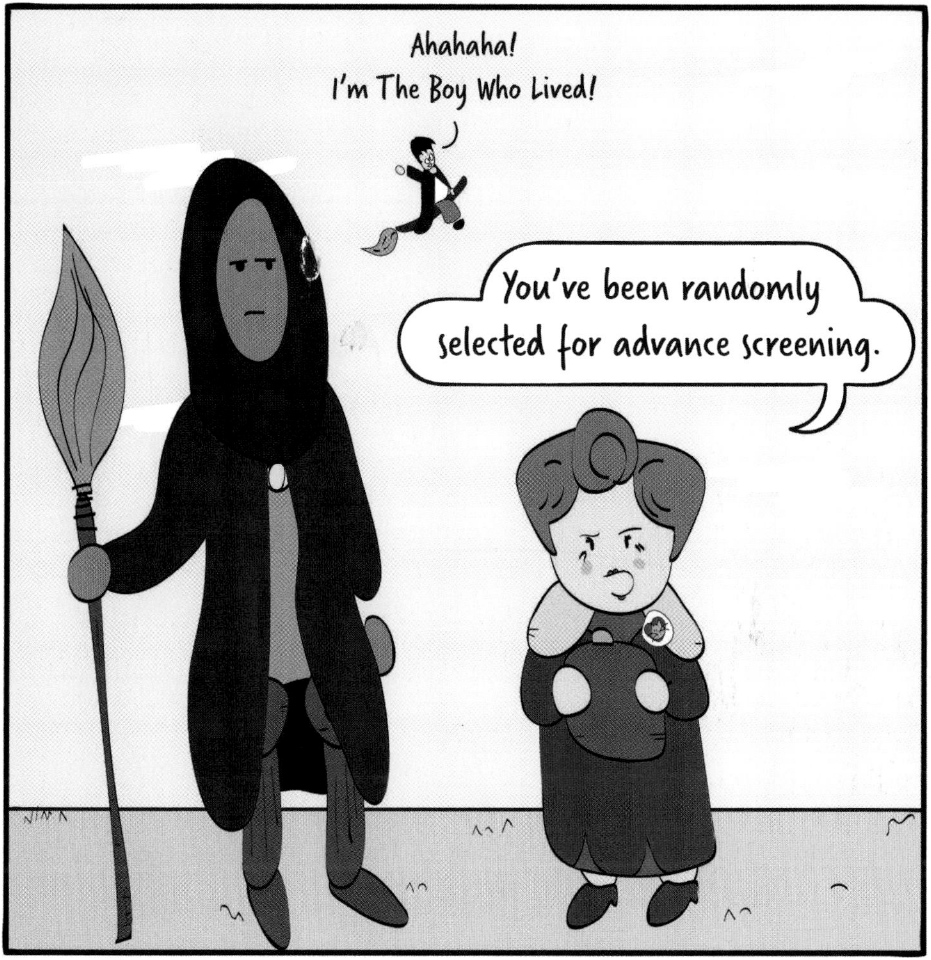
Ahahaha!
I'm The Boy Who Lived!
You've been randomly selected for advance screening.

Don't you ever wish you could just look normal?
Look, if you didn't want to come to Comic-Con with me, you coulda just said.

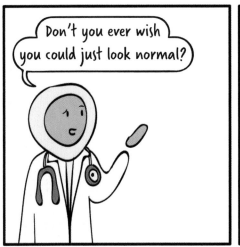

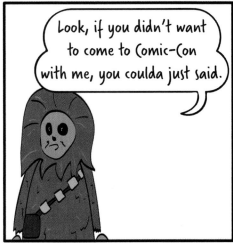

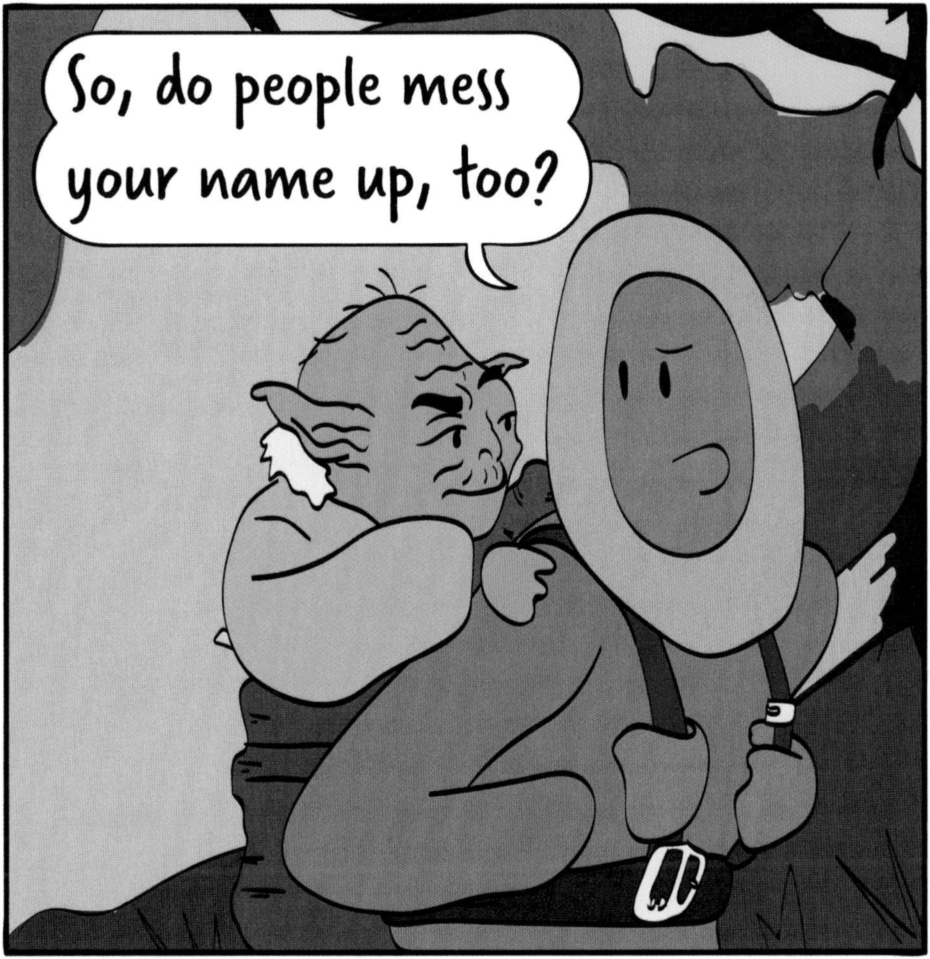
So, do people mess your name up, too?

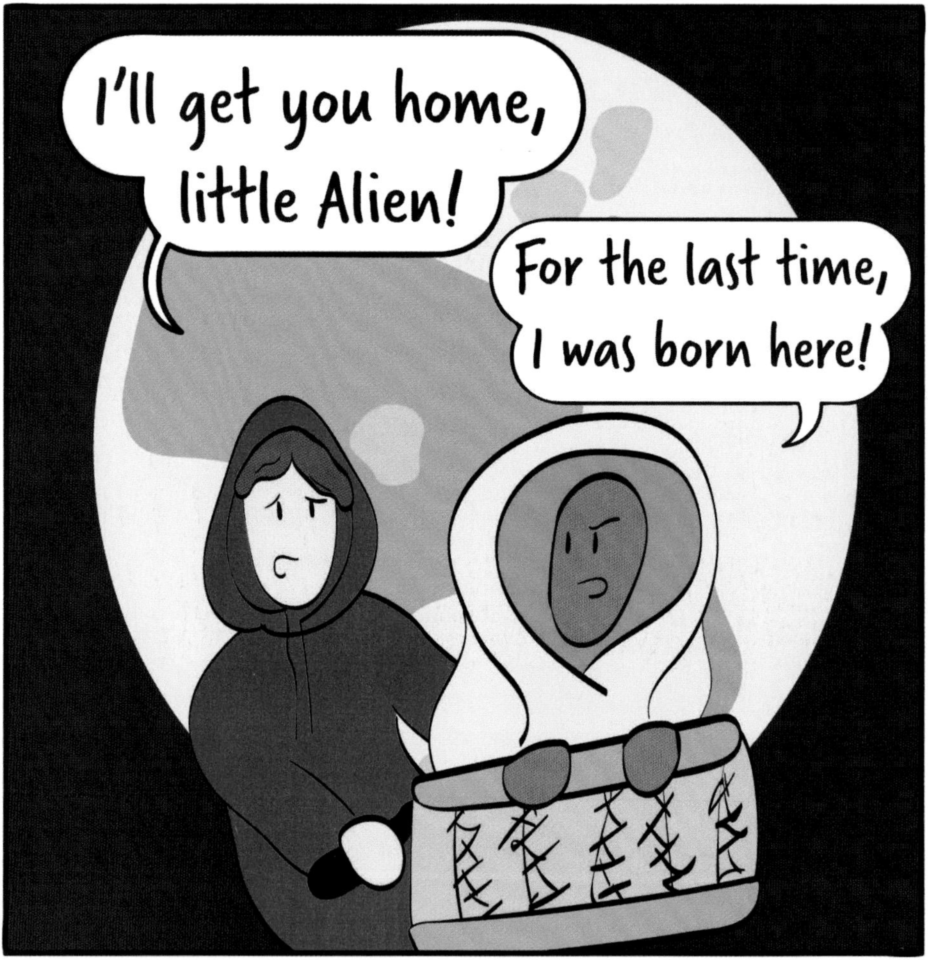
I'll get you home, little Alien!
For the last time, I was born here!

oh sweet, a Muslim! please be normal. please be normal. please be normal.
Allahu Akbar!
BOOM

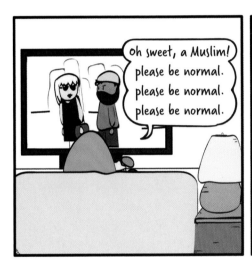

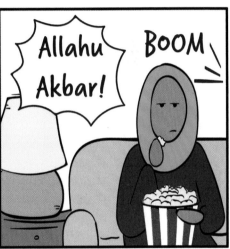

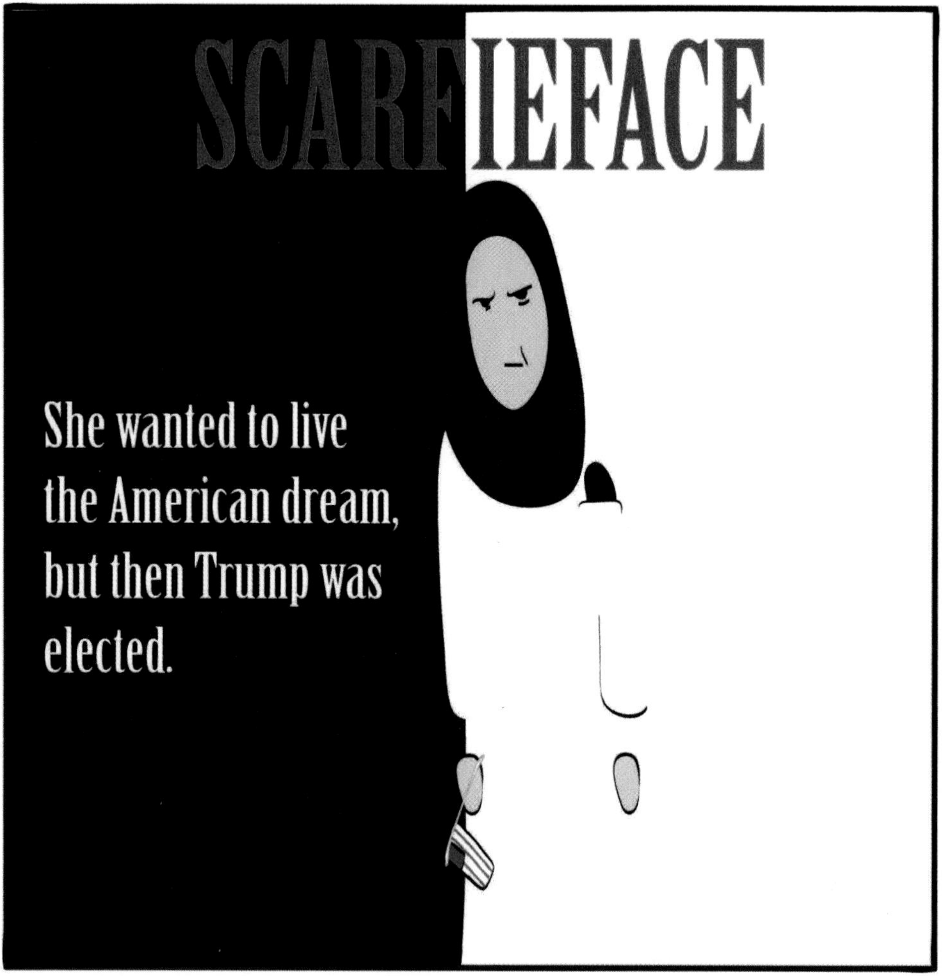
SCARFIEFACE
She wanted to live the American dream, but then Trump was elected.

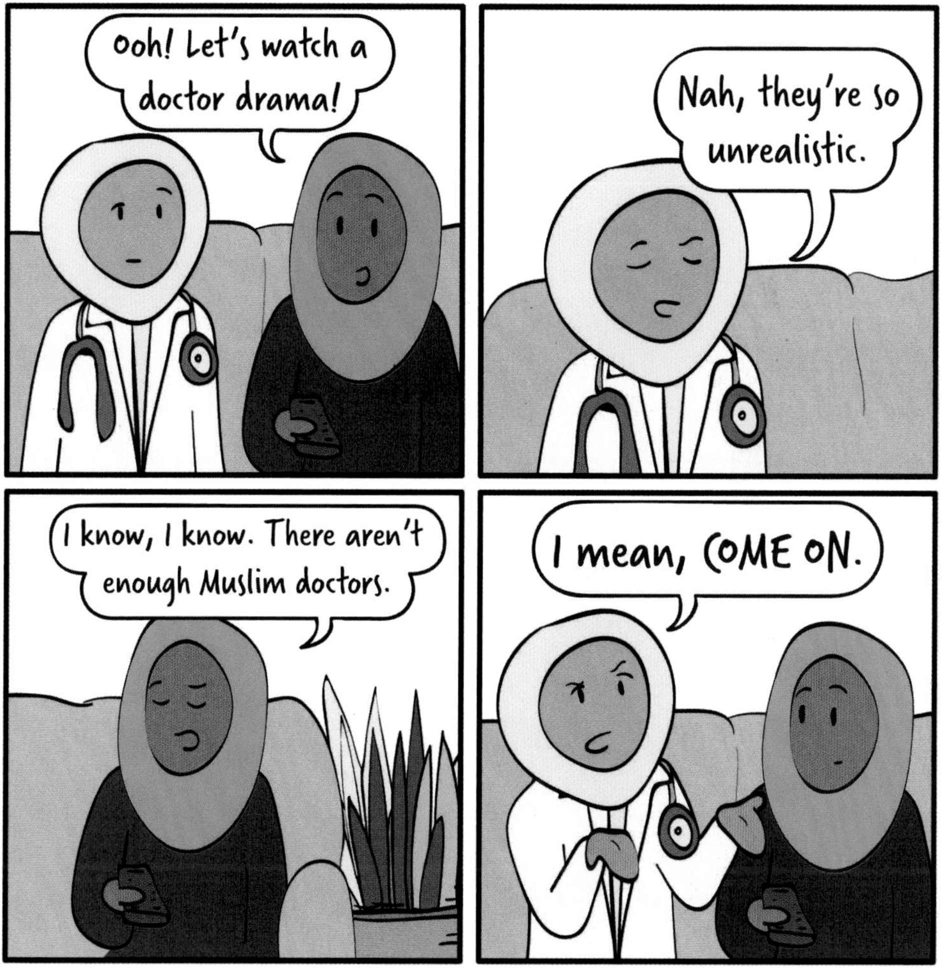
Ooh! Let's watch a doctor drama!
Nah, they're so unrealistic.
I know, I know. There aren't enough Muslim doctors.
I mean, COME ON.

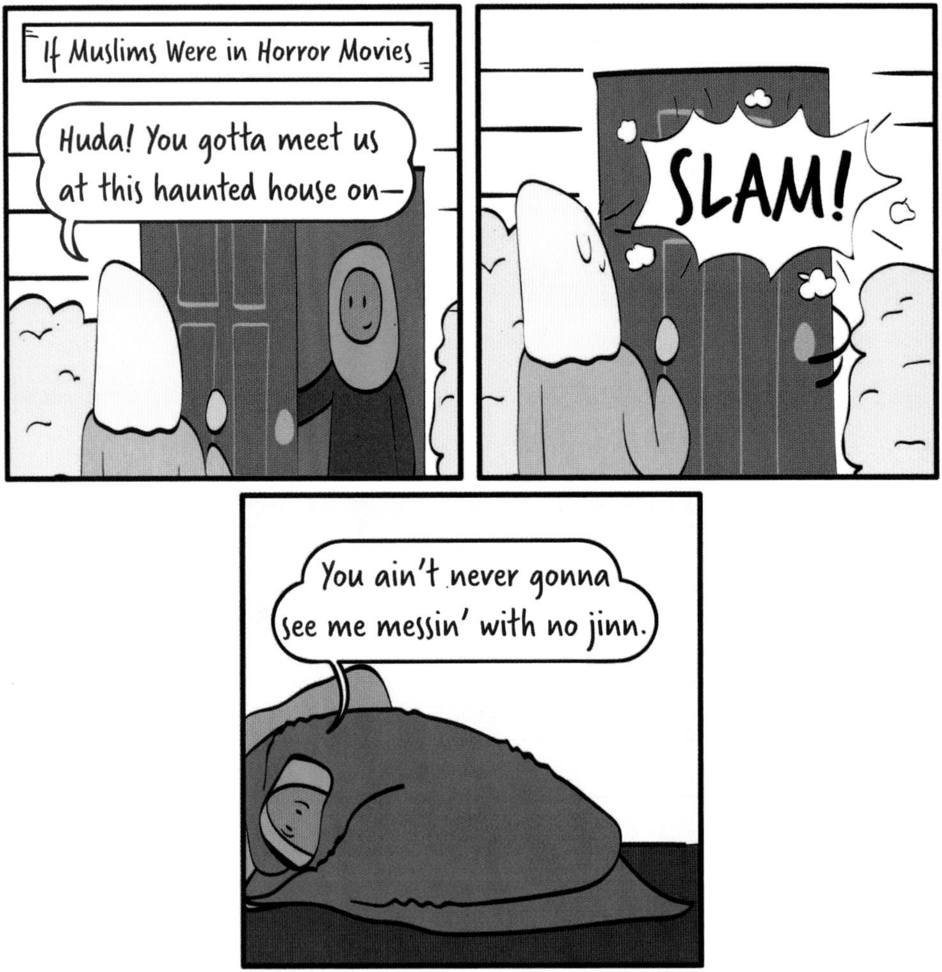
If Muslims Were in Horror Movies
Huda! You gotta meet us at this haunted house on—
SLAM!
You ain't never gonna see me messin' with no jinn.

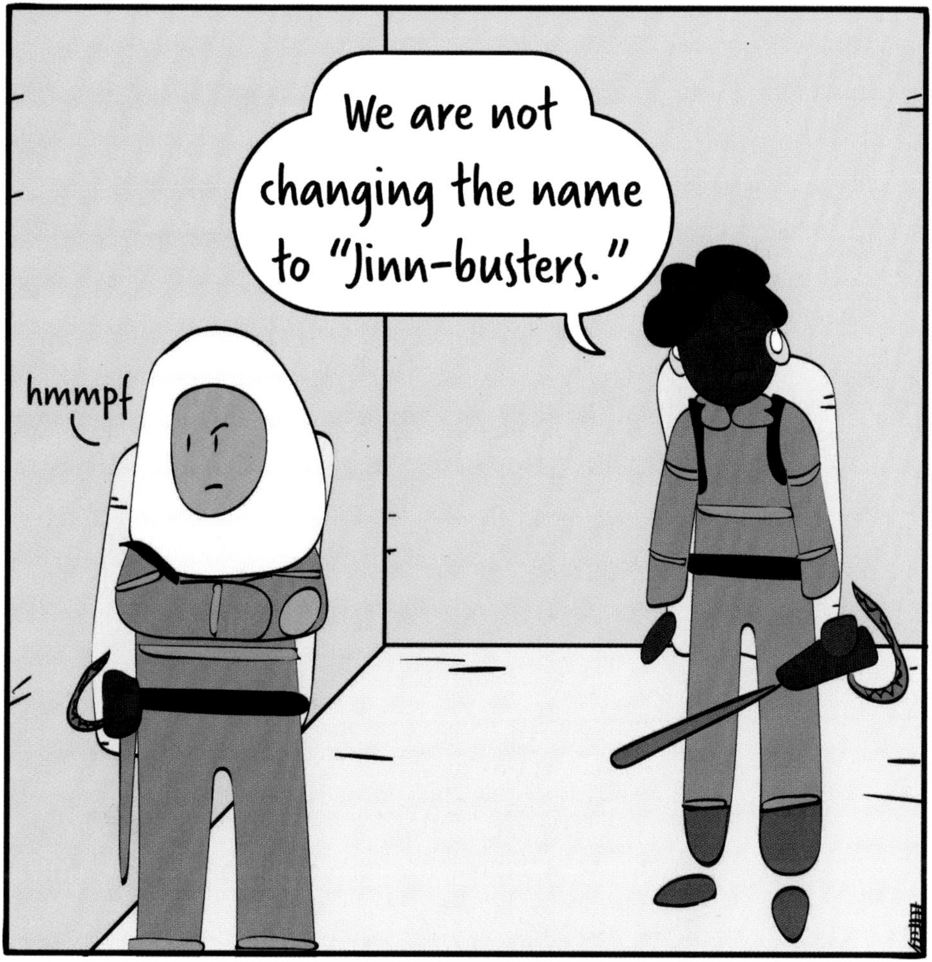
We are not changing the name to "Jinn-busters."
hmmpf

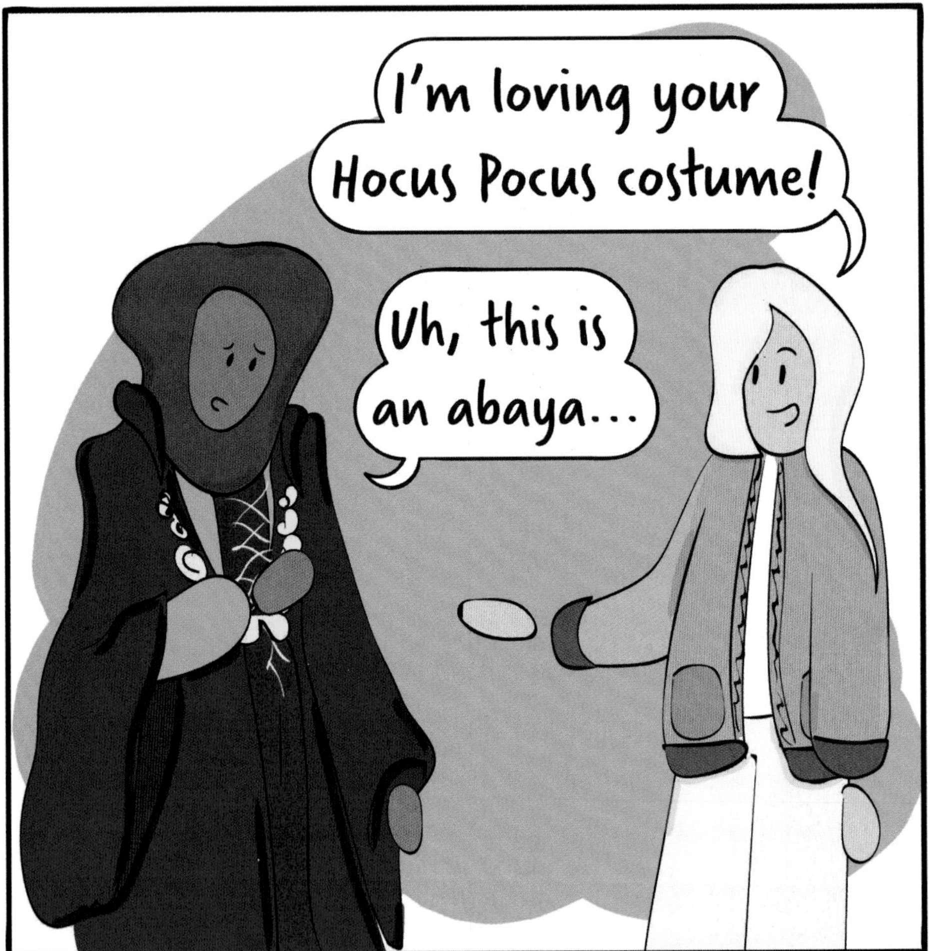
I'm loving your Hocus Pocus costume!
Uh, this is an abaya...

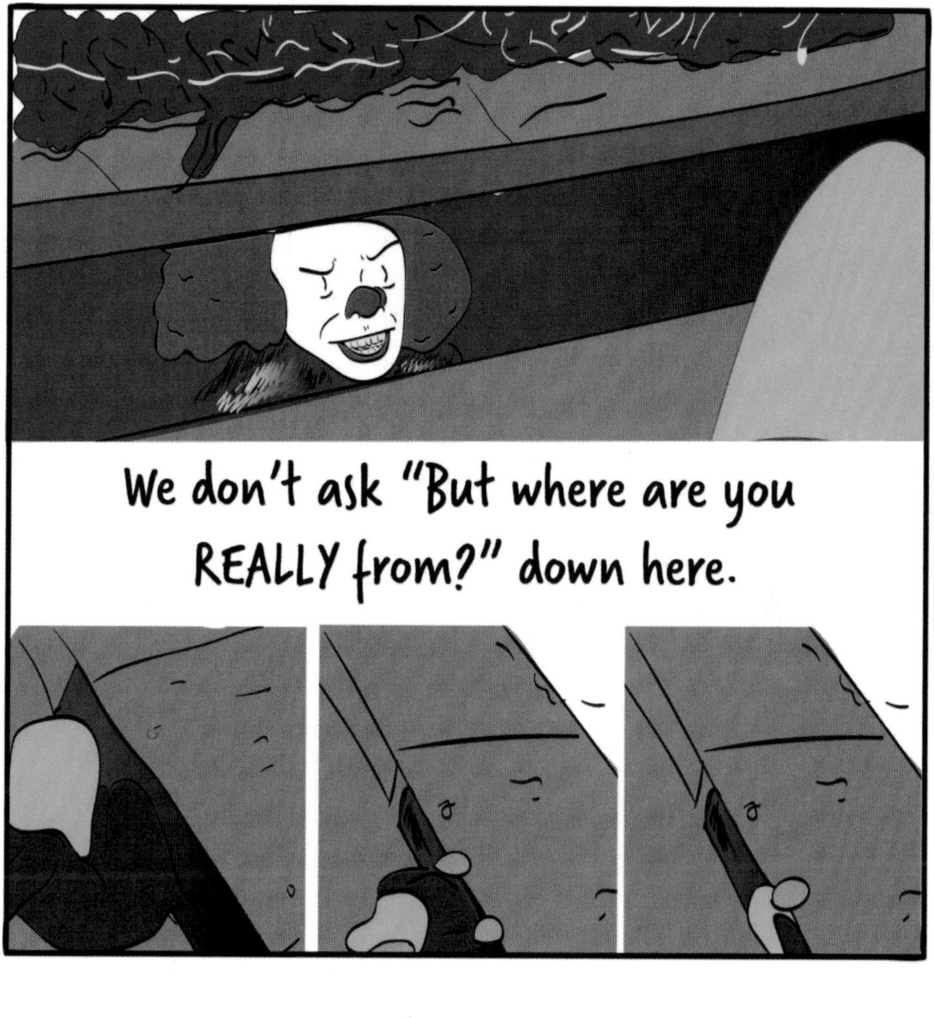
We don't ask "But where are you REALLY from?" down here.

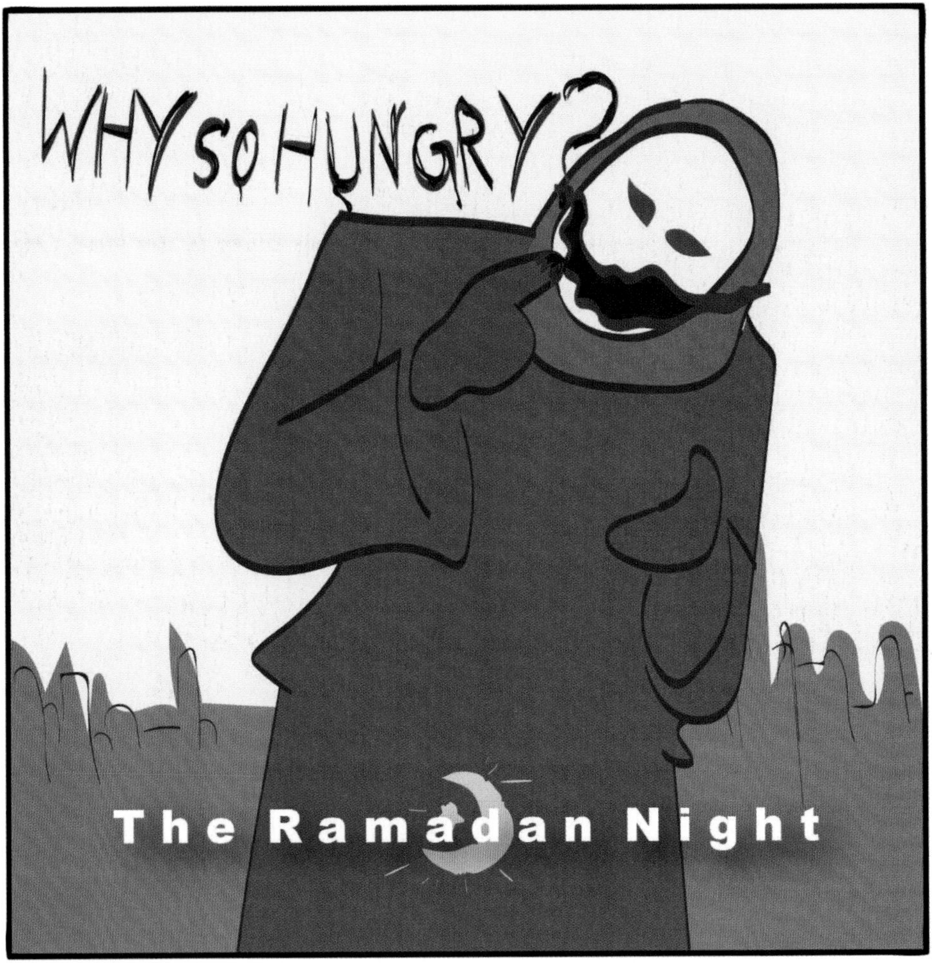
WHY SO HUNGRY?
The Ramadan Night

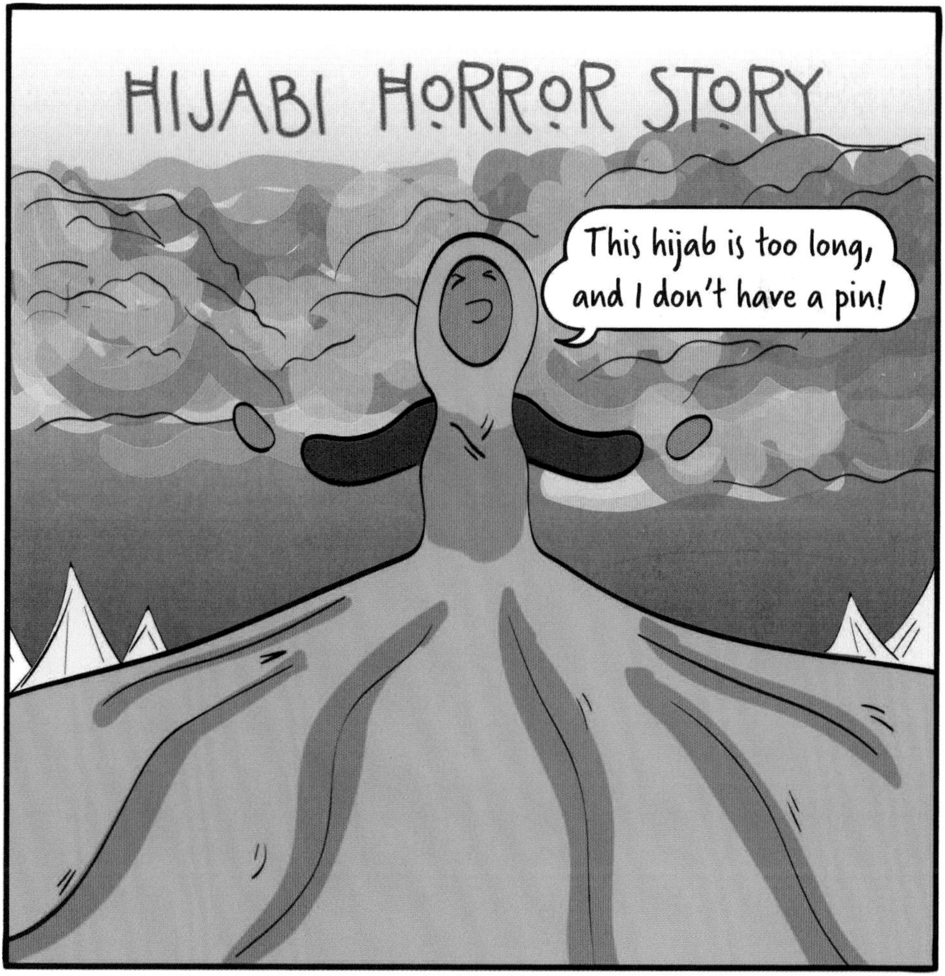
HIJABI HORROR STORY
This hijab is too long, and I don't have a pin!

You're the superhero of my dreams!
Gehad!
ACK!
Now is NOT the time!

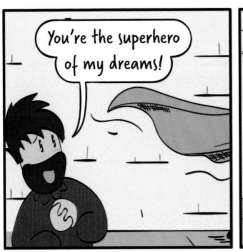

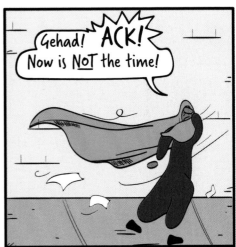

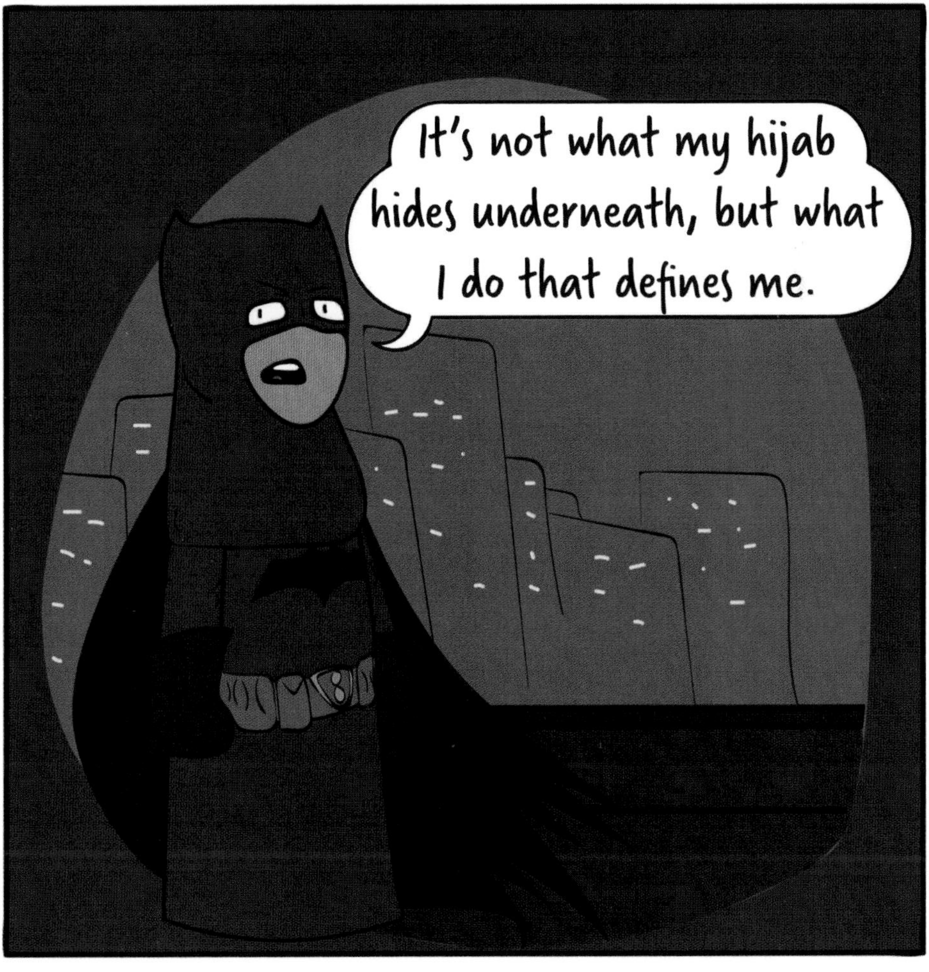
It's not what my hijab hides underneath, but what I do that defines me.

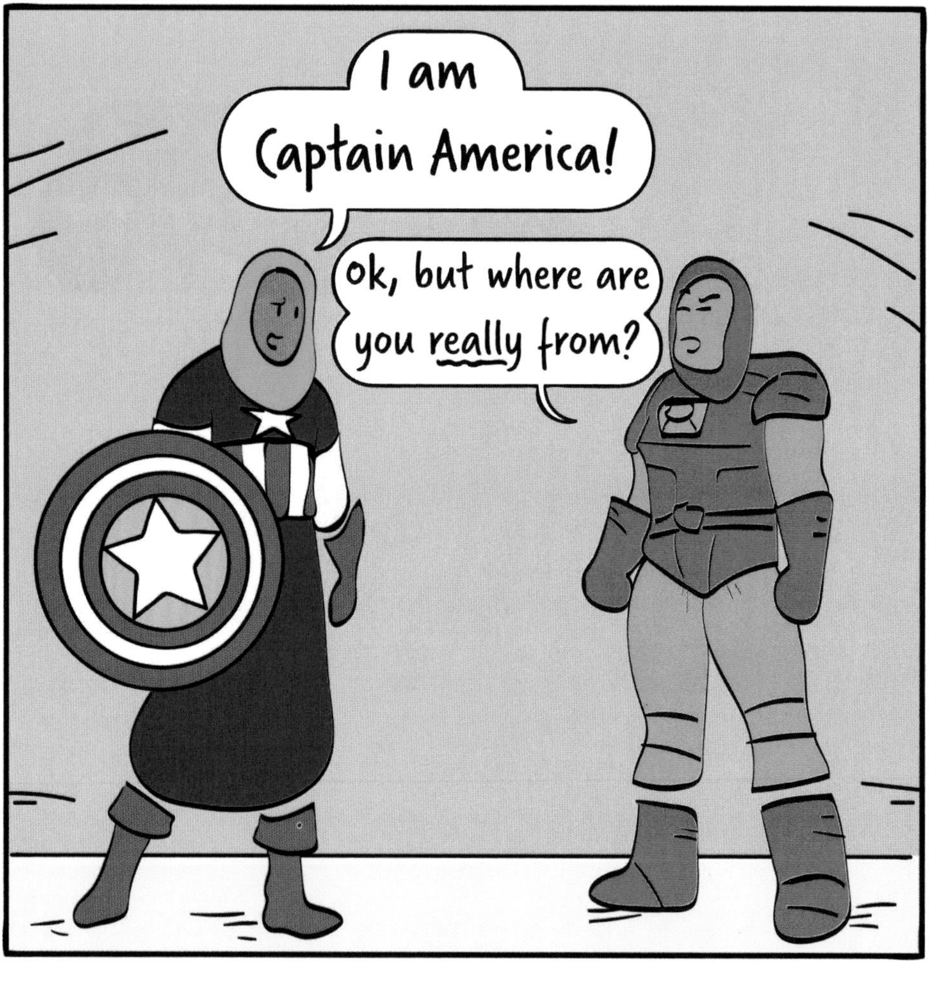
I am Captain America!
Ok, but where are you really from?

Chapter 6: It Never Hurts to Hope

No doubt there are nice people out there, too.

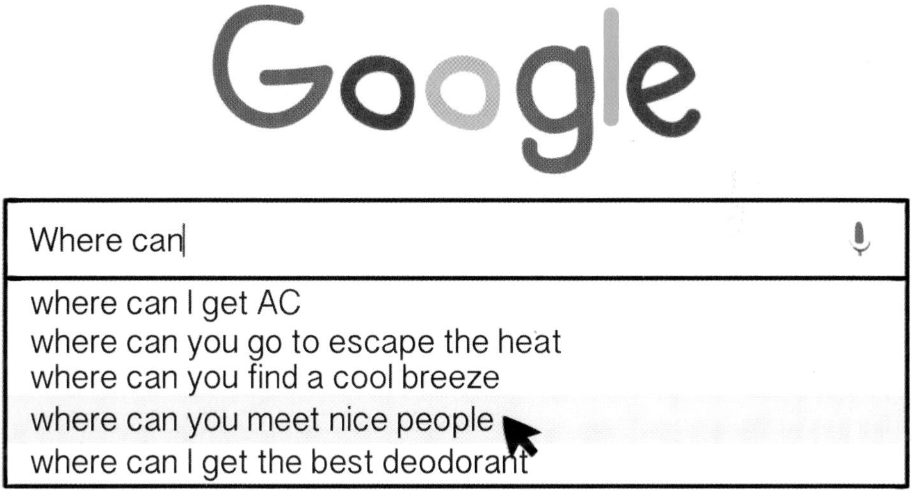
Google
Where can
where can I get AC
where can you go to escape the heat
where can you find a cool breeze
where can you meet nice people
where can I get the best deodorant

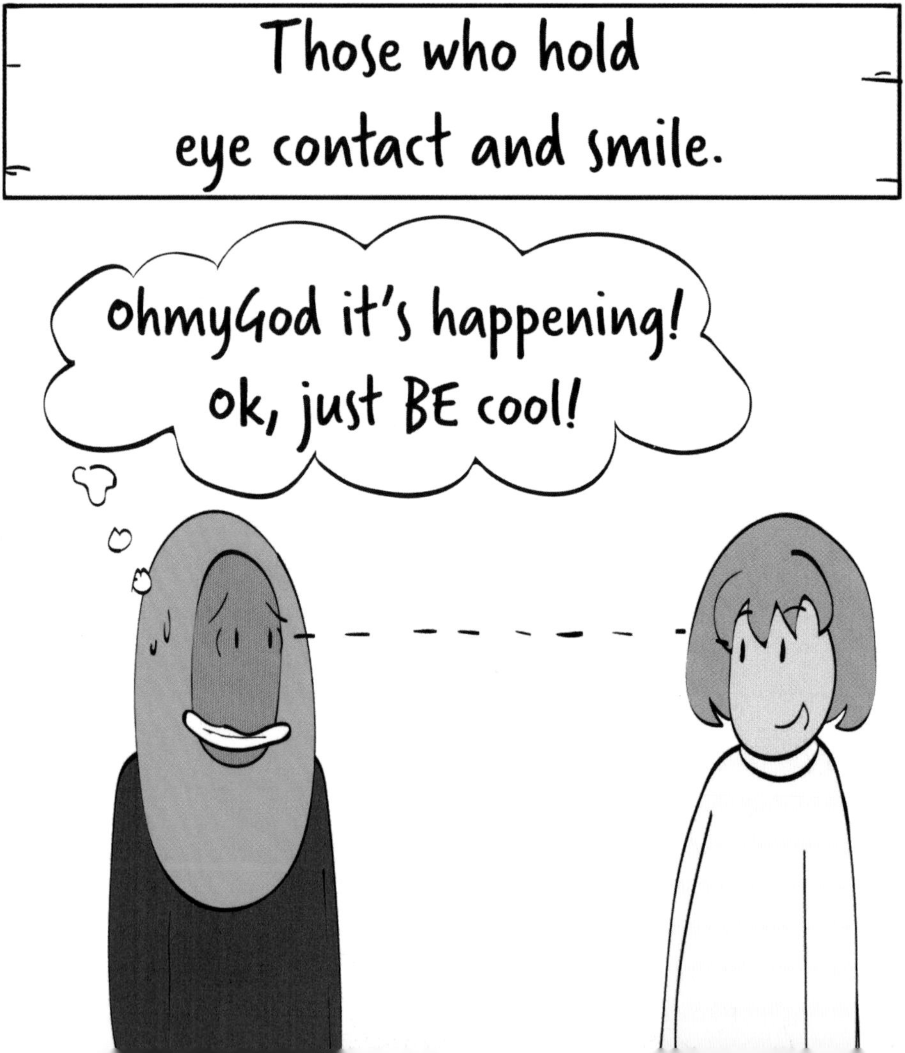
Those who hold
eye contact and smile.
ohmyGod it's happening!
ok, just BE cool!

Their small acts of solidarity don't go unnoticed.

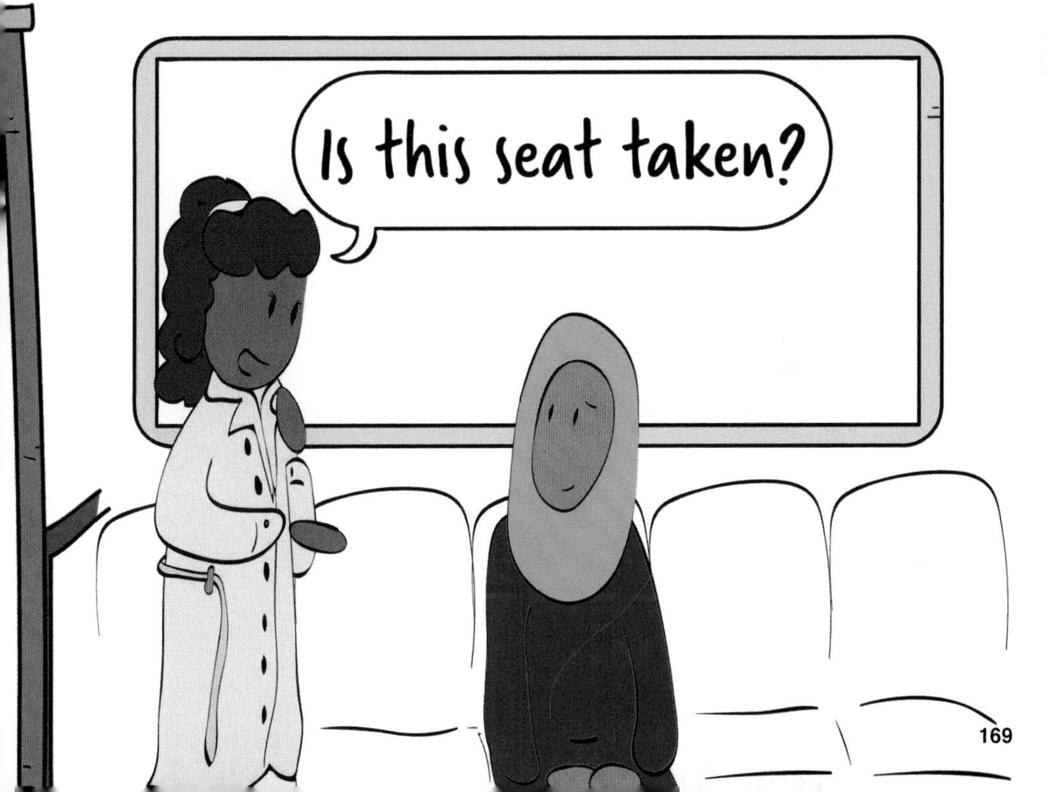
Is this seat taken?

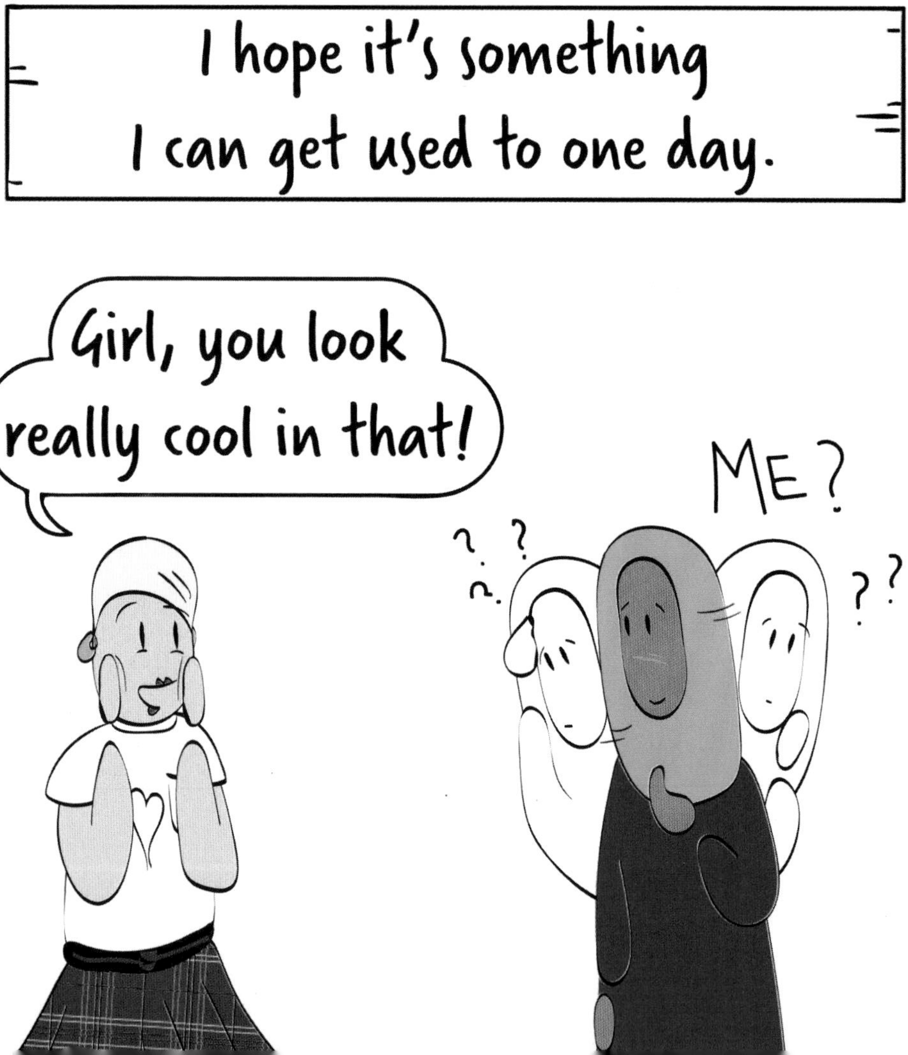
I hope it's something
I can get used to one day.
Girl, you look really cool in that!
ME?

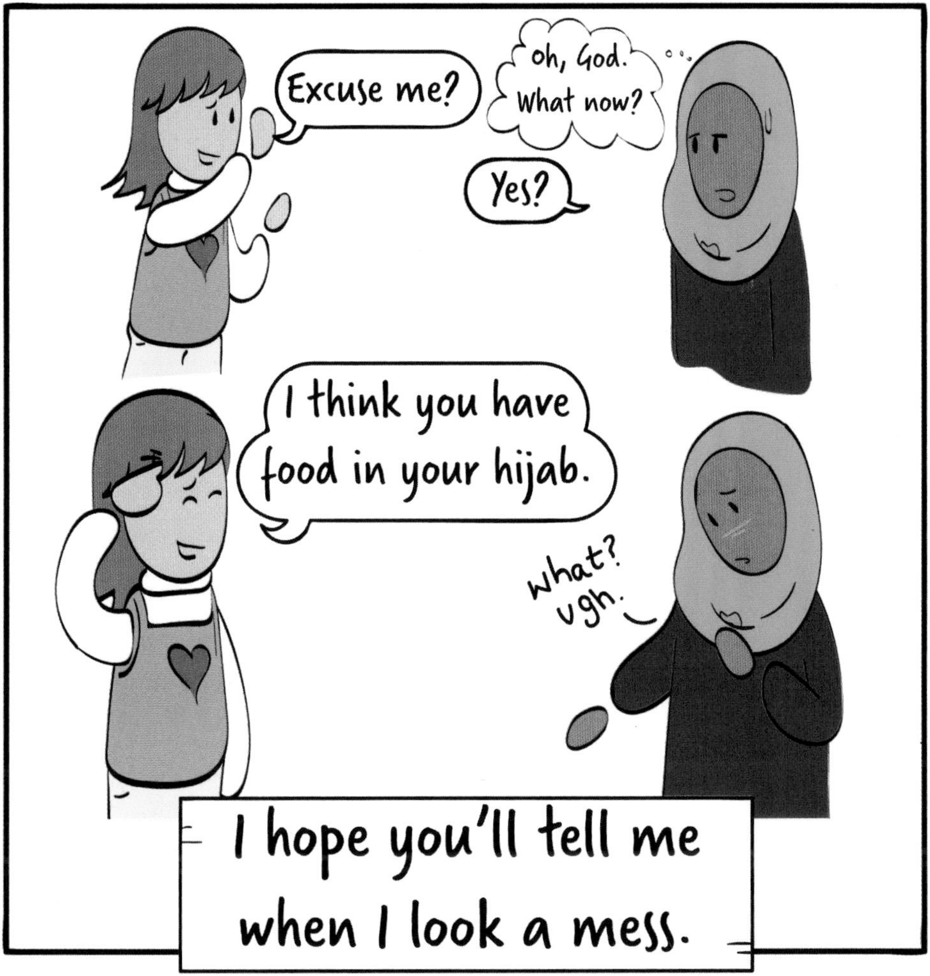
Excuse me?
Oh, God. What now?
Yes?
I think you have food in your hijab.
what? ugh.
I hope you'll tell me when I look a mess.

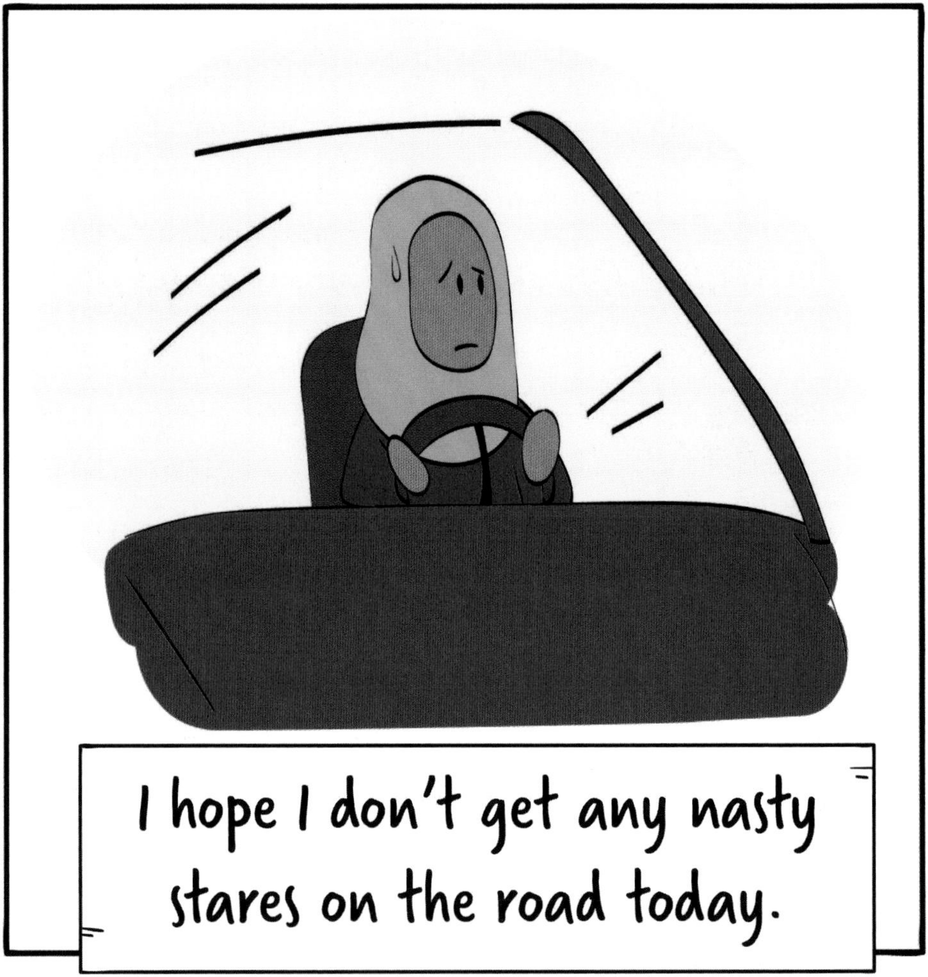
I hope I don't get any nasty stares on the road today.

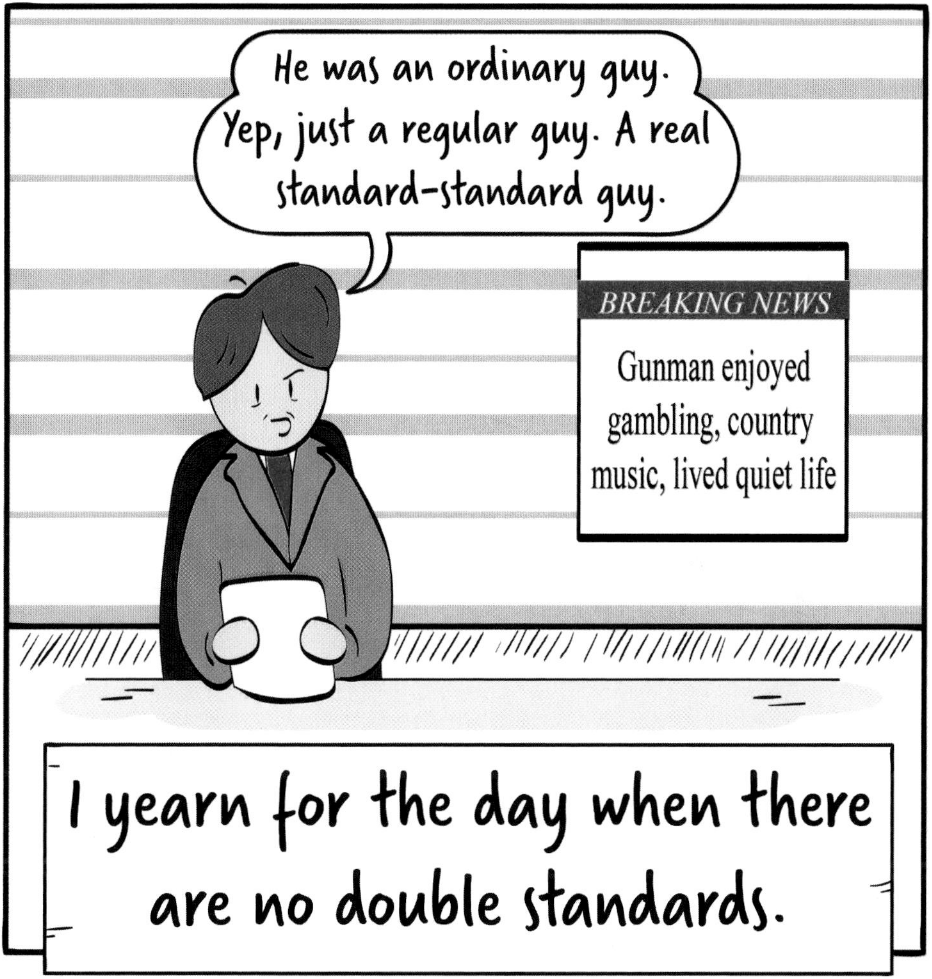
He was an ordinary guy. Yep, just a regular guy. A real standard-standard guy.
BREAKING NEWS
Gunman enjoyed gambling, country music, lived quiet life
I yearn for the day when there are no double standards.

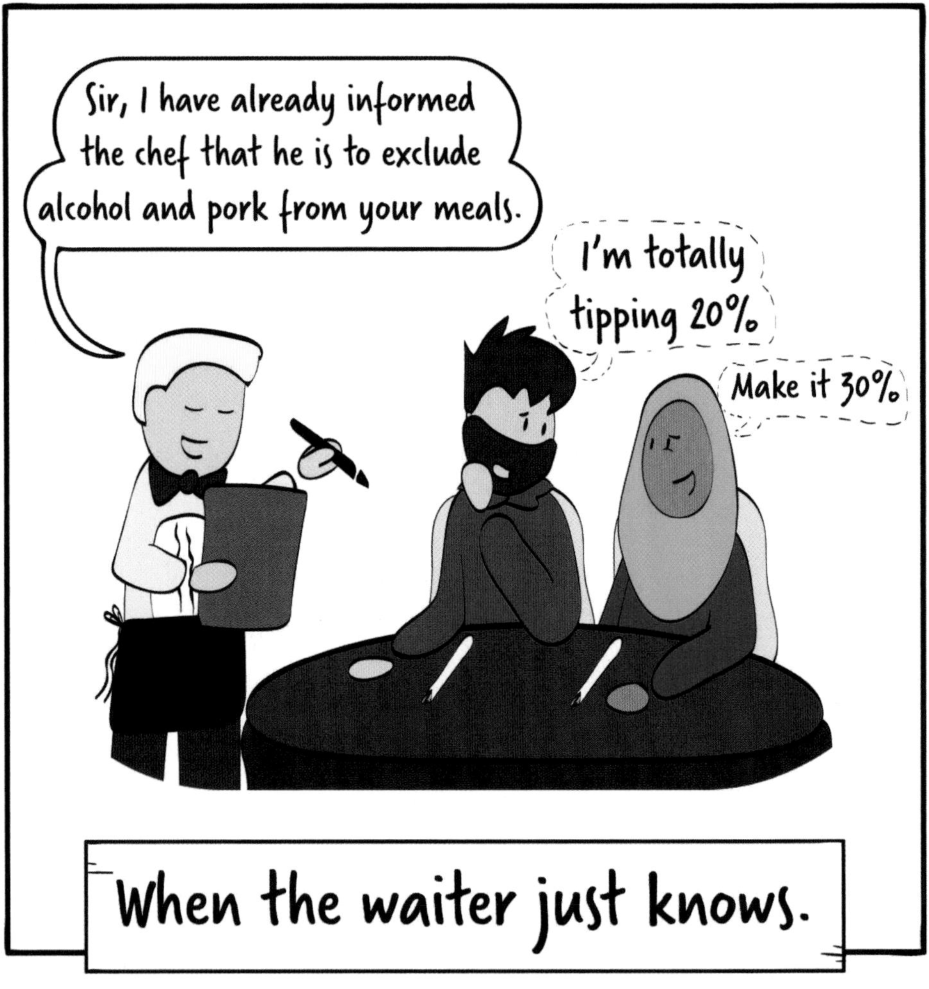
Sir, I have already informed the chef that he is to exclude alcohol and pork from your meals.
I'm totally tipping 20%
Make it 30%
When the waiter just knows.

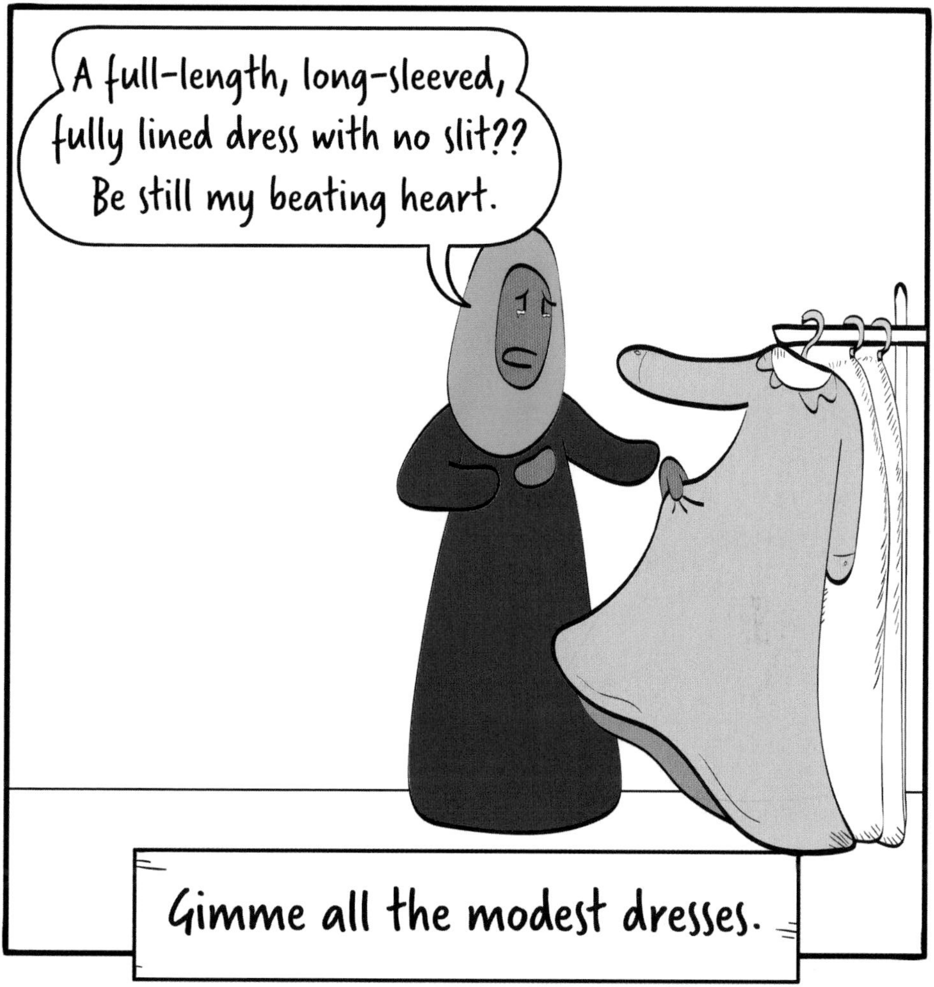
A full-length, long-sleeved, fully lined dress with no slit?? Be still my beating heart.
Gimme all the modest dresses.

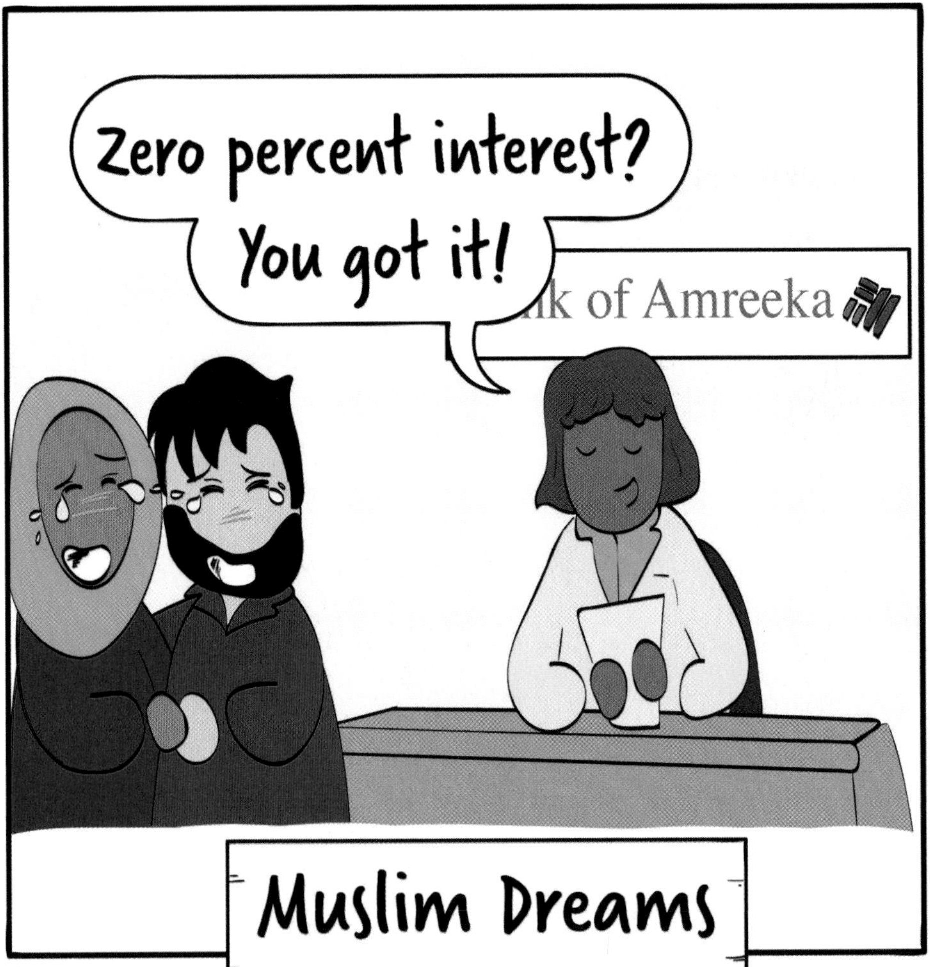
Zero percent interest? You got it!
k of Amreeka
Muslim Dreams

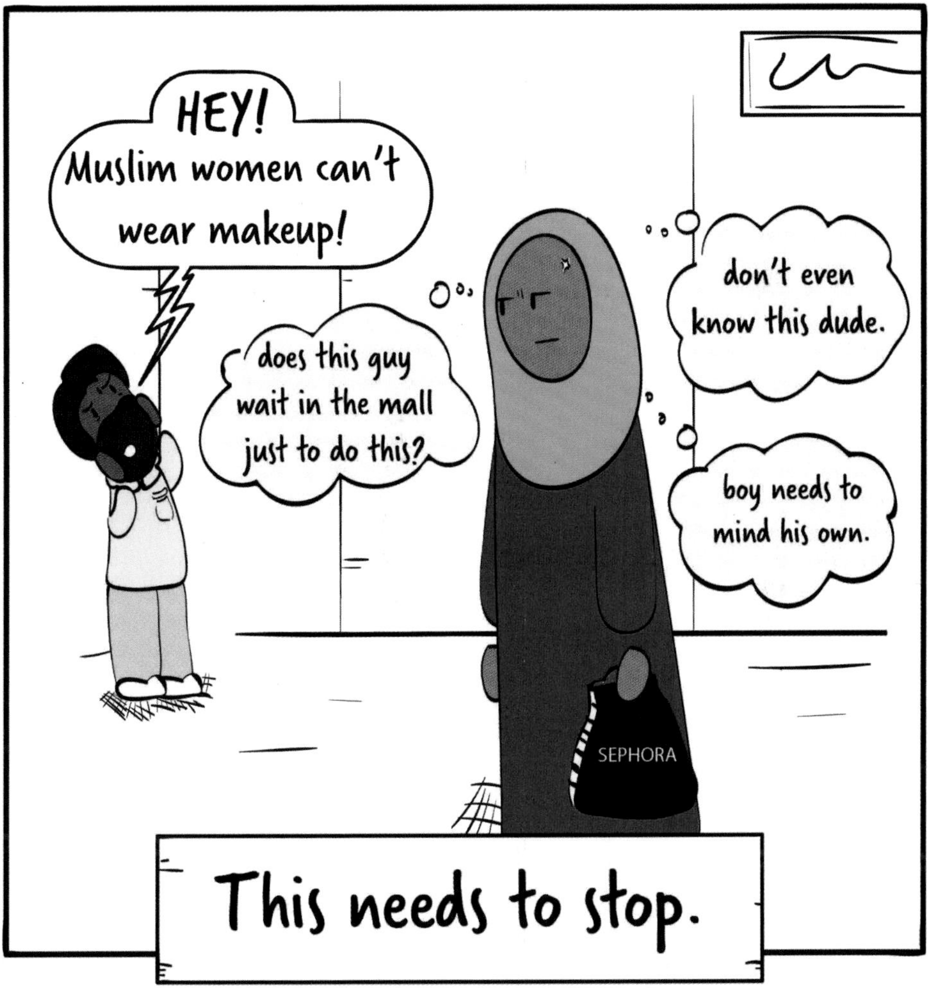
HEY!
Muslim women can't wear makeup!
does this guy wait in the mall just to do this?
don't even know this dude.
boy needs to mind his own.
SEPHORA
This needs to stop.

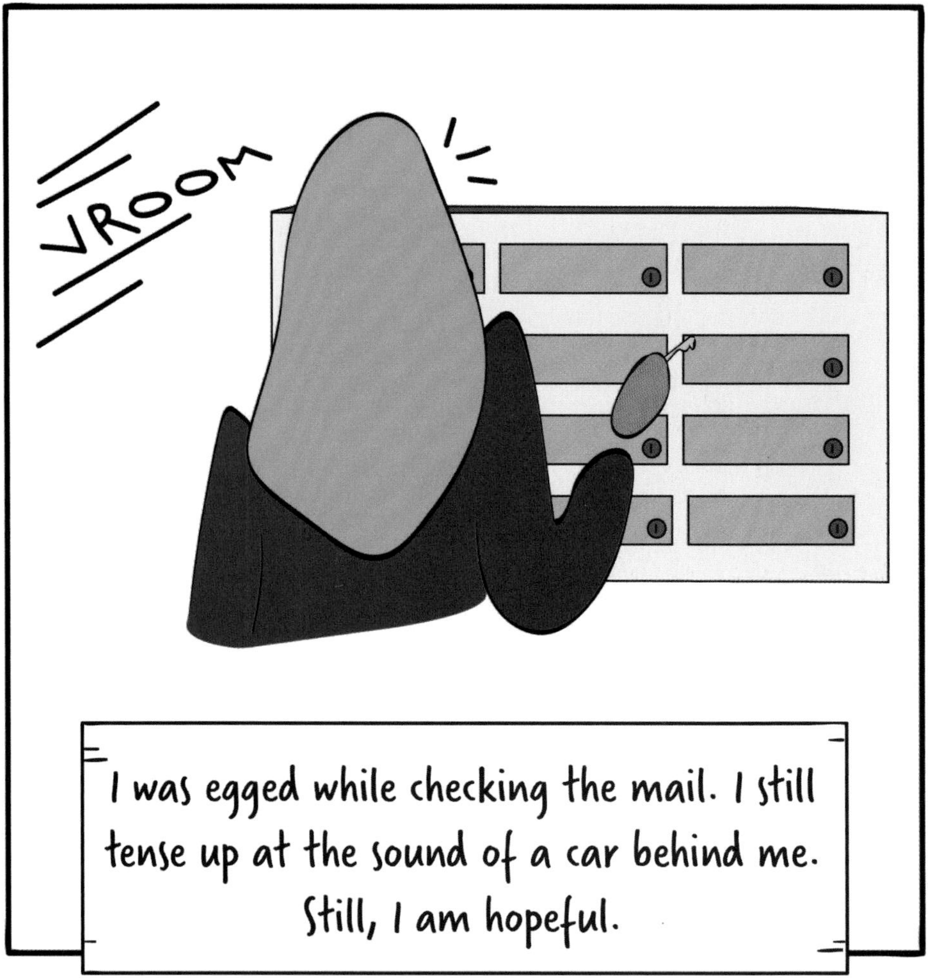
VROOM
I was egged while checking the mail. I still tense up at the sound of a car behind me. Still, I am hopeful.

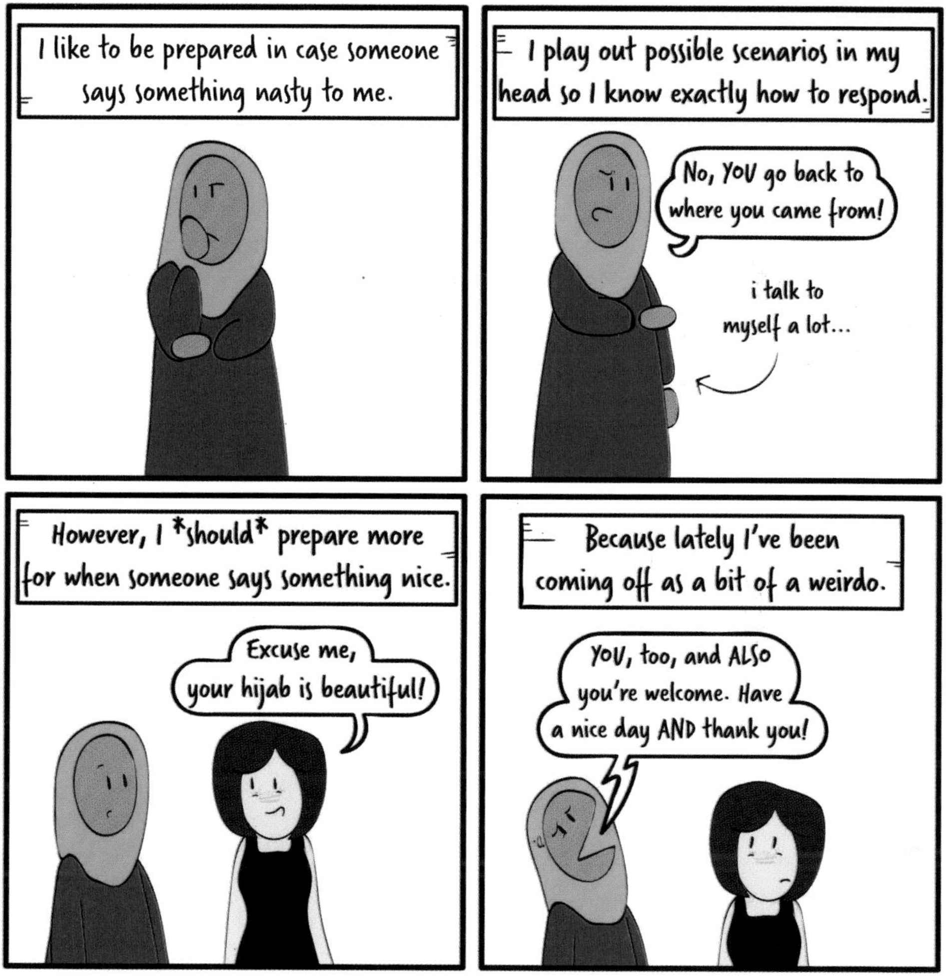
I like to be prepared in case someone says something nasty to me.
I play out possible scenarios in my head so I know exactly how to respond.
No, YOU go back to where you came from!
i talk to myself a lot...
However, I *should* prepare more for when someone says something nice.
Excuse me, your hijab is beautiful!
Because lately I've been coming off as a bit of a weirdo.
YOU, too, and ALSO you're welcome. Have a nice day AND thank you!

You look beautiful. Muslims are so lucky they don't have to wear makeup.
ahahaha thanks.
Should I tell her?
actually wearing two layers of foundation, blush, and mascara.

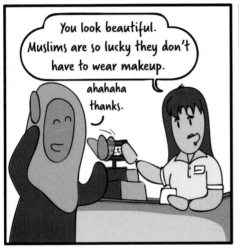

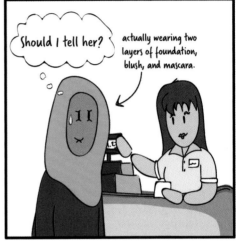

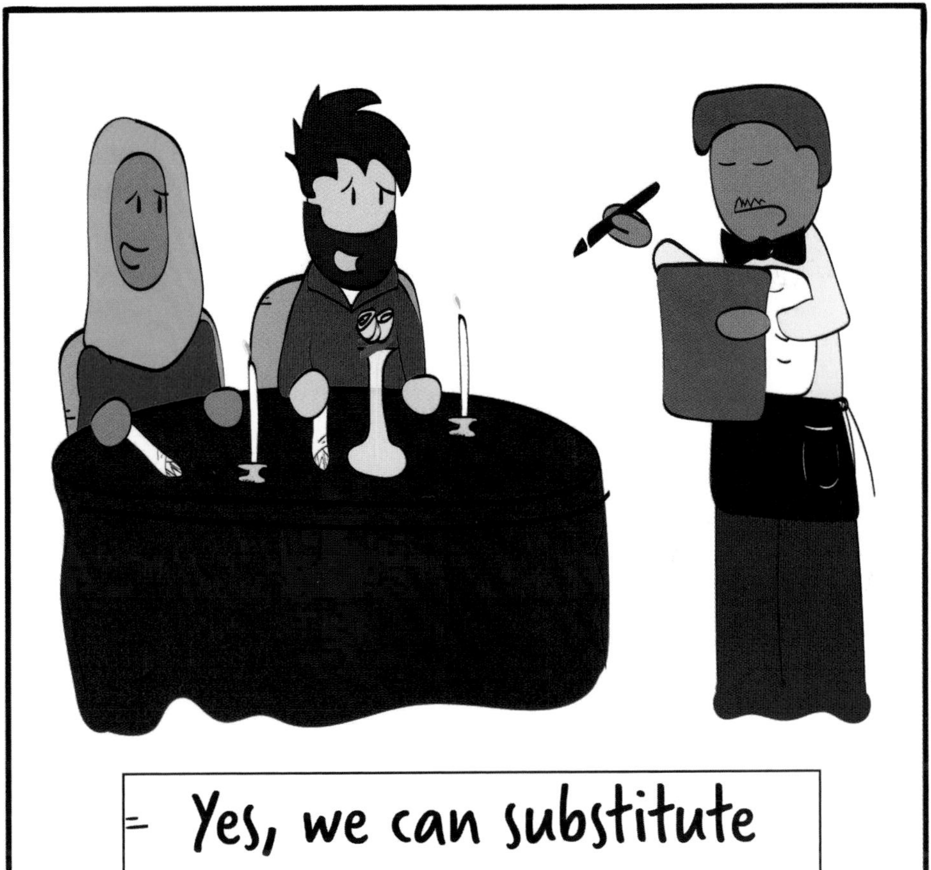
Yes, we can substitute that with turkey bacon.

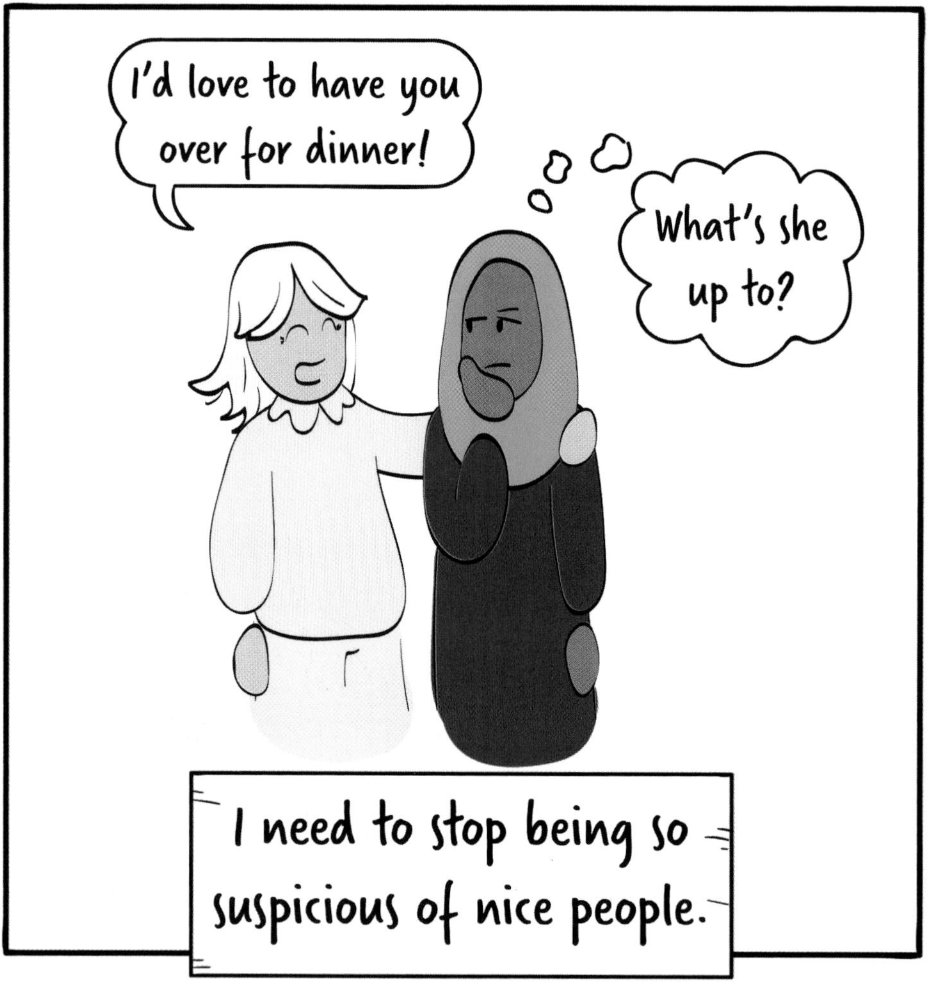
I'd love to have you over for dinner!
What's she up to?
I need to stop being so suspicious of nice people.

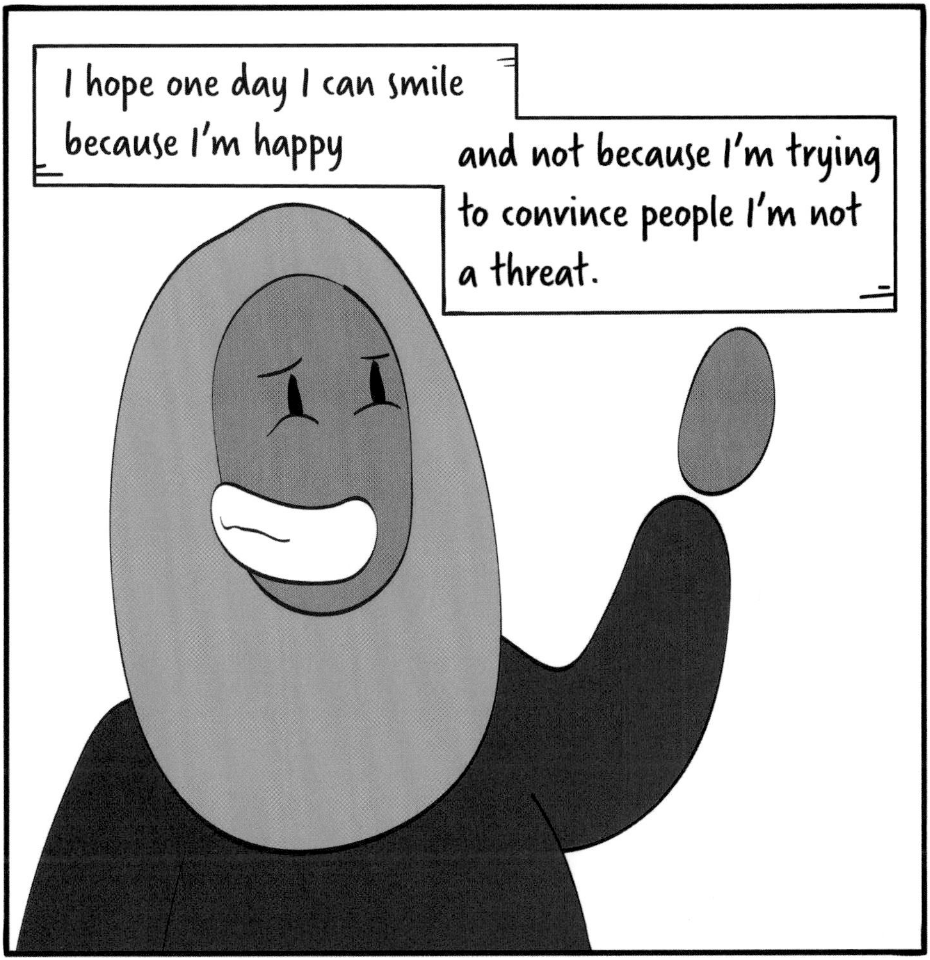
I hope one day I can smile because I'm happy
and not because I'm trying to convince people I'm not a threat.

I heard something on the news today about Muslims that didn't make sense, so I did some research and pretty easily found out how wrong they were!
✓ doesn't jump to conclusions
✓doesn't expect me to educate her
✓doesn't want praise for doing the bare minimum
A-Are you OK?

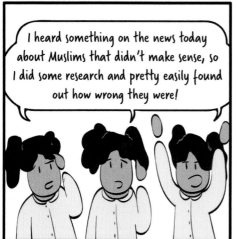

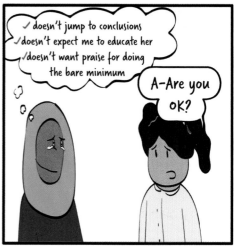

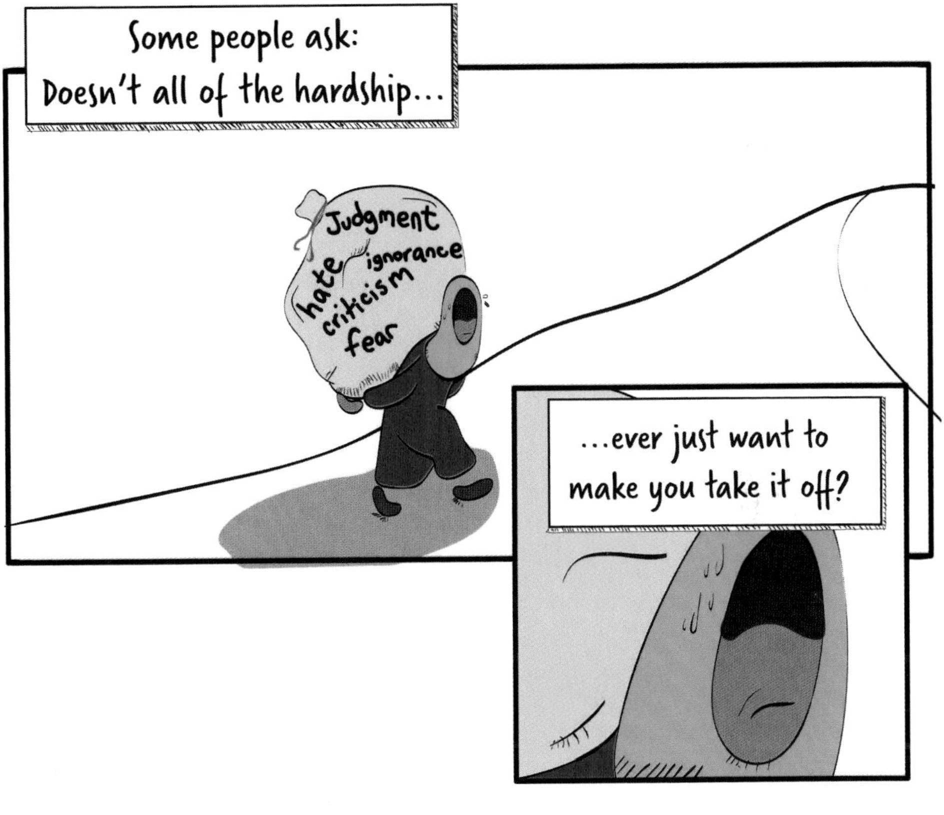
Some people ask:
Doesn't all of the hardship...
Judgment
hate
ignorance
criticism
fear
...ever just want to
make you take it off?

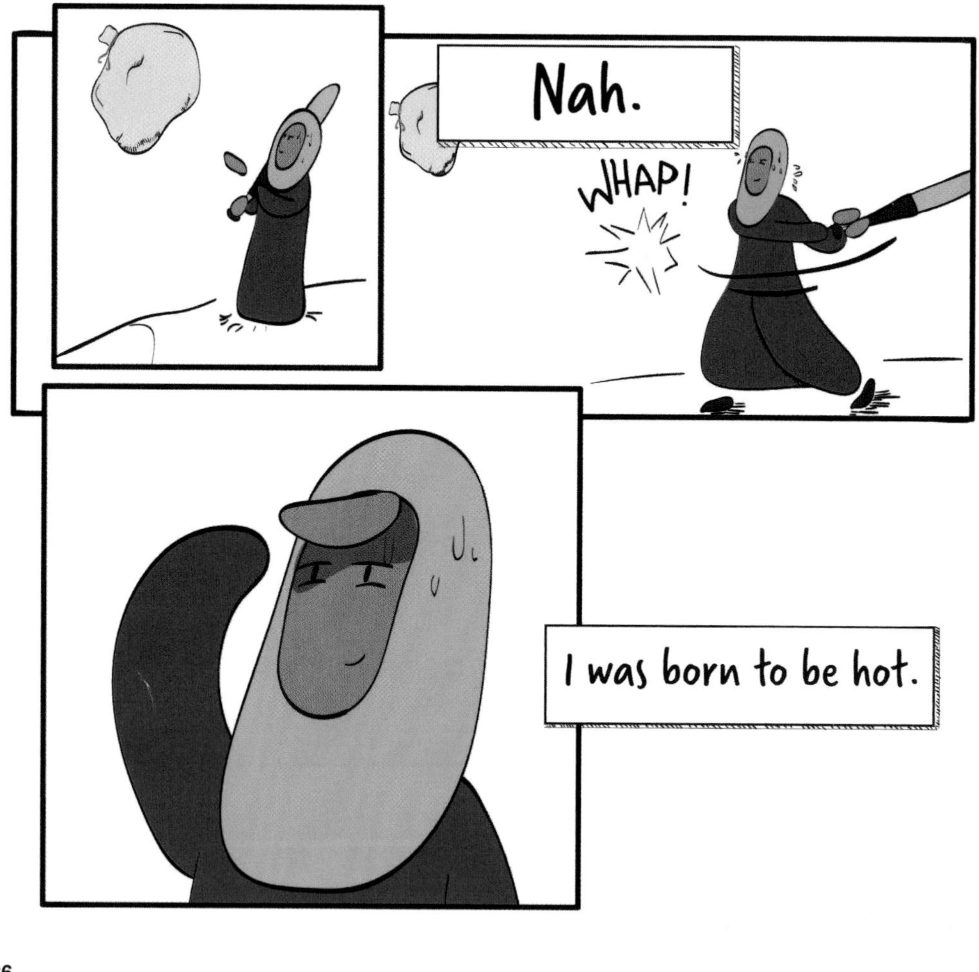
Nah.
WHAP!
I was born to be hot.

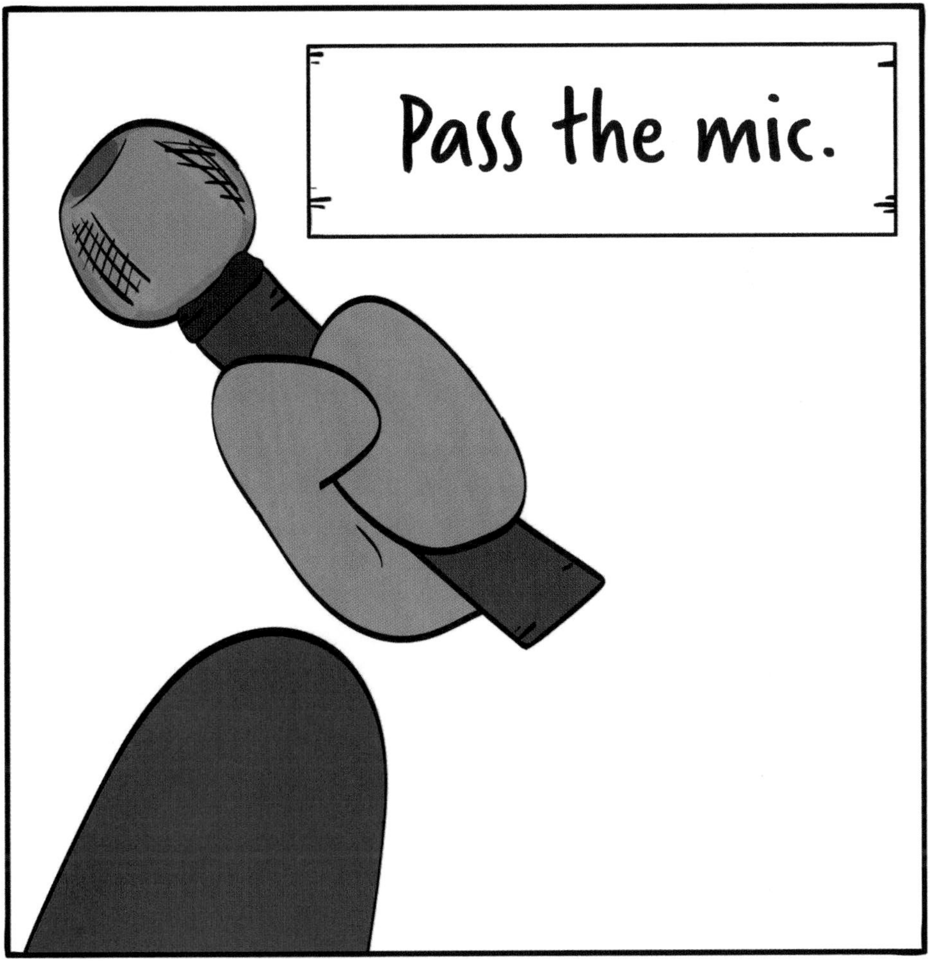
Pass the mic.

Glossary

Abaya: (n) Long-sleeved, fully lined dress-like garment worn by some Muslim women.

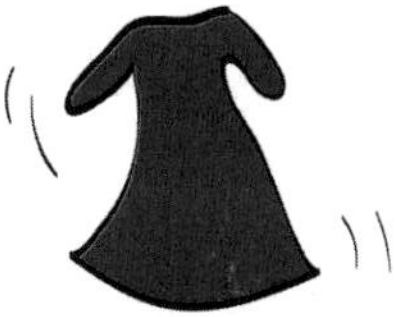

Allahu Akbar: Arabic phrase used by Muslims everywhere, multiple times a day, that means "God is greater than anything."

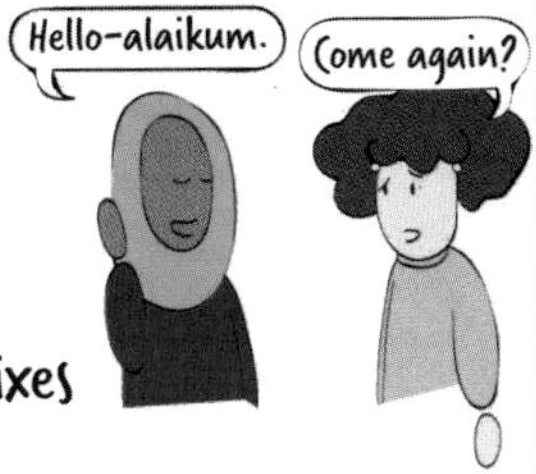
Hello-alaikum.
Come again?

Arabeesi: (n) A language whose made-up words are half Arabic/half English, or are mainly Arabic words that begin or end with English prefixes or suffixes.

Aunty: (n) Term used to refer to any older matriarchal figure (not actual Aunt; is usually very nosy).

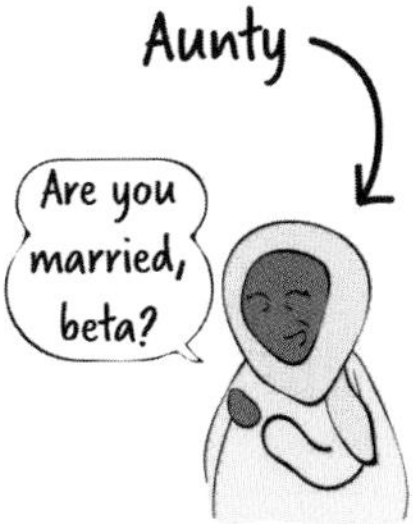
Aunty
Are you married, beta?

Beta: (n) Urdu word that means "son" but can also be used as a term of endearment for both boys and girls. Usually used by an elder to refer to a youth.

Gehad (or Jihad): (n) An Arabic word referring to a praiseworthy struggle that is for a greater cause. It includes the struggle for personal development and growth.

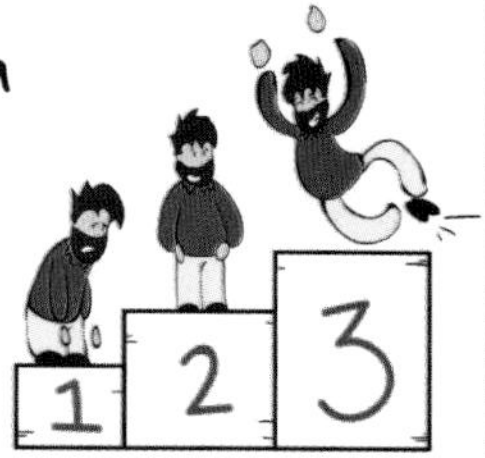
1
2
3

Halal: (adj) An Arabic word that refers to what is permissible under Islamic law. Most often heard regarding the preparation of meat.

حلال

Hijab: (n) Arabic word that refers to the piece of cloth that covers a Muslim woman's hair. Not all Muslim women wear it, and it does not equate religiosity. Also referred to as a scarf. (yes, you may compliment a woman on her hijab!)

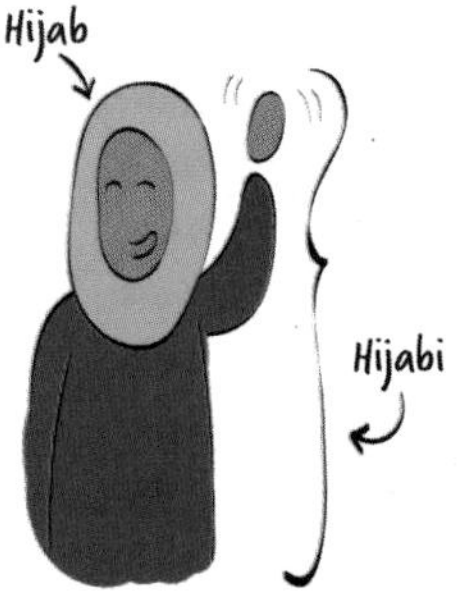
Hijab
Hijabi

Hijabi: (n) Slang word referring to a Muslim woman who wears the hijab.

InshaAllah: An Arabic phrase meaning "if God wills." When Muslim parents use this phrase on their kids, it usually means a big fat "no."

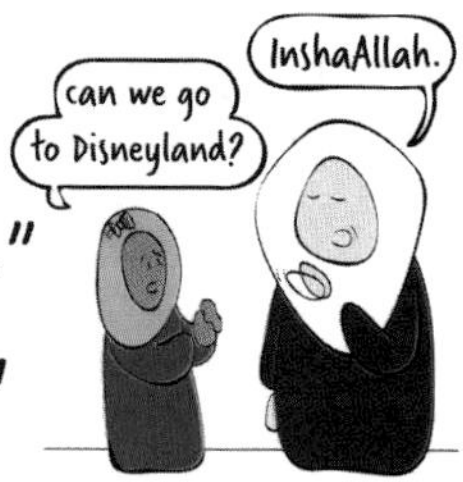
can we go to Disneyland?
InshaAllah.

Jinn: (n) An Arabic word referring to the creations of God that exist parallel to humans. They are capable of tremendous physical strength and can possess humans. They may also appear in either human or animal form and can be either good or evil. TL;DR issa ghost.

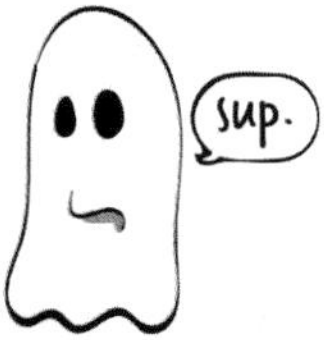
sup.

Maghrib: (n) An Arabic word referring to the fourth prayer of the day that Muslims offer at sunset. If a Muslim is fasting, Maghrib is the time at which she breaks her fast.

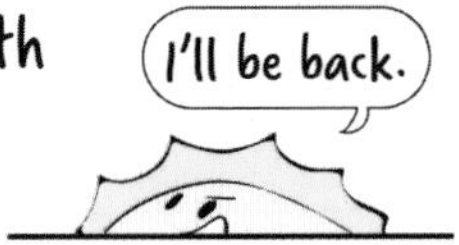
I'll be back.

Masjid: (n) An Arabic word that literally translates to "place of prostration." In short: it's where Muslims pray.

Moozlum/Moslem/Mozlem: (n) Mispronunciation of the word Muslim. It's a soft "S" guys, c'mon!

Muslim: (n) Follower of the religion of Islam.

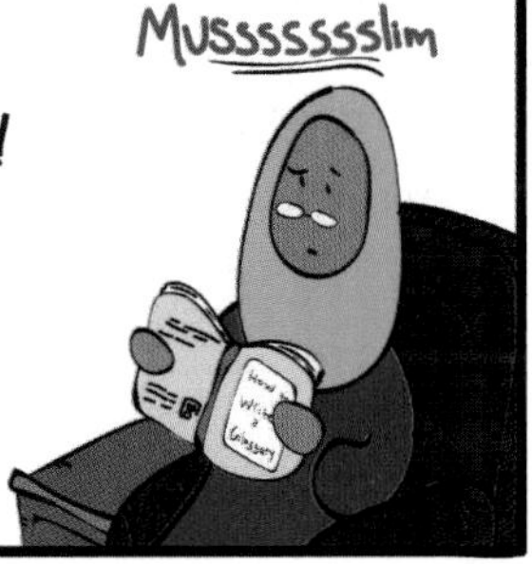
Musssssslim

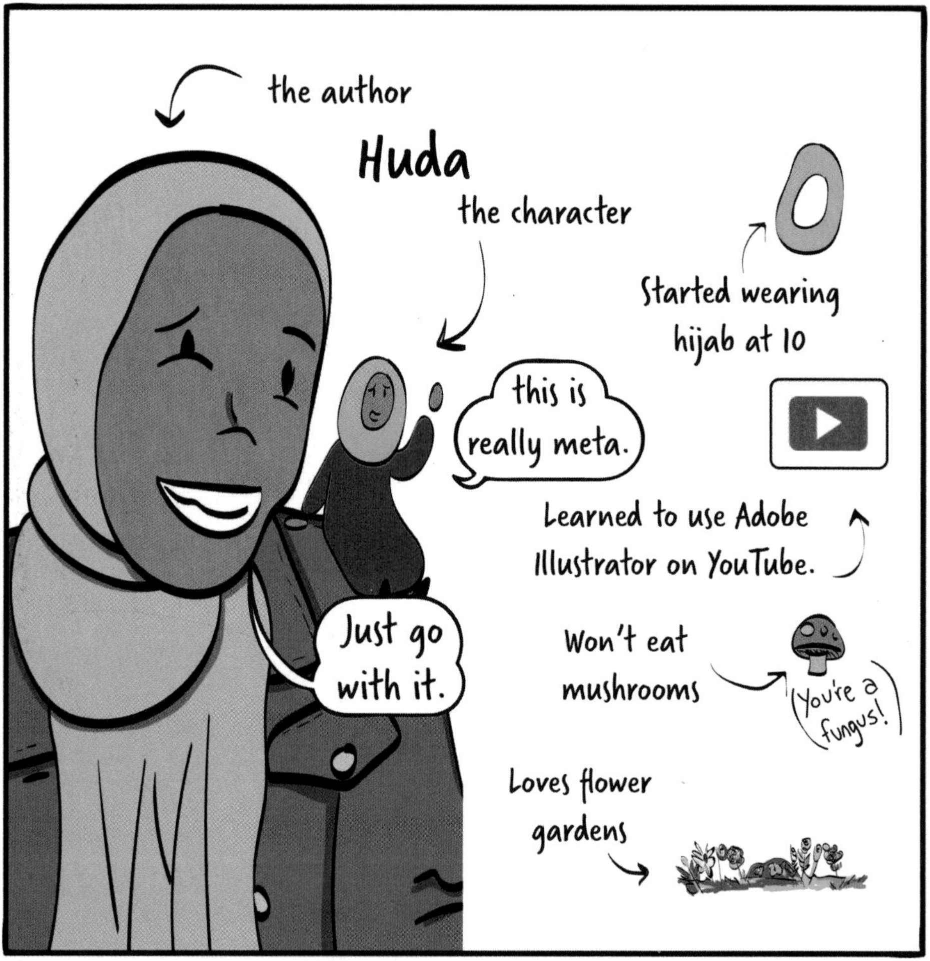
the author
Huda
the character
Started wearing hijab at 10
this is really meta.
Learned to use Adobe Illustrator on YouTube.
Just go with it.
Won't eat mushrooms
You're a fungus!
Loves flower gardens